THE GUITAR IN TUDOR ENGLAND

Few now remember that the guitar was popular in England during Queen Elizabeth and Shakespeare, and yet it was played from the royal co common tavern. This ground-breaking book, the first entirely devote renaissance guitar in England, deploys new literary and archival material, ι with depictions in contemporary art, to explore the social and musical wοιιd of the four-course guitar among courtiers, government servants and gentlemen. Christopher Page reconstructs the trade in imported guitars coming to the wharves of London, and pieces together the printed tutor for the instrument (probably of 1569), which ranks as the only method book for the guitar to survive from the sixteenth century. Two chapters discuss the remains of music for the instrument in tablature, both the instrumental repertoire and the traditions of accompanied song, which must often be assembled from scattered fragments of information.

CHRISTOPHER PAGE is a Fellow of the British Academy, Professor of Medieval Music and Literature in the University of Cambridge and from October 2014 Gresham Professor of Music at Gresham College, London for three years. He holds the Dent Medal of the Royal Musical Association awarded for outstanding services to musicology. In 1981 he founded the professional vocal ensemble Gothic Voices, which now has twenty-five CDs in the catalogue, three of which won the coveted Gramophone Early Music Record of the Year award. In 2012, he was a founder member of the Consortium for Guitar Research at Sidney Sussex College, an affiliate of the Royal Musical Association. He has published many books and articles on early music, most recently a major study, *The Christian West and its Singers: The First Thousand Years* (2010).

MUSICAL PERFORMANCE AND RECEPTION

General editors

JOHN BUTT AND LAURENCE DREYFUS

This series continues the aim of Cambridge Musical Texts and Monographs to publish books centred on the history of musical instruments and the history of performance, but broadens the focus to include musical reception in relation to performance and as a reflection of period expectations and practices.

Published titles

Playing with History: The Historical Approach to Musical Performance
JOHN BUTT

Palestrina and the German Romantic Imagination: Interpreting Historicism in Nineteenth-Century Music
JAMES GARRATT

Eight Centuries of Troubadours and Trouvères: The Changing Identity of Medieval Music
JOHN HAINES

The Keyboard in Baroque Europe
CHRISTOPHER HOGWOOD (ED.)

The Modern Invention of Medieval Music: Scholarship, Ideology, Performance
DANIEL LEECH-WILKINSON

Performing Brahms: Early Evidence of Performance Style
MICHAEL MUSGRAVE AND BERNARD SHERMAN (EDS.)

Stradivari
STEWART POLLENS

Beethoven the Pianist
TILMAN SKOWRONECK

The French Organ in the Reign of Louis XIV
DAVID PONSFORD

Bach's Feet: The Organ Pedals in European Culture
DAVID YEARSLEY

Histories of Heinrich Schütz
BETTINA VARWIG

Engaging Bach: The Keyboard Legacy from Marpurg to Mendelssohn
MATTHEW DIRST

The Musical Work of Nadia Boulanger: Performing Past and Future between the Wars
JEANICE BROOKS

The Guitar in Tudor England: A Social and Musical History
CHRISTOPHER PAGE

THE GUITAR IN TUDOR ENGLAND

A Social and Musical History

CHRISTOPHER PAGE

CAMBRIDGE
UNIVERSITY PRESS

CAMBRIDGE
UNIVERSITY PRESS

University Printing House, Cambridge CB2 8BS, United Kingdom

One Liberty Plaza, 20th Floor, New York, NY 10006, USA

477 Williamstown Road, Port Melbourne, VIC 3207, Australia

314-321, 3rd Floor, Plot 3, Splendor Forum, Jasola District Centre, New Delhi-110025, India

79 Anson Road, #06-04/06, Singapore 079906

Cambridge University Press is part of the University of Cambridge.

It furthers the University's mission by disseminating knowledge in the pursuit of
education, learning and research at the highest international levels of excellence.

www.cambridge.org
Information on this title: www.cambridge.org/9781107519374

First published 2015
Reprinted 2016
First paperback edition 2017

A catalogue record for this publication is available from the British Library

Library of Congress Cataloging in Publication data
Page, Christopher, 1952–
The guitar in Tudor England : a social and musical history / Christopher Page.
pages   cm. – (Musical performance and reception)
Includes bibliographical references and index.
ISBN 978-1-107-10836-3
1. Guitar – England – History – 16th century.   I. Title.
ML1015.G9P34   2015
787.870942´09031–dc23
2014046560

ISBN 978-1-107-10836-3 Hardback
ISBN 978-1-107-51937-4 Paperback

For Anne . . .

Nulle chose, tant soit douce,
Ne te sçauroit esgaler,
Toi qui mes ennuis repousse
Si tost qu'ils t'oyent parler.

Ronsard, 'A sa guiterre'

. . . and for Ewart and Marie

Last night I lay a-sleeping, there came a dream so fair;
I stood in old Jerusalem beside the temple there.

Anglican hymn

Contents

Figures

Tables

Music examples

Acknowledgments

This book, for all its failings, although not the first book I have written, is certainly the first where I have been constantly aware that many people outside university life, narrowly defined, possess profound and extensive knowledge of the material: knowledge which it is not always easy to access using standard research techniques or to find in peer-reviewed publications. They include independent scholars, scholar-performers and many others who will surely find that I have made more than my share of mistakes, or have been guilty of too many simplifications. I offer this book to them with a good heart and with the necessary apology. Special thanks are due to Peter Forrester, Chris Goodwin, Erik Stenstadvold and James Westbrook who read the entire book in typescript. Peter Forrester also allowed me to reproduce his photograph of the overmantel at Hengrave Hall, a document he was the first to bring to my attention, and he alerted me to the panel in the Victoria and Albert Museum. Chris Goodwin has been a constant source of advice and wise counsel, most generously offered, while Erik Stenstadvold and James Westbrook have been my indispensable guides for some years now in all matters of guitar history. I am immensely grateful to this tetrarchy of scholars for their sharp eyes and their sound judgement.

I owe a special debt to Joyce Tyler for sharing with me letters, documents and notes compiled by her late husband James Tyler, deeply missed by all that love early plucked instruments. I would also like to make special mention of Monica Hall who, with great kindness, read several chapters and accompanying appendices at a time when she had much else to preoccupy her. Michael Fleming was always generous with his advice and shared many materials with me. John Milsom kindly read an early draft of the chapter on song. Alexander Batov patiently explained to me why strumming seems to work so much better on the renaissance guitar than on the lute. David Skinner, as always, gave crucial help in the management and editing of digital images. Phil Robins read the entire text and removed many infelicities (I am of course responsible for any that remain). I owe a special debt to Nicholas Rogers, archivist of Sidney Sussex College, Cambridge, for his boundless erudition. Steven Collee supplied me with a photograph of his residence at Ruffyneshill in Kent, and Paul Sparks provided a crash course in the history of the *mandore*. Editors of as yet unpublished volumes in the series Records of Early English Drama kindly sent me any references to gitterns that they had encountered in their documents. Peter Blayney responded to an enquiry about the Stationers' Company with a letter of four single-spaced pages. That kind of generosity is virtually impossible to repay.

For advice on specific documents and issues I am grateful to Gavin Alexander, Susan Brigden, Charles Burnett, John Caldwell, Helen Cooper, Claire Daunton, the late Frank Dobbins, John Downing, Peter Duckers, Elizabeth Evenden, Tom Freedman, Paul Griffiths, Peter Holman, David King, Andrea Kirkham, Frank Koonce, Michael Lowe, Darryl Martin, Edward Martin, Philip Mead of Toddington, Katie Nelson, Jason Scott-Warren, Matthew Spring and Edward Wilson-Lee. Among librarians, archivists and museum staff I offer special thanks to Kathy Adamson (Royal College of Music), Penny Fussel (Worshipful Company of Drapers), James Gibson (Rochester Bridge Trust), Jenny Hand (Northampton Museum and Art Gallery), Kate Hay (Victoria and Albert Museum), Jane Hughes (Pepys Library, Cambridge), Sue Hurley (archivist of the Stationers' Company), Nicholas Humphrey (Victoria and Albert Museum), Dirk Leyder (National Archives, Brussels), Erin McHugh (Doctoral Museum Assistant at the Royal College of Music), Georgianna Ziegler (Folger Shakespeare Library), and the staffs of Lambeth Palace Library, Bristol Records Office, the Cathedral Archives (Canterbury), Cheshire Records Office (Chester), Essex County Record Office (Chelmsford), Hampshire County Record Office (Winchester), Isle of Wight Records Office (Newport), Leicestershire, Leicester and Rutland Record Office (Leicester), The National Archives (London), Norwich Archive Centre and the Stadtbibliothek/Stadtarchiv, Trier. The staff of Cambridge University Library provided good-humoured and valuable assistance day after day. I am grateful to Vicki Cooper of Cambridge University Press for believing in the book, and to Fleur Jones and Beata Mako, also of the Press, for their hard work on my behalf. I owe a special debt to Andrew Dawes for his work as copy-editor. I am very grateful to Alistair Warwick for taking such care with the musical examples. The reader may be assured that any faults of consistency or presentation which remain are mine alone.

And so I come at last to my wife Anne, who over the last two years must have heard every piece of sixteenth-century guitar music there is, played on the replica four-course guitar she bought me to mark a significant birthday. She shares the dedication of this book with my parents, long gone, who met and married, during the Second World War, in the earthly Jerusalem.

Note on music examples

In order for the examples to be readily playable by modern guitarists, all have been transcribed assuming a four-course guitar in E and using the tenor octava clef customary for notating music for the guitar. The reader is asked to remember that, as far as we may discern, sixteenth-century guitars were often (but by no means invariably) relatively small instruments – the guitar was 'a diminutive of the lute', in the words of one French renaissance commentator – and that the sounding pitch of the music represented in the examples would generally have been appreciably higher than shown, perhaps a fourth or more above the written pitch. On the other hand it will become clear during the course of the book (and it is otherwise well established) that there were also larger guitars in sixteenth-century England whose sounding pitch may have lain approximately in the range suggested by the transcriptions.

The transcriptions do not indicate either unison courses or octave strings.

The tablatures have been transcribed using the following system of equivalences, where the first two lines of the table represent standard sixteenth-century practice:

Abbreviations

BCI	*Books in Cambridge Inventories*, E. S. Leedham-Green, 2 vols. (Cambridge, 1986)
BDECM	*Biographical Dictionary of English Church Musicians*, A. Ashbee, D. Lasocki, assisted by P. Holman and F. Kisby (Aldershot, 1998)
BJHM	*Basler Jahrbuch für historische Musikpraxis*
EEBO	*Early English Books Online* http://eebo.chadwyck.com
EEPF	*Early English Prose Fiction* http://collections.chadwyck.co.uk
EM	*Early Music*
EMH	*Early Music History*
ESTC	*English Short Title Catalogue* http://estc.bl.uk
FEW	Wartburg, Walther von, *Französisches etymologisches Wörterbuch: eine Darstellung des galloromanischen Sprachschatzes* (Bonn, 1922–)
FoMRHI	Fellowship of Makers and Researchers of Historical Instruments, Bulletins and Communications www.fomrhi.org
GSJ	*Galpin Society Journal*
HMC	Historical Manuscripts Commission
IJMH	*International Journal of Maritime History*
JAMS	*Journal of the American Musicological Society*
JEGP	*Journal of English and Germanic Philology*
JLSA	*Journal of the Lute Society of America*
JRMA	*Journal of The Royal Musical Association*
LEME	*Lexicons of Early Modern English* http://leme.library.utoronto.ca
LSJ	*Lute Society Journal*
MED	*Middle English Dictionary*, ed. H. Kurath and S. M. Kuhn, 20 vols. (Ann Arbor, University of Michigan Press, 1952–2001) http://quod.lib.umich.edu/m/med/
ML	*Music and Letters*
MQ	*Musical Quarterly*
NQ	*Notes and Queries*

ODNB	*Oxford Dictionary of National Biography*, ed. H. C. G. Matthew and B. Harrison, 61 vols. (Oxford, 2004) www.oxforddnb.com
OED	*Oxford English Dictionary*, 2nd edn in 20 vols. (Oxford, 1989) www.oed.com
PL	*Patrologiae Cursus Completus Series Latina*, ed. J. P. Migne, 217 vols. (Paris, 1844–45) with 4 vols. of indices (Paris, 1862–64) http://pld.chadwyck.co.uk
PMLA	*Proceedings of the Modern Language Association*
RBT	Archives of the Rochester Bridge Trust
RECM	*Records of English Court Music*, ed. A. Ashbee, 9 vols. (Snodland and Aldershot, 1986–96)
RISM	*Répertoire International des Sources Musicales*
RMARC	*Royal Musical Association Research Chronicle*
TNA	The National Archives, Kew

Introduction

I

'Keep close your friend's letters, for craft and malice never reigned more'.[1] This is the warning that one friend gave to another in 1587, but it would have been good advice at any time in the sixteenth century. Those who sent letters on personal or political business under the Tudors had every reason to fear the 'craft and malice' of spies, and some resorted to ciphers and secret tokens. One such was Edward Courtenay, First Earl of Devon. In the winter of 1553–4, when he was widely believed to be the best match for Princess Elizabeth, Courtenay found himself 'the rallying point for every major conspiracy' against her half-sister, Queen Mary.[2] To communicate with his allies, Courtenay hit upon a device that was unusually ingenious even by the standards of Elizabethan duplicity. He took a *guiterre* and marked it with a cipher known to his principal associate, Peter Carew. The deceit was soon discovered, however, and became common knowledge at court. The news reached two imperial ambassadors who reported it to their master, Charles V, a ruler with a deep political interest in the fortunes of the restored Catholic monarchy in England. The ambassadors assured the Emperor that Queen Mary and her Privy Council, having interrogated various suspects, now believed

that it was certain the guilt of the said Courtenay was established by several other prisoners, that he was a knowing and consenting participant in the said sworn agreement, [and that] he had a cipher inscribed on a *guiterre* for use with Peter Carew . . .[3]

---

[1] Mildred Burghley to Sir William Fitzwilliam, 24 March 1587, quoted in Daybell, 'Secret Letters'. I have modernised the spelling.

[2] Bartlett, '"The Misfortune that is wished for him"', 1. For more recent work on Courtenay, see Overell, *Italian Reform and English Reformations*, esp. 61–80, and *ODNB*, 'Courtenay, Edward'.

[3] '. . . qu'il estoit certain le dite Cortenai estoit convaincu par plusieurs autres prisonniers, qu'il estoit participant saichant et consentent de la dite conjure, qu'il avoit un ziffre avec pierre caro tailée sur une guiterre . . .'. Brussels, National Archives, Audience, n° 384, f. 591v. This episode is mentioned (on the basis of the printed paraphrase in the *Calendar of State Papers*) by Marsh, *Music and Society*, 181. The report was all the more believable since such 'deceitful traffique', in the words of Tudor diplomat Sir James Melville, was common. Francis Walsingham, the royal spymaster, often used secret tokens and devices to verify whether couriers were bringing news from trustworthy informants (Alford, *The Watchers*, 82–3, 119 and 197). Plotters devised a range of methods to communicate in

1

These details ring true, for both of the suspects were musicians. Edward Courtenay was remembered after his death as a talented performer on the lute, and Peter Carew made music with Henry VIII.[4] What is more, the practice of inscribing a guitar with a symbol or *ziffre* of purely personal (as opposed to treasonable) significance was not unusual in the sixteenth century; a poem by Pierre de Ronsard celebrates a *guiterre* marked with his lady's name and his own *en chifre*.[5] In this respect, as perhaps in others, Edward Courtenay and Peter Carew were guilty as charged.

Their stratagem would never have been considered, let alone attempted, if there were anything unusual or odd about courtiers sharing a *guiterre*, or giving one as a present, during the early 1550s. Courtenay and Carew were hiding their cipher in plain sight. The ambassadors' letter may therefore be said to reveal an indisputably courtly context for the *guiterre* in England, shedding a welcome light on musical life at the Tudor court. But what kind of instrument is meant?[6] In sixteenth-century French, the term *guiterre* was a synonym of both *guiterne* and (a rarer word) *quinterne*. The author of a treatise published in Poitiers in 1556 regarded all three as names for a plucked and fretted instrument with three double courses plus a single top string or *chanterelle*.[7] During the 1550s, two publishing partnerships in Paris issued elegant volumes of tablature for what is undoubtedly the instrument that the author had in mind; Adrian Le Roy and Robert Ballard called it the *guiterre*, the form found in the ambassadors' letter, while Robert Granjon and Michel Fezandat used the term *guiterne*. All four of the prints issued by the latter team depict this *guiterne* as a plucked instrument with incurved sides, a single circular sound-hole, frets and a fixed bridge: a true guitar as that term will be understood in this book (Figure 1).[8]

secret, for example letters sealed in wine bottles with specially marked corks, and notes on black paper left in the dark corner of a privy (Orlin, *Locating Privacy*, 254, n.) An inscribed guitar would not necessarily attract attention, since the men and women of Tudor England were accustomed to seeing symbols and text on walls, beams, pots and other surfaces where they would often now count as graffiti (Fleming, *Graffiti and the Writing Arts*).

[4] When Sir Thomas Wilson gave the funerary oration for Courtenay at Padua in 1556 he mentioned the earl's skill with the lute, in a humanistic context, also praising his fluency in Spanish, French and Italian, together with his knowledge of *philosophia* and the art of drawing. Strype, *Ecclesiastical Memorials*, vol. I, 550; vol. II, 420–7, at 422: 'Testudinem vero sonorisque intervallis, et temperata varietate contrectavit, absolutam ut in illo diceres perfectionem.' Peter Carew became a favoured companion of Henry VIII when that king had a mind to sing 'certain songs they called fremen songs, as namely "By the bank as I lay" and "As I walked the wood so wild"'. The source is Hooker's biography of Carew. See Maclean, *The Life and Times of Sir Peter Carew*, 38–40. For Carew's involvement in political events, see Wagner, *The Devon Gentleman*, 153–236.

[5] Céard, Ménager and Simonin, eds., *Pierre de Ronsard*, vol. I, 930.

[6] For the medieval gittern as a pear-shaped, plucked and fretted instrument whose body, neck and peg-box were carved from a single block, see Appendix F.

[7] *La maniere de bien et iustement entoucher les Lucz et Guiternes*, 96–7.

[8] Brown, *Instrumental Music*, 1551₁, 1552₅, 1552₆ and 1553₄. All have been issued in facsimile by Editions Chanterelle (Tyler, ed., *Simon Gorlier and Guillaume Morlaye*). In this book I accept the conclusion of Meucci, 'Da "chitarra italiana" a "chitarrone"', that the *Chitara da sette corde* for which

Figure 1. The title page of Robert Granjon and Michel Fezandat, *Le Premier Livre de Chansons, Gaillardes, Pavannes, Bransles, Almandes, Fantaisies, reduictz en tabulature de Guiterne par Maistre Guillaume Morlaye ioueur de Lut*, second edition (Paris, 1552). Brown, *Instrumental Music*, 1552₅.

The music master and songwriter Thomas Whythorne (d. 1595) relates in his remarkable autobiography that he learned the 'Gyttern' while a young man in London during the late 1540s and into the 1550s. At the time, he maintains, the instrument known by that name was still considered 'stranʒ', meaning that it was unusual and probably also foreign.[9] Whythorne's testimony is indirectly supported by many documents from the second half of the sixteenth century, the period when references to the 'gittern' (in various spellings) begin to proliferate in a wide range of English documents. Import records, for example, show that the government did not levy a duty on 'gitternes' in 1545 but decided it should do so thirteen years later, suggesting that the trade in legally imported gitterns rose to the level where it came to official notice at some point between 1545 and 1558. Inventories of property drawn up for probate show gitterns appearing among the possessions of Cambridge

Melchiore de Barberiis published four tablatures in 1549 was a small instrument with a lute-shaped body, not a four-course guitar (Brown, *Instrumental Music*, 1549₂).

[9] Osborn, ed., *The Autobiography*, 19. For further discussion of the term, see 160.

scholars for the first time in 1559–60, even though such inventories are available (and rich in references to instruments) from the mid-1530s. Perhaps the choice document, however, is the record that shows Queen Elizabeth received a boxed set of three 'Getternes' as a New Year present in 1559. The gift was offered on behalf of the most famous instrument maker of early Elizabethan England, and (better still) the Queen asked for the instruments to be brought to her rather than simply stored or passed on to another. She evidently wished to see the three gitterns, and even perhaps to play them.

At about the time when the Queen received these three 'Getternes' we begin to find music in English sources, written in French lute tablature, for a four-course or four-string instrument tuned guitar-wise to a rising fourth, major third and fourth. This is the string arrangement and tuning of the *guiterre* and *guiterne* for which the French publishers issued their books in the 1550s. The pieces in the English sources show no lack of panache, as a saltarello from the Osborn Commonplace Book of *c.* 1560, with its florid play on the upper strings or 'fine, minikin fingering', demonstrates (Example 1).[10] As if to complement the appearance of such confident music, images of relatively small guitars begin to appear by the late 1560s in works of art produced for English patrons, mostly by continental artists and craftsmen, including two of the most opulent depictions of a renaissance guitar to survive from sixteenth-century Europe (see Chapter 1).

By far the simplest explanation for what we find in documents, musical sources and works of art is that the new 'gittern' of the late 1540s onwards in England was the *guiterne/guiterre* of contemporary France, namely the four-course guitar. We shall soon encounter an English gentleman, of high rank in the Tudor government, who bought a 'gyttron' after a diplomatic visit to France in 1550. A tutor for the four-course guitar, probably published in 1569, bears the running title 'An instruction to the *Gitterne*' (emphasis mine) on most of its surviving pages, following its French model. As the latest Parisian fashion in amateur musicianship, the four-course guitar would have commended itself to gentlemen and others in England with an avid taste for imported French goods and fashions. This does not mean, however, that the term 'gittern' implies a guitar of the kind shown in Figure 1 whenever it appears in a sixteenth-century source; it would be contrary to common sense (and to the nature of Tudor documents) to assume so. There are, to be sure, some sources where the meaning is assured, but in general we do better to interpret the documents in terms of shared

---

[10] Ascham, *Toxophilvs*, Sig. Cij^v.

Example 1.   'Salt[a]rello', from the Osborn Commonplace Book (Beinecke Rare Book and Manuscript Library of Yale University, Osborn Music MS 13), f. 42 (old foliation), f. 46 (new foliation). The original can be viewed in the Digital Library of the Beinecke at http://beinecke.library.yale.edu. For the first four notes of measure 3, the tablature indicates a-g-a-b♭, which seems unidiomatic for this repertory and has no counterpart in the 'galliard to salt[a]rello' which immediately follows in the MS and has exactly the reading given here at the corresponding place. I assume that the scribe inadvertently wrote the tablature letters on the third course instead of the second, with the result that the phrase appears in the manuscript a major third too low.

themes and concerns without pressing any single source too hard for what it may reveal about the guitar.[11]

II

The guitar in Tudor England has never before been made the sole subject of a monograph.[12] That is not altogether surprising; the sources of music for the instrument are sparse and there seems to be no evidence that it was ever used in consort, like the cittern. Yet the ambassadors' letter quoted above captures much that gives the history of the Tudor guitar its special character and interest.[13] Unlike the lute, the guitar was never dependably gentle in the Elizabethan sense of possessing an assured lineage or a right to respect. Its allure arose from the competing attractions of the decent and the disreputable, the simple and the sophisticated. The *guiterre* of Edward Courtenay and Peter Carew was used (if not necessarily played) by two of the highest courtiers in the land, and yet the guitar can also be found in the hands of apprentices fleeing their masters, of impoverished tricksters, of Inns of Court gallants and alehouse wastrels. It yielded readily to players who wished to do little more than strum chords, but it could also accommodate musicians who sought a more demanding repertoire. To the higher gentry and nobility, the guitar was a fashionable object with some appealingly low associations, rather like a printed translation of Boccaccio's *Decameron*. To those lower down the social scale it was a relatively inexpensive purchase, but one whose connections were enticingly select, like a pair of scented gloves.

The period from the accession of Edward VI in 1547 to the end of Elizabeth's reign in 1603 encloses, with some neatness, a distinct phase in the history of the renaissance guitar. As mentioned above, the sixteenth-century instrument was generally equipped with seven strings disposed as

[11] According to *La maniere de bien et iustement entoucher les Lucz et Guiternes*, published in 1556, at 96, 'depuis douze ou quinze ans en ça, tout nostre monde s'est mis a Guiterner', which places the beginnings of the craze in the early 1540s. Facsimile in Saint-Arroman and Dugot, *Méthodes et Traités, Luth*, vol. I, 25–53. In a series of studies, John Ward maintained that the gittern of Tudor documents might equally well be the wire-strung gittern, effectively a treble cittern tuned guitar-wise, mentioned in seventeenth-century sources. See *Sprightly and Cheerful Musick*, 6–16, and *Music for Elizabethan Lutes*, vol. I, 24–9. In a review of the latter, Sayce (in my view rightly) deems that Ward 'gets into a tangle that transcends the boundaries of common sense ...' with this proposal. Ward's argument is dismissed (perhaps somewhat briskly) by Tyler in Tyler and Sparks, *The Guitar and its Music*, 25, n. See here Appendix F.

[12] For previous scholarship on the renaissance guitar in England, see Ward, *Sprightly and Cheerful Musick*, 6–21, 107–8 and 109–29, and *Music for Elizabethan Lutes*, vol. I, *passim*, but esp. 24–9; Heartz, 'An Elizabethan Tutor for the Guitar'; Tyler and Sparks, *ibid.*, 24–9. Gill, *Gut-Strung Plucked Instruments*, 4–8, mentions some essentials, albeit without much documentation, and his account is not confined to England. One of the principal iconographical sources, the Eglantine Table now at Hardwick Hall, is usefully studied (but before cleaning) in Collins, 'A 16th-Century Manuscript in Wood'.

[13] The modern term 'renaissance guitar' is to my mind satisfactory. No special problems have been created by the passage of the term into widespread use.

three double courses and a single *chanterelle*. By the 1620s, many players in England, as elsewhere in Europe, had adopted the five-course guitar. One may speak of 'Europe' advisedly here, for the social and musical history of the guitar in early modern England belongs in a European context. According to John Milsom, most accounts of Tudor music,

especially those written by English-born authorities, proceed as if sixteenth-century England were a country largely untouched by the music of continental Europe, at least until the generation of William Byrd and Thomas Morley. They pay little attention to the cohort of foreign musicians that has long been known to have served the Tudor court from the reign of Henry VII onwards, and they do not consider the easy access English musicians must have had to foreign repertories through the burgeoning medium of print.[14]

The first traces of the guitar in England include the inventory by a *Netherlandish* lute player of instruments in the royal keeping called '*Spanishe* vialles' and an inlaid table produced by craftsmen who were probably *Germans* or *Flemings* serving an *English* patron. The most sophisticated playing in *England*, insofar as we can reconstruct it, was partly an emanation of *French* practice. The cultivation of the guitar under the Tudors can only be understood in relation to 'the music of continental Europe', the influence of 'foreign musicians' and 'the burgeoning medium of print' evoked by Milsom.

The purpose of this book is to frame a social and musical history of the guitar in Tudor England by gathering the relevant literary, archival and pictorial documents in a more comprehensive manner than has yet been attempted. This is to claim a good deal, for the late John Ward marshalled an impressive array of material in his *Sprightly and Cheerful Musick* (1978–81) and later in *Music for Elizabethan Lutes* (1992).[15] Ward's expertise and interests, however, and his encyclopaedic (if sometimes confusingly disposed) knowledge, lay principally in the domain of tablature sources for stringed instruments, together with Elizabethan verse, song and balladry, so it is understandable that he did not look far into the unpublished wills and probate inventories found in many County Record Offices. Such documents are our principal source for the ownership of musical instruments, and major repositories (such as those at Leicester and Norwich) house many hundreds of them. Nor did the depth of Ward's studies, in his chosen fields, give him frequent opportunity to delve into what was then

---

[14] 'Caustun's Contrafacta', 30. Milsom was writing in 2007, since when the situation has changed in ways that make the cosmopolitan history of the guitar in Tudor England more comprehensible. See, for example, Dumitrescu, *The Early Tudor Court and International Musical Relations*.

[15] These studies, notably the latter, were generally very well received by members of Ward's own constituency, the musicological fraternity. The view from at least one scholar-performer, however, although as erudite as any the book received, was notably different. See the trenchant review of *Music for Elizabethan Lutes* by Sayce. For a preliminary report on a source that Ward missed, see Goodwin, 'The Earliest English Lute Manuscript?' Goodwin is preparing a further study of this manuscript.

the Public Records Office, now The National Archives at Kew. Documents from The National Archives (TNA) such as letters, lists of imports by shipment and inventories of property have all yielded information that has been deployed in the following chapters. One might add that Ward never saw, because he could not, the principal iconographical source for the Elizabethan guitar in all its splendour, shown in marquetry on the Eglantine Table of *c.* 1567. For this, Ward used a very accomplished but fallible nineteenth-century drawing.[16] It is also of account that Ward was only able to give passing notice to two further leaves from the only known Elizabethan tutor for the four-course guitar, 'An instruction to the Gitterne', which came to light very late in his studies. Four folios of this book survive in all, two of them in the United States, two of them in England, and together they form the earliest surviving material from any European book actually published as a guitar tutor.[17]

When those printed leaves are placed with the corpus of music for the guitar in English manuscript sources, the total repertoire is still decidedly modest. Fortunately, we may add the five guitar books published in the 1550s by the partnership of Adrian Le Roy and Robert Ballard, for these elegant volumes made their way to England as a set some time in the second half of the sixteenth century. Yet despite this modest store of material, the music in certain sources preserved in England – the Osborn Commonplace Book of *c.* 1560 and 'An instruction to the Gitterne' – is of considerable musical and historical interest. While the tablatures for the guitar printed in sixteenth-century France and Spain mostly treat the instrument as a reduced and miniaturised lute, the Osborn Commonplace Book and 'An instruction to the Gitterne' both offer music that suggests how a great deal of guitar playing was conducted in the sixteenth century and in a mostly unwritten tradition, namely by the player strumming sequences of block chords.

This requires a brief sketch of the continental context. The fashion for intricate finger-style music on the four-course guitar in the manner of the lute, as far as the four courses of the instrument would allow, and as far as notated sources reveal it, arose on the continent in the 1540s and lasted until at least the 1570s when it gradually faded away.[18] The subsequent spread of the *five*-course guitar throughout Europe facilitated (and no

---

[16] Ward used the best available substitute: Jewitt's drawing of 1882, which he reproduces in *Music for Elizabethan Lutes*, vol. I, Fig. 11. The drawing, in many ways an impressive piece of work since it was made long before the table was cleaned, nonetheless (1) underestimates the depth of the instrument, (2) suppresses all surface details showing the grain and nature of the woods used, (3) redraws the design of the rose, (4) places the fixed bridge at an incorrect angle and makes it appear too massive, (5) leaves the viewer uncertain as to whether or not the original shows the seven strings in courses and (6) as reproduced by Ward, occludes the place of the guitar in the overall decorative scheme.

[17] Ward mentioned these leaves in his correspondence, and I gladly acknowledge the assistance I have received from these letters, copies of which were kindly passed to me by Peter Duckers and Joyce Tyler.

[18] No music for any kind of guitar survives from the sixteenth century in printed form later than the 1570s. Brown, *Instrumental Music, passim.*

doubt in part inspired) a shift of interest among guitarists towards forms of solo performance and accompaniment using block chords: the player repeatedly swept all or most of the five courses at once, varying the stroke and perhaps interweaving plucked chords of sparser texture. As the sixteenth century passed to the seventeenth, music for the guitar in this brushing style was extensively recorded in manuscript and print as guitarists created a notation-based culture unapologetically geared to the characteristic idioms and instant appeal of their instrument. Means were found to cultivate such brushing play and to sketch its elements either in tablature or in various dedicated one-letter-per-chord systems devised to notate dance music or accompaniments for songs in a simple and succinct manner.[19]

Another way to describe these developments would be to say that highly literate finger-style playing of the kind indicated in the French prints of the 1550s, or the academic counterpoint composed for the guitar by a composer such as Miguel de Fuenllana,[20] was a learnèd irruption into an existing culture of strumming play that remained in place when the fashion for elaborate music in the finger-style manner faded; the developments of real historical importance towards the end of the century were therefore the rise of the five-course guitar to create richer strummed chordal blocks and the enhanced literacy of that practice by *c.* 1600. The Osborn Commonplace Book and 'An instruction to the Gitterne' provide very early glimpses of this brushed and chord-based play at a time simultaneous with that of the lute-style tradition.

A final word should be said, about the plan of the book. Chapter 1 explores the pictorial record of instruments that may be unhesitatingly classified as guitars. Chapter 2 seeks to uncover more about the Tudor owners and players of such instruments using material mostly gathered from archives. Chapter 3 considers the ways in which those individuals obtained their instruments from dealers and importers, while Chapter 4 explores how they might learn to play with the aid of a unique survival, 'An instruction to the Gitterne', licensed to be printed in 1568/9. Chapters 5 and 6 turn to music for the four-course instrument that was either copied in England or was known there, dividing the material into purely instrumental items (Chapter 5) and accompanied songs (Chapter 6). This separation is to some extent artificial, but it is nonetheless required by the different patterns of survival in each case. Our access to the

[19] Hall and Yakeley, 'El estilo castellano'; Hill, 'L'accompagnamento *rasgueado* di chitarra'; Tyler and Sparks, *The Guitar and its Music.*
[20] The models for the guitar music published by Fuenllana in his *Libro de Musica para Vihuela* (1554) lie with intabulations of works by such distinguished masters of counterpoint as Morales, Guerrero, Gombert and Josquin, made for the vihuela. Fuenllana accordingly offers music of textbook scrupulosity, with points of imitation and progressive thickening of the texture that are clearly based upon the linear independence and integrity of vocal models. See, for example, the 'musica para guitarra' in *Libro de Musica para Vihuela,* f. 164v.

instrumental music of Tudor guitarists is relatively good; for English song accompanied by the guitar, however, we are in a much less fortunate position. Literary documents nonetheless reveal that such material must once have existed, and the task is therefore to proceed on the basis of hints in tablature and literary texts. Finally, Chapter 7 explores the autobiography of a musician who learned to play the gittern as a young man in London. It is good fortune indeed that the author of the earliest autobiography in English was a Tudor guitarist.[21]

---

[21] In a poem on the Battle of Lepanto (1571), James VI of Scotland imagines a Venetian chorus giving thanks for their victory with an ensemble including 'gutornes', while a biting satire on Archbishop John Hamilton of St Andrews tells how he fled to France in 1540–3 and learned 'with guthorne for to dance'. James VI, who later became King of England as James I, is presumably envisaging the court music he knew, while John Hamilton was in France in the very dawn of the fashion for the guitar at the French court. In their different ways, these Scottish sources are of considerable interest, and with such materials to hand the reader of this book is entitled to ask why the account is devoted to England only (I do not read Welsh, so could not venture into the principality). I am not well versed in either the history or the abundant literature of early modern Scotland, whereas I have spent a lifetime as a teacher of medieval English literature and its historical context reaching well into the sixteenth century with authors such as Skelton, More and Surrey. My second reason for omitting Scottish material is that I share the weakness of most writers who, once they have begun a book, find themselves keen to finish it. This project has already taken three times as long as I expected, and work in Scottish archives would have extended it further still. Finally, this book tells an essentially London story, or at least one that moves within the 'golden triangle' of London, Oxford and Cambridge. It would be unfortunate indeed if a history of the renaissance guitar in Scotland, with so rich a background in Franco-Scottish contacts and court politics, were to become a satellite to the largely English and metropolitan narrative that unfolds here.

CHAPTER I

Imagery

I

Depictions of musical instruments on the walls, ceilings and stairways of
Elizabethan houses, as they survive today, are considerably less common
than the ghosts who are reputed to haunt the rooms. No doubt those
unhappy spirits are grieving for the destruction of their former homes.
Many houses built during the 1500s passed to descendants of the original
owners, or to purchasers, who decided that the Tudor fixtures had 'out-
stood their time' and should be removed. The history of many domestic
buildings after the death of Elizabeth in 1603 is therefore a sorry tale of
destruction by those who had only a qualified regard for architecture
deemed to be 'Elizabethan', a term rarely used until the later 1700s. To
an eye of the eighteenth century, accustomed to landscaped gardens,
Tudor-period mansions gave scant attention to the beauty of landscape
'which was then but little or not at all regarded',[1] while their external
plasterwork looked poor beside stucco. In an age of floor carpets, they were
apt to seem draughty and inhospitable. If funds allowed, whatever was
deemed to be antiquated or useless was demolished and replaced with new,
or rebuilt, in a contemporary taste that better expressed the prosperity and
influence of the new owner; wainscoting was taken down and sold off, wall
paintings covered over and panelling removed or covered with painted
paper.[2]

---

[1] From the Revd Sir John Cullum's detailed description of the Elizabethan mansion of Hawstead
Place, seat of the Drury family, in Suffolk (Cullum, 'The History and Antiquities of Hawsted', in
Nichols, ed., *Bibliotheca topographica Britannica*, vol. VIII, 139).

[2] Compare the (surely only lightly fictionalised) account of such vandalism in the fifth chapter of
Jerome K. Jerome's celebrated comic novel, *Three Men in a Boat*, first published in 1889, concerning
the Elizabethan or Jacobean panelling in a house in Kingston upon Thames: 'From the stairs, they
went into the drawing-room, which was a large, bright room, decorated with a somewhat startling
though cheerful paper of a blue ground. There was nothing, however, remarkable about the
apartment, and my friend wondered why he had been brought there. The proprietor went up to
the paper, and tapped it. It gave forth a wooden sound. "Oak," he explained. "All carved oak, right
up to the ceiling, just the same as you saw on the staircase." "But, great Cæsar! man," expostulated my
friend; "you don't mean to say you have covered over carved oak with blue wall-paper?" "Yes," was
the reply: "it was expensive work. Had to match-board it all over first, of course. But the room looks
cheerful now. It was awful gloomy before."

11

This work could be very thoroughly done. It was the proud boast of Sir Richard Worsley in 1720 that he had left 'not . . . one stone standing' of the Elizabethan house he had inherited at Appuldurcombe, on the Isle of Wight (Figure 10).[3] Even when there was no such thorough demolition, a house could suffer much from the vicissitudes of dynastic fortunes. When a member of the gentry or nobility acquired another estate by marriage, a house might fall into disrepair as their centre of political and paternalistic influence shifted to a different region of the country. Eventually, the furnishings of the neglected house might be dispersed and the building itself left to decay. At about the time when Richard Worsley was demolishing Appuldurcombe, for example, to replace it with a building more to his taste, the contents of Toddington Manor in Bedfordshire were dispersed on carts; the panelling went to a local inn, and a magnificent carved overmantel to a nearby mansion. In this way, a major source for the history of the Tudor guitar was rescued from oblivion (Figure 8).

Despite the ravages of fortune and neglect, however, there are some surviving depictions of an instrument that seems to be making its first English appearance in the 1560s, for no earlier examples are known. Before we proceed, however, it will be wise to establish what we seek. On one hand, there are some stable typological criteria to apply: we are looking for images of plucked instruments with incurved sides tending towards a figure eight, a single circular sound-hole, a fretted neck, a fixed bridge and a flat or slightly rounded back. (We may expect to find cases where some of these features are 'hidden', notably the back.) On the other hand, however, these consistent features may sometimes be expected to combine with an important *variable*, namely *overall size*, prompting the question of whether the instrument shown is a guitar or a vihuela, the Spanish counterpart to the lute and an instrument that meets all of our typological criteria.

Viewed in terms of political history, this appears to be an issue that can hardly be avoided. Given that the Seventeen Provinces of the Netherlands passed to the Spanish Crown in 1556 it is a considerable simplification to speak of the vihuela as a 'Spanish' instrument; contemporary events probably disseminated it from Granada to Groningen. We might add Greenwich, since Philip II of Spain married Queen Mary of England in 1554; it would be remarkable if the culture of the vihuela, so lovingly and diligently described by the Franciscan friar Juan Bermudo in the *Declaracion de instrumentos musicales* of 1555, did not come to the English court with Spaniards in the entourage of their king, indeed with some of the friars that accompanied the Spanish monarch to London.[4]

---

[3] See Appendix B (1565).

[4] Henry Machyn saw these friars in London during early December 1554 as they sang in a grand liturgical procession of the Spanish royal household. Nichols, ed., *The Diary of Henry Machyn*, 78.

In organological terms, however, it is not so clear that we need any more than the broadest notion of how any 'vihuelas' in circulation in Tudor England might have differed from guitars. For the most part, the representations that come into question in this chapter either depict four-course instruments or they are not sufficiently detailed to make the number of strings clear. Only one shows an instrument held by a human figure, and it appears to be quite within the size range commonly associated today, rightly or wrongly, with the four-course guitar of the sixteenth century (Figure 8). There is also a terminological issue. As far as we can establish, English-speakers of the Tudor period called all the instruments that meet our criteria 'gitterns',[5] for there are only sporadic traces of any alternative nomenclature. An important document from 1547 lists 'foure Gitterons ... caulled Spanishe vialles' (see Appendix B), and while this certainly looks like an attempt to introduce 'vihuela' terminology into English the text is an inventory, a class of document where a precision not normally attempted in speech was often necessary. What is more, if the instruments in question could be called both 'gitterons' and 'Spanishe vialles' in informal usage then the two terms were in some measure synonymous, which does not suggest that they were firmly associated with diagnostic criteria. Furthermore, the question of whether the vihuela was 'known in England' during the Tudor period, and might therefore have found its way into 'English' art, is not a very profitable one, at least when put in those terms, for the genealogies of the works explored in this chapter are too complex for them to be regarded as English in any profound sense. We shall find evidence in the next chapter of gitterns (to

[5] When we turn to the principal authority on the Spanish vihuela, Juan Bermudo's *Declaracion de instrumentos musicales* (1555), we find that it has more to say about the diffuseness of the border between *guitarra* and *vihuela* than its definition. Bermudo describes a standard tuning for what he calls the 'common' *vihuela* (Book IV, Ch. 55), but that is not strictly speaking diagnostic because he expects good players to devise their own (IV, 59). The common *vihuela* has six courses, but that is not strictly diagnostic either because some have seven (IV, 62). The *guitarra* commonly has four courses (IV, 65), but that is not a distinguishing feature because some have five, and while a *guitarra* can be expected to be smaller than a *vihuela* (IV, 65) there is 'a new small *vihuela*' which is 'good for a large *guitarra* strung with six courses' (IV, 60). Bermudo's remarks nonetheless suggest some of the criteria that guided informed Spanish-speakers in their choice of term. Although there were some smaller vihuelas and some larger guitars, the word *guitarra* generally meant an instrument that was smaller, *mas corto* ('more short'), and therefore likely to be higher in tessitura, than those which called for the name *vihuela*. The term *guitarra* was also appropriate when the contrapuntal textures were in two or at most three parts, rather than in the denser counterpoint of advanced compositions for the *vihuela*. Bermudo is quite clear that 'one [plays] two-part and occasionally three-part music on this *guitarra*', meaning a standard four-course instrument tuned in the manner of the 'moderns' to a rising fourth, major third and fourth (IV, 65). The *guitarra* was also more closely associated with what Bermudo terms 'struck music', presumably referring to strumming. In the constant interplay between sequences of sonorous block chords and counterpoint, which energises so much that takes place in sixteenth-century music, the kingdom of the *guitarra* was the former, of the *vihuela* the latter, but both could meet in the middle. The terms 'vihuela' and *guitarra* were therefore a means to integrate a number of contextual judgements about the size, musical textures and playing technique of waisted and fretted plucked instruments. See the works by Alcalde, Dugot and Ballot, and J. Griffiths in the bibliography.

use the contemporary term) built in different sizes, and even in sets like consorts of viols.[6]

Tudor iconography of the guitar[7]

1. An engraved portrait of Robert Dudley, Earl of Leicester, in The Bishops' Bible, printed in London in 1568. The engraving has been attributed to the Mechelen artist Franz Hogenberg (Figures 2 and 4).

2. A woodcut of a four-course guitar printed by Marin Mersenne (*Harmonie universelle*, 1636), which is virtually identical to another given by Pierre Phalèse (*Selectissima . . . in guiterna ludenda carmina*, 1570) derived from Adrian Le Roy's lost manual for the four-course guitar. There is good reason to suppose that the image passed to the English translation of that manual registered with the Stationers' Company in 1568/9 and published by James Rowbothum (Figures 18 and 20).

3. An inlaid table of *c.* 1567, the 'Eglantine Table', now at the Elizabethan mansion of Hardwick Hall, near Chesterfield, in Derbyshire (Figures 5 and 6).

4. A painted overmantel in the Summer Parlour (now the Dining Room) at Hengrave Hall in Suffolk, showing two guitars, a larger and a smaller, among other string and wind instruments. Of uncertain date, but probably later sixteenth century, and almost certainly retouched (Figure 7).

5. A painted panel (probably an overmantel) of carved and gilded oak, showing Apollo and the Muses, now in the Victoria and Albert

---

[6] I have reluctantly decided to omit from this discussion (1) the plucked instrument shown on the title page of *The Psalter or Psalmes of Dauid Corrected and pointed as they shal be song in Churches . . . gathered out of the booke of Common prayer, confirmed by Act of Parliament, in the fyrst yere of the raigne of our soueraigne Lady Quene Elizabeth*, printed by William Seres (1563, available on *EEBO*) and later used again. The instrument does not show enough of the necessary features to be considered relevant here, especially since the context in which it appears is so markedly generic. I have also omitted (2) the depictions that might be interpreted (but questionably) as bowed guitars, such as the instrument shown on the reverse of the portrait of Sir Christopher Hatton, dating from the early 1580s and now in Northampton Museum and Art Gallery (reproduced in Ward, 'The English Measure', 15). For further and enlightening discussion of this issue see Holman, *Four and Twenty Fiddlers*, 70–1. If such representations are deemed to be the result of a confusion in the artist's mind, the question arises of whether the disorder lies in showing a guitar played with a bow or a small viol(in) equipped with the wrong kind of bridge. Perhaps the latter is the more likely explanation, but these instruments might be a late survival of the bridgeless proto-viols that are traceable in Valencian and other Southern sources towards (and in some cases beyond) the year 1500. Woodfield, *The Early History of the Viol*, remains an important discussion of this question, notably for its gallery of pictorial sources. I have also omitted, albeit reluctantly, the images of guitar-like instruments in the 'St Andrews Psalter' or 'Wode Partbooks' (Scotland, 1562–92, with early-seventeenth-century additions), not because they are Scottish, but because the instruments depicted, though resembling guitars in some important respects, are several times indicated as 'violes' in the accompanying text. The richness of musical iconography in this source deserves a detailed study to itself.

[7] Enquiries addressed to the owners of nearly 150 houses in England with Elizabethan remains, and Fellows of the Society of Antiquaries of London (devoted to the study of 'the material past') via their newsletter, *Salon*, failed to produce any more such images of guitars. Nothing relevant is listed in the Luborsky and Ingram *Guide to English Illustrated Books, 1536–1603*. It is to be hoped that more images will come to light in the future.

Museum, London (A.12–1924). Commonly dated to the late sixteenth century (? *c.* 1580). Probably from the manor house at Toddington, Bedfordshire, built in the 1570s and subsequently totally rebuilt (Figure 8).

6. Drawings of two triumphal arches built for the entrance of James I to London in March 1603, devised by Stephen Harrison and engraved by William Kip (*The Arch's of Triumph Erected in honor of the High and mighty prince James the first of that name*; first edition 1604) (Figure 9).

The earliest example appears in the border of an engraving used for the first edition of The Bishops' Bible, the densely illustrated English translation of the Scriptures commissioned by Archbishop Matthew Parker and issued by the London printer Richard Jugge in 1568. A prefatory page to Part II of the volume, containing the biblical books from Joshua to Job, presents a mildly mannerist portrait of Robert Dudley, Earl of Leicester, attributed to Franz Hogenberg (Figure 2). Like a great many engraved title pages and portraits in continental books and prints, the decorative scheme presents what is essentially a Roman trophy or victor's battlefield display of captured arms and booty. Yet although the decoration is generic, the emblematic force of such elements could be revived when they wove a laurel, so to speak, for the individual shown in the accompanying cartouche, in this case a royal favourite.

The image is one of several that present Dudley in a manner appropriate to the favour he enjoyed, but which also emphasise the loyalty of a magnate whose father was executed after an abortive attempt to divert the throne from the Tudor line. Dudley and his brother Ambrose had to rebuild the family's reputation for being DROIT ET LOYAL, 'true and faithful', in the words of the motto at the base of the engraving. The military associations of the surrounding decoration, notably the armour, are therefore by no means inert; Dudley 'conceived his actions and martial ambitions within the French aristocratic code of the *noblesse d'epée*, which emphasised blood and social hierarchy as prerequisites for royal service and placed martial and natural law above civil and common law'.[8] He accordingly appears within the cartouche armed and holding the baton of a military commander, ready to serve his Protestant sovereign in the struggle against the Catholic powers of Europe, as he was later to do in the Dutch War of Independence. The portrait forms the prefatory image to the book of Joshua, the Israelite warrior numbered among the Nine Worthies, a favoured subject for Elizabethan mural paintings and civic pageantry. It is partly in that

---

[8] Mears, 'Courts, Courtiers, and Culture in Tudor England', 706.

Figure 2.   Robert Dudley, Earl of Leicester. Engraving, probably by Franz Hogenberg,
used for The Bishops' Bible (London, 1568), preface to Part II. From the copy in Trinity
College, Cambridge, C.5.8. Reproduced by permission of the Master and Fellows.

illustrious guise, as a Joshua for Protestant England in the later 1560s,
that Dudley appears here.[9]

At the top left of the picture, by a pair of dividers and a setsquare, is
another instrument for accurate measurement, a guitar:

[9] See Reader, 'Tudor Mural Paintings', reproducing an example recovered from a demolished building
in Amersham, originally a private house. For the Nine Worthies in mid-Tudor pageantry, see
Nevinson, 'A Show of the Nine Worthies', and on French precedents, Scheller, 'Gallia Cisalpina:
Louis XII and Italy 1499–1508'.

Specifications

- Although a book of music lies across the body and mostly obscures the waist, there is no doubt about the intended form.
- The fixed bridge and central sound-hole, with decorative rose, can be clearly seen.
- There are five strings, apparently single, and no frets.
- The sickle-shaped peg-box, without a carved human or animal head, shows three pegs.
- The shallow body appears to taper towards the base.

The presentation of the guitar has clear affiliations to materials in continental model books; the angle at which the instrument leans, and the device of decoratively obscuring the middle area of the soundboard with an overlaid object, both have precise parallels in the 1572 model book of Hans Vredeman de Vries, *Panoplia seu armamentarium* (Figure 3, the lower region of the file on the far left). This does not alter the fact that a guitar and a music book are here presented among the decorative accoutrements considered fitting for a portrait of an English nobleman. What is more, enlargement of the image discloses something easily missed by the naked eye: the open book of notation which lies over the instrument shows a four-

Figure 3.   Ornaments from Hans Vredeman de Vries, *Panoplia seu armamentarium* (Antwerp, 1572). Reproduced from Hollstein, *Dutch & Flemish Etchings, Engravings and Woodcuts 1450–1700*, vol. XLVIII.

Figure 4.   Detail of Figure 2.

line grid with markings which must be intended, given where the book
rests, to represent a printed or manuscript collection of tablature for the
four-course guitar (Figure 4).

II

The most lavish depiction of a guitar, not only from renaissance England
but also from sixteenth-century Europe, appears on the Eglantine Table,
now in the late-Elizabethan mansion of Hardwick Hall in Derbyshire
(Figures 5 and 6). This is a 'table' in the common Elizabethan sense of a
solid board or panel to carry a painting, or in this case elaborate
marquetry.[10] According to John Shute, who toured Italy in 1550, 'fine
woodes in marketrey' should be deployed 'as shal be thought plesaunt and

---

[10] For the term 'table' in this sense see Foister, 'Paintings and Other Works of Art', 275, and Cooper,
    Citizen Portrait, 26. The Table was cleaned and restored between November 1995 and March
    1997, but the conservation report does not suggest that the guitar was materially affected during the
    process. I am grateful to Dr Nigel Wright of Hardwick Hall for showing me the report. For studies,
    see Collins, 'A 16th-Century Manuscript in Wood', and Segerman and Abbot, 'Stringed
    Instruments on the Eglantine Table', both of which were published before cleaning. See also
    Grijp, 'Fret Patterns of the Cittern'. For commentary by art historians, see Wells-Cole, *Art and
    Decoration*, 250 and Plate 218. The Eglantine Table may be the 'inlayde table in the windowe' of
    the withdrawing chamber in 1601 (Levey, *Of Household Stuffe*, 47–8). The embroideries at the Hall
    have a richer bibliography than the Table and illuminate the social and political aspects of the
    opulence of Hardwick. See, for example, Levey's study mentioned above and Pick, 'The Worthy
    Ladies of Hardwick Hall'.

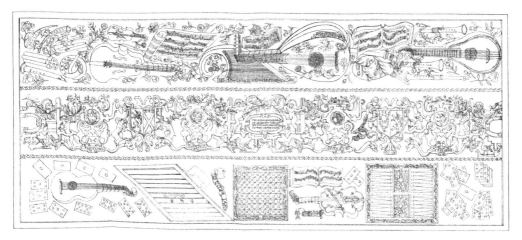

Figure 5.   The layout of the decorative scheme on the surface of the Eglantine Table.
Drawing by Llewellyn Jewell in *The Reliquary*, July 1882.

necessary for nobles and mighty princes', and that is certainly the case here.
The work was made for Elizabeth of Shrewsbury (d. 1608), better known
as Bess of Hardwick.[11] In 1567 Bess married her fourth husband George
Talbot, Earl of Shrewsbury, and the Table was probably made to commemorate their union, for the Talbot motto PREST ◊ D'ACOMPLIR is
displayed there in a prominent fashion.

The dense ornamentation makes extravagant use of strapwork, of the
scrolls characteristic of German *Rollwerk* and of vigorous grotesquerie.
Crowded among these elements are a guitar, a lute, a cittern, a harp and
several viols (or fretted violins) shown in exquisite but not always dependable detail, together with a bagpipe, cornetti, shawms, a recorder and an
S-shaped trumpet. The result is a lavish emblem of harmony and nuptial
concord, but also a reminder of the rich musical sounds that could be heard
in the life of a great house during a procession to dinner, perhaps, when
music was played in the great chamber, or when musicians came to the
door on New Year's morning. Nonetheless, the decorative scheme does not
only emphasise the secular pleasures of the nobility, often censured for
their 'gitternes, violes, and other instruments';[12] there is also a four-part
anthem by Thomas Tallis, *O lord in thee is all my trust*, duly attributed to
that master on part of an open scroll but texted no further than the first
seven words.

---

[11] Shute, *The First and Chief Groundes of Architectvre* (1563), Sig. Fi*. Hardwick ('new') Hall cannot
be the original home of the Table, for work began on that house only in 1590. The most likely
location immediately before Hardwick Hall is Chatsworth. For Bess herself there is Durant, *Bess of
Hardwick.*
[12] Bruto (trans. W. P.), *The Necessarie, Fit, and Conuenient Education of a yong Gentlewoman* (1598)
Sig. Hviij.

The Eglantine Table and the engraving of Robert Dudley are both indebted for their iconography to imported continental prints. The model book of Hans Vredeman de Vries, mentioned above, shows tangled instruments arranged in parallel files very reminiscent of the Eglantine Table (Figure 3); something very similar should probably be counted among the models that the Table craftsmen employed. They also acknowledged the Elizabethan fondness for enriched surfaces and (by continental standards) flattened figures to be seen in contemporary portraiture either by English artists or by continental painters aware of Tudor taste.[13] That susceptibility is even more marked in the two-dimensional birds, flowers and unicorns of Elizabethan embroidery, to which the makers of the Eglantine Table may also be indebted. Their work resembles the design of a magnificent carpet, dated 1579, also kept at Hardwick Hall, divided like the Table into three equal and self-contained files that run lengthwise.[14]

In terms of craftsmanship and technique, as opposed to iconography and design, the models for the Table lie with the Italian *intarsiatori*, the craftsmen in marquetry who exploited techniques for creating the illusion of three dimensions in two.[15] Sometimes, as at S. Maria in Organo in Verona, they chose complex polyhedrons, surpassingly delicate examples of the joiner's art, foreshortened by distance and subtly transformed in appearance by a slight tilt; more often, however, the *intarsiatori* selected objects of attractive form and admonitory value: an hourglass to inspire intimations of mortality, a book as a summons to learning or prayer. Musical instruments attracted these craftsmen because they were complex, fragile and refined artefacts of beguiling shape that could be read in various ways, some of them certainly admonitory. They appear lying on shelves or leaning within the compartments of fine cabinets whose doors have swung open towards the viewer, a favourite device of *trompe l'oeil* artistry ever since. Notable instances include the celebrated work at Urbino, Mantua and Gubbio, together with choirstalls in the cathedrals of Savona and Genoa; these all have *trompe l'oeil* depictions of musical instruments from a formative period in Western European lutherie.[16]

---

[13] See Frye, 'Ways of Seeing in Shakespearean Drama and Elizabethan Painting'; Gent, '"The Rash Gazer"'; Kury, '"Glancing Surfaces"'; Hazard, *Elizabethan Silent Language*, esp. 77–108; and Cooper, *Citizen Portrait*, esp. Ch. 1.

[14] Wells-Cole, *Art and Decoration*, Plate 430.

[15] The bibliography on this topic is naturally very extensive. White, *The Birth and Rebirth of Pictorial Space*, and Edgerton, *The Renaissance Rediscovery of Linear Perspective*, are fundamental works in English. For some more recent studies, see the papers in Dalai Emiliani, ed., *La Prospettiva rinascimentale*; Kuhn, 'Measured Appearances' and Sinisgalli, ed., *La prospettiva*.

[16] Pellini, *Strumenti musicali in tarsie italiane*; Bartoletti, ed., *Il coro ligneo della Cattedrale di Savona*; Cheles, 'The Inlaid Decorations of Federico da Montefeltro's Urbino Studiolo'.

The movements of ambassadors, often with substantial followings, may have allowed some potential patrons from England to view marquetry of this quality, and so may the presence of exiled English noblemen in Italy during the reign of Queen Mary.[17] There seems to be no documented case of Italian grand-scale intarsia being imported, or otherwise brought home, and it is difficult to imagine how any could have been transported; most of the known examples form part of relatively immoveable assemblages such as a panelled room or a set of choirstalls, rather than the kind of object that might be given as a diplomatic gift, such as a chest or a chair with an inlaid back.[18] Yet if the objects did not travel, the traditions of craftsmanship did move northwards, and a route can be traced in stages reaching northwards from Italy through German-speaking lands to England and especially to London.

By the last decades of the fifteenth century, craftsmen in Trentino and Tyrol were producing intarsia work of high quality under the influence of artists further south; the second decade of the sixteenth brings furniture with intarsias depicting polyhedrons, strikingly reminiscent of the best Italian precedent, from as far north as Nuremberg, with inlay of equal quality emerging from Neuburg, Ulm and Mainz.[19] The best available explanation for the quality and ambition of the Eglantine Table therefore probably lies with the several hundred immigrants from Germany and the Low Countries, craftsmen in cabinet making and furniture, who are traceable in England during the later sixteenth century, mostly south of the Thames in Southwark to elude regulation by the authorities of the city of London. They are variously called *scrynmaker* ('joiner', 'cabinet maker'), *kistmaker* ('maker of chests') and 'turner', and listed as natives of Flanders, Brabant, Germany, Cologne and Cleves, among other locations in Northern Europe. One might therefore ask of the Eglantine Table, as of some other great examples of Elizabethan furniture: 'Where could such a confection have been made except London, and where in London other than the Liberty known as Southwark [where] the expelled talents of Flanders, Holland and North-Western Germany gathered?'[20]

---

[17] Bartlett, 'The English Exile Community'. See further the same author's *The English in Italy 1525–1558*, and Overell, *Italian Reform and English Reformations*.

[18] There is one famous example of a chest with illusionistic intarsia being given as a diplomatic gift, namely the 'Plus Oultra' cabinet of *c.* 1530, now in the Victoria and Albert Museum, London, and possibly made for the apartments of the Emperor Charles VI in the Castello di Gonzaga when he visited Mantua. No such gift is known to have come to England.

[19] Kreisel, *Die Kunst des deutschen Möbels*, vol. i, 80–103, 'Die Intarsienkunst der spätrenaissance', including Abb. 113 (chest with intarsia, early sixteenth century, Tirol), 133, 158, 181 (ivory inlay of abstract shapes, including polyhedrons; possibly from Nuremberg, second quarter of the sixteenth century), 184 (Neuburg, *c.* 1560), 193–4, 195, 197–9, 200 (Ulm, 1569), 204 (Mülhausen), 214 (Innsbruck, *c.* 1570–80), 215 (? Tirol, 1560), 217–8 (Tirol), 273 (Mainz, *c.* 1555).

[20] Forman, 'Continental Furniture Craftsmen'. See also Pettegree, *Foreign Protestant Communities*, and Luu, 'Natural-Born versus Stranger-Born Subjects'.

Figure 6.   The guitar shown in marquetry on the Eglantine Table, now at Hardwick Hall, Derbyshire. Probably made to commemorate the marriage of Elizabeth ('Bess') of Hardwick to George Talbot, Earl of Shrewsbury, in 1567. Photograph by Marzena Pogorzały.

As Figure 6 reveals, the indebtedness of the Eglantine Table crafts-men to Italian precedent has its limits. They make no attempt to show the instruments in a feigned cupboard, or in any other kind of illusio-nistic space, and almost without exception each instrument is shown as if it were a heraldic emblem presented frontally, usually with a slight suggestion of depth and volume arising from a tilt that is often incon-sistent with the frontal view. The representation of the guitar provides a clear example. The soundboard is shown as if viewed from directly above, but the ribs imply a tilt. The bridge is viewed from above but also from slightly behind; the fingerboard is shown frontally but the neck is given a tilt that gradually increases until the peg-heads on the far side of the peg-box from the viewer become invisible. This is very much Elizabethan work.

Specifications
- The total length is 530 mm, the sounding string length 370 mm, the width of the wider bout 180 mm and of the narrower 143 mm. The depth, at its widest, is 25 mm.
- There are seven strings, presumably to be understood as a four-course arrangement with single *chanterelle*.
- There is the corresponding number of pegs, but the seven strings are not disposed into their courses.

- Comparison between the *chanterelle* and the lowest strings suggests an attempt to distinguish between a lighter and a heavier gauge on an instrument set up for a right-handed player.
- The elaborate rose is placed appreciably closer to the bridge than in contemporary continental representations.
- The junction of body and neck is curiously massive and shows no sign of a heel. The craftsmen have differentiated between the wood of the soundboard and that of the ribs, perhaps choosing materials employed by contemporary luthiers; the former appears to be made of spruce or pine. The neck, peg-box and ribs may be of maple.
- The fingerboard is distinguished by the use of a different timber, darkened with hot sand.
- The behaviour of the strings beyond the nut is impossible on an instrument tuned for play.

Prior to manufacture, the design of the guitar would have been drawn actual size on paper so that each component could be cut out and glued onto veneer that was either the required colour by nature or could be made so by dyeing or singeing. Once the design was cut out with a knife, the shaped veneer would be laid on the surface of the board and its outline traced on the bare top prior to excavation of the table surface with a sharp blade or shoulder knife. The motifs would then be glued in place and pressed during drying. Once dry, the surface would be scraped to ensure a uniform smoothness, polished and varnished.[21] In this process, the initial drawings were made with varying reference to actual instruments, or with only intermittent regard to the results of visual inspection; for the guitar, this even extends to elements that yield easily to measurement, such as the placement of the frets; no attempt has been made to copy the fretting to be seen on an instrument fit for use. Five virtually equidistant frets are shown reaching considerably further along the neck than they should and with inaccurate spacing, the error mounting as the frets proceed.

The fingerboard of an instrument built with these proportions could have accommodated eight frets, perhaps nine. The images of guitars in the French guitar books of the early 1550s, and the engraving traceable to Adrian Le Roy's lost guitar tutor, show eight frets (Figures 1, 18 and 20); in 1546, Alonso Mudarra required ten for the *guitarra* and Juan Bermudo, just under a decade later, also expected ten, although he allowed that 'small instruments, or those that play simple music, use only five or six'.[22] If the Hardwick Hall guitar is shown actual size, it is indeed a small instrument: a double-course Tudor ukulele.[23]

---

[21] I am grateful to Dr Nicholas Humphrey, Curator (Furniture, Textiles and Fashion Deptartment) at the Victoria and Albert Museum, London, for advice on these matters.

[22] Mudarra, *Tres Libros de Mvsica*, f. 71; Bermudo, *Declaracion*, Book IV, Ch. 65.

[23] The sole surviving example of what is probably an English cittern, now in the National Music Museum, Vermillion, South Dakota, has a scale length of 340 mm (inventory No. NMM 13500).

Figure 7.   Detail of the painted overmantel in the Summer Parlour
(now the Dining Room) at Hengrave Hall in Suffolk. Photograph by
Peter Forrester.

III

A painted overmantel at Hengrave Hall in Suffolk, formerly the home of
the Kitson family, shows an assemblage of musical instruments, on either
side of the pediment, that includes two guitars (Figure 7). The heraldry in
the centre of the piece displays the arms of Kytson impaling Cornwallis,
suggesting that the painting was done to celebrate the marriage of Thomas
Kytson II to Elizabeth Cornwallis in 1560, or perhaps the birth of their two
children if two images of infants in swaddling clothes held by mermaids
represent their offspring of 1563 and 1566. The complex heraldry indicates that shields were added to the painting at various times, and that
the mural as it now appears must therefore be the work of many decades.
The arms include Gage (with the badge of a baronet) quartering Darcy; the
earliest person entitled to these arms was Sir Edward Gage, created a
baronet in 1662.[24]

Specifications

- The larger guitar has a sounding string length of 380 mm, and the depth
  of the ribs at the heel is approximately 30 mm. No frets are visible and
  there are five strings, possibly repainted at some stage.

---

[24] For advice on these matters I am indebted to Edward Martin of the Suffolk Institute of Archaeology
and History, and to Dr Andrea Kirkham.

- The smaller instrument has a sounding string length of 320 mm, and the ribs at their deepest measure approximately 30 mm, considerable for its size.
- Two frets are visible on the smaller instrument after the nut.
- The smaller guitar has three strings and five pegs, the larger five strings and no visible pegs. The number of strings may have no precise significance, especially in view of the likelihood that there has been some degree of repainting.
- The sickle-shaped peg-box visible on the smaller guitar, with carved head, has a parallel in The Bishops' Bible and the Eglantine Table.
- Both guitars show a position for the sound-hole considerably more in accord with continental examples than at Hardwick Hall. (The serpentine sound-holes, somewhat reminiscent of the viol or violin, on the larger guitar may be a later addition.)
- The effects of time and over-painting make it difficult to assess the quality of the work when originally done, for many superficial details have been worn away – if they were ever painted – including the design of the rose on each instrument and the higher frets on the smaller guitar. Nonetheless, there are few traces to suggest first-class or metropolitan work and it therefore seems likely that this was a provincial production from the beginning.

Very little can be relied upon in these two depictions, but unless the two guitars were added later than the sixteenth century, which there is no reason to suspect, the overmantel shows that guitars of contrasting sizes were known in England, a valuable complement to the documentary record (which we shall soon encounter) showing that guitars were sometimes built in sets.

A considerably more lavish depiction appears on a carved panel of oak, now in the Victoria and Albert Museum in London, which shows Apollo and the Muses with musical instruments (Figure 8). Taken together with its frame, which is possibly of later date, this substantial piece measures 121 cm in height and 178 cm in breadth. In 1754, or thereabouts, the work was carted to Hockliffe Grange in Bedfordshire as William Wentworth, Earl of Strafford, dispersed some of the furnishings from the decayed Elizabethan manor house at Toddington, not far away. In all probability, therefore, Toddington was its original home. This was the seat of the Cheyney family in the later Elizabethan period, and if the date of *c.* 1580 commonly assigned to the overmantel is correct then it was made for Sir Henry Cheyney or for his widow Jane, to whom the property passed upon his death in 1587.[25] It would certainly have formed a luxuriant

[25] I am most grateful to Mr Philip Mead of Toddington for showing me a facsimile of a memoir of the late Major Cooper Cooper from *The Bedfordshire Advertiser* for Friday, 21 January 1898. This documents (1) the demolition of most of Toddington Manor in the first decades of the eighteenth century; (2) the sale of furnishings, including the overmantel, by the owner of the site, Earl Strafford, in 1745; (3) the purchase of the overmantel by an ancestor of Sir Richard Gilpin of

Figure 8.   Terpsichore with a guitar. Detail of the Apollo and the Muses panel, probably
from Toddington Manor, Bedfordshire. Late sixteenth century. © Victoria and Albert
Museum, London.

addition to a magnificent house, of forty-five hearths, where the royal court
was received on two occasions.[26]

Specifications

- The instrument has six strings, evidently intended to represent gut since
  the rope-like surface, arising from the twisting process, is shown in an
  exaggerated form on part of the highest course near the plucking hand,
  and perhaps on part of the lowest.
- The circular sound-hole, centrally placed, is filled with a foliate design,
  parts of which are visible with gilding.
- The depth of the body is greatest in the middle and tapers down to the
  neck, as to the foot, where the absence of a heel suggests (but does not

Hockliffe Grange; (4) the movement of the panel to Hockliffe Grange where it was placed in an
adjacent building called 'The Temple of the Muses'; and (5) the purchase of the piece, after Gilpin's
death, by Major Cooper Cooper of Toddington in 1882. The article also refers to a brochure 'On
the wood-carving of Toddington Manor', by Major Cooper Cooper, addressed to 'my very old
friend, Sir Richard T. Gilpin . . .'. Mr Mead informs me that the publisher was H. G. Fisher of
Woburn, and that the brochure appeared in 1885 (private communication, 21 April 2014). No
other trace of the brochure has so far been found.

[26] See the remarkable digital reconstruction of the Tudor house by Alan Higgs, http://slimshader.co.
uk/cheney's%20palace.pdf.

necessarily indicate) construction from an excavated block in the manner of the medieval gittern.

- There are no frets on the surface of the flush fingerboard, nor is there any trace of them looping around the surprisingly extended neck as may be seen on the lute depicted on this same overmantel.
- The string fastening is 'concealed' by the player's right hand.
- The back of the instrument could not be viewed.

The theme of Apollo and the Muses holding an array of musical instruments, with the Muses posed as a group around the god, has a long history in Tudor art beginning with a design for a pageant in the coronation procession of Ann Boleyn in May 1533, commonly attributed to Holbein. The chief but not the only source of the tradition, on a European scale, is Raphael's *Parnassus* in the Vatican, widely known beyond Rome from Marcantonio Raimondi's print *c.* 1514–20.[27] Later versions known in England include an alabaster panel, of exquisite quality, marked with the royal arms and the initials ER, now at Hardwick Hall and probably dating from the 1570s.[28] The Toddington overmantel may be of the same period. Both pieces are assuredly the work of foreign craftsmen resident in England since they far exceed what is known of native ability just as they depart from all but the most educated contemporary English taste. In contrast to the carved screen at Burton Agnes (*c.* 1600–10), or the hall screen at Speke (*c.* 1560), where somewhat flattened figures face outwards 'in an ordering governed by iconographic rather than visual relationships and rationalized by the principle of symmetry rather than of linear perspective',[29] the modelling of Apollo and his entourage here shows a relatively advanced knowledge of anatomy. The sense of bodily mass and balance in each figure is captured with an assured technique and the illusion of antique garments that ruck and fold is expertly managed.

The musical instruments comprise a guitar, two antique lyres, a treble viol or violin, a recorder, an oboe, a triangle, a lute and a hurdy-gurdy. There are signs of repair, sometimes revealed by hairline cracks in the wood, and since the recorder is modelled after a baroque instrument it must replace a lost original that was inserted into the composition. (The other wind instrument appears to be an oboe, for the bore is certainly conical, and the turning looks baroque.) After Apollo himself, the guitarist is the dominant figure in the group; she has one foot raised as if dancing, which identifies her as Terpsichore. Her guitar appears to be undamaged save for the loss of most of the gilding, some patches of which remain.

---

[27] Reproduced in Thompson, 'Poets, Lovers, and Heroes', 16.
[28] Wells-Cole, *Art and Decoration*, 253–4, and Figs. 426 and 427.
[29] Evett, 'Some Elizabethan Allegorical Paintings', 156.

It may seem surprising to find a guitarist in such antique company, but there is some precedent in the fifty engraved cards forming the so-called '*Tarocchi* of Mantegna'. Neither playing cards nor tarot, but perhaps 'a didactic game or simply an instructional booklet',[30] these prints emerged during the third quarter of the fifteenth century and were a major source for the transmission of Italian renaissance imagery to Northern Europe. Some show the Muses with various musical instruments, and the image of Terpsichore standing with a guitar, or a guitar-shaped instrument, was an established element in the tradition.[31] Furthermore, the presence of a guitarist on the Toddington overmantel does not seem so strange viewed in continental terms. The demotic air the guitar could possess in some contexts did not prevent Spanish writers from equating it with classical and biblical references to the *cithara*; Juan Pérez de Moya's *Philosofia secreta* (1585) evokes 'la guitarra de Orpheo', while Hieronymo Roman y Zamora gives the *guitarra* to Apollo in his *Republicas del mundo* (1595).[32] In France, Simon Gorlier maintained in 1551 that the Ancients were long content 'with such instruments as the *Guiterne*, which they called Tetrachordes', an allusion to the instrument of Mercury.[33] Gorlier's contemporary, the anonymous author of *La maniere de bien et iustement entoucher les Lucz et Guiternes*, noted that the four-course guitar 'strongly resembles the tetrachord of Mercury . . . which Boethius describes in the first book of his *De Musica*'.[34] The genetic relationship between the French words *guiterre/guiterne* and the Latin *cithara*, or Greek *kithara*, inspired some to suppose that the guitar was derived from the lyre of the Ancients. Pierre Trichet can still report this opinion as late as *c.* 1640, albeit with a disclaimer saying that he does not endorse it.[35] The Toddington overmantel is the supreme visual expression, in European art, of an antique context for the renaissance guitar.

IV

With the beginning of the Jacobean period, guitars appear in two drawings of the triumphal arches built for the passage of James I through London in

---

[30] Thompson, 'Poets, Lovers, and Heroes', 14. See also Seznec, 'Apollo and the Swans'.

[31] For examples see http://warburg.sas.ac.uk > iconographic database > gods and myths > muses > individual > Terpsichore.

[32] Juan Pérez de Moya, *Philosofia secreta*, 219; Hieronymo Roman y Zamora, *Republicas del mundo* (1595), vol. II, 301.

[33] Tyler, ed., *Simon Gorlier and Guillaume Morlaye, Le Troysieme Livre*, preface.

[34] *La maniere de bien et iustement entoucher les Lucz et Guiternes*, 96. Facsimile of the text in Saint-Arroman and Dugot, *Methodes et Traités, Luth*, vol. I, 25–53. The text is translated with commentary and good bibliographical introduction, including facsimiles and editions, in Reeve, 'A Mid Sixteenth-Century Guide to Fret Placement'. The author, however, did not believe the claim, based by some on the Spanish form *guitarra*, that the gittern was similar to the *cithara* of the ancient Greeks.

[35] For Trichet's comments see Saint-Arroman and Delume, *Méthodes et Traités, Guitare*, vol. I, 16.

Figure 9.   Detail of one of the triumphal arches built for the entrance of James I to London in March 1603, devised by Stephen Harrison and engraved by William Kip (*The Arch's of Triumph Erected in honor of the High and mighty prince James the first of that name*; first edition, 1604). Photograph by Michael Fleming.

March 1603. Devised by the 'joyner and architect' Stephen Harrison, they were drawn and engraved by William Kip for Harrison's *The Arch's of Triumph Erected in honor of the High and mighty prince James the first of that name* (first edition, 1604).[36] One instrument appears in 'The Deuice called *Hortus Euporiae*' or 'Garden of Plentie', built at the little conduit in Cheapside (Figure 9). On the left-hand side the nine Muses (without Apollo) appear seated holding a guitar, bass viol, lute, flute, cornet, antique lyre, cittern, hautboy and open book of music. The fingerboard and peg-box of the guitar are entirely obscured, but the incurved sides, a section of the ribs and the fixed bridge are visible. Another guitar appears in 'The Deuice called *Nova foelix arabia*', built at the great conduit in Cheapside. Here eleven musicians – seemingly real players, not wooden figures or

[36] For the engravings in this book, see Bergeron, 'Harrison, Jonson and Dekker', and Stevenson, *The City and the King*, Ch. 3, *passim*.

painted images – were placed in the uppermost tier of the arch, beneath the balustrade, playing various instruments with the guitar appearing in the immediate neighbourhood of a bass viol and a lute. (There may be a suggestion of a plectrum, strange though that may seem at this date.) Some or all of these musicians were presumably involved in the 'excellent Musicke' that was played just before the king moved on from this arch to the next. In a decorative context such as this, it is very uncertain whether this is evidence for the use of the guitar in consort, something for which English sources of the Tudor period provide no other evidence.

* * *

All the representations surveyed in this chapter draw upon the visual vocabulary of Western European art that expanded dramatically in the century between 1450 and 1550 and reached England through the circulation of printed books, the northward dissemination of Italian styles and techniques, the thriving trade in Flemish prints and the arrival in London of immigrant craftsmen, especially from Germany and the Low Countries.[37] The influence of Northern mannerism, with its elements of grotesquerie and strapwork like curling belts or scrolls of leather, can be seen in most examples, while the decorative motif of instruments stacked or piled in abundance, developed in Italian intarsias and Flemish prints, lies behind several examples. It is doubtful whether these representations can be called 'English' in any respect save that they were made for English patrons and show signs, here and there, of accommodation to Elizabethan taste. With the possible exception of the overmantel at Hengrave Hall, an elaborate but unrefined piece that may be native work, everything is either definitely or probably the work of continental artists. Since references to the gittern are fairly abundant in the literary and archival sources of the Marian and Elizabethan period, there is no requirement to draw the radical conclusion that the visual record has no bearing upon circumstances in England. It is precisely the cross-Channel connections revealed by the transmission of such continental iconographic models and lineages that make England's participation in the European culture of the renaissance guitar plausible.

---

[37] In addition to works cited in the notes above, see esp. Corbett and Lightbown, *The Comely Frontispiece*, and Wells-Cole, *Art and Decoration*; Ewing, 'Marketing Art in Antwerp'.

CHAPTER 2

Who owned a gittern?

Item by estimation iiij oz. of broken silver
Item a gitterne
Item xij paier of sheates and one sheate
Inventory of Dennys Bucke (1584)

I

Visitors to the house of Dennys Bucke, a yeoman in the Norfolk
village of Great Walsingham, might catch the sound of a gittern
beneath the cries of the geese that were loose in his yard. A few
decades earlier, prisoners taking exercise in the Tower of London, or
sitting by an arrow-slit window, could hear the sound of a fellow
captive playing the gittern. More such scenes can be recovered, or
legitimately imagined, for after 1550 references to the gittern begin
to multiply in many kinds of literary and archival records. (These
references are calendared below in Appendix B, to which the reader
is referred for details of all dated citations in this chapter.) Read in
broad context, this increase of material reflects a rise in the volume
of maritime trade that brought many new commodities, including
gitterns, to the Port of London. The mounting output of shipyards
in London, Ipswich and elsewhere during the later 1550s testifies
to the health, in England, of what has been called 'the modern,
novel and innovative sector' of most European economies during
the sixteenth century.[1] Those in a position to benefit purchased
imported looking-glasses, desks, perfumed gloves, musical instru
ments and many other commodities on a scale probably unknown,
in many cases, to their grandparents. The prominence of the gittern
in written sources after 1550, relative to the half-century before, also

---

[1] Scammell, 'British Merchant Shipbuilding'. Muldrew, *The Economy of Obligation*, 20–21, contests
the more pessimistic assessment in Jones, *Birth of the Elizabethan Age*. See also Unger, 'Shipping
and Western European Economic Growth', 88, and for further discussion Ball, *Merchants and
Merchandise* and Brenner, *Merchants and Revolution*.

reveals the special place that this portable, relatively inexpensive and companionable instrument had earned, together with the cittern, in a literate amateurism that began to gather strength in the 1500s (see Chapter 4). As a result of both developments, maritime and musical, even university men ceased to be the impecunious clerks of Chaucer's imagination, with no possessions save their books. A student who entered Trinity College, Cambridge in 1564 possessed 'a gitterne in a case' when he died, carefully kept with other valuables that included two small gold rings and a silver spoon (Appendix B, 1605).

The seminal period for the introduction of the gittern into England lies in the years around 1550. Some of the evidence for that interpretation has already been cited in the Introduction; we may now add more from the Books of Rates for the Customs House. These volumes were issued by the government, in print or manuscript, to standardise duties on imported merchandise for the benefit of the Crown; in something resembling alphabetical order, the books list the commodities brought into the Port of London and value them in consignments, often of a dozen or a gross, so that the officials will know the duty to be paid.[2] A much smaller section of each book then gives the outward rate on exports. The earliest surviving printed list, dating from 1545, contains the following entries for instruments and strings, but there is no sign of a gittern:

Table 1. Stringed instruments and strings in *The rates of the custome house bothe inwarde and outwarde the dyfference of measures and weyghts and other co[m]modities very necessarye for all marchantes to knowe newly correctyd and imprinted* (1545).

	£	s	d
Clarycordes the payre		2	
Harpe strynges the boxe		10	
Leutes with caces the dossen		48	
Leute stringes called mynikins the groce			22
Vials the pece		4	
Virginales the payre		3	4

[2] The core study of the Rate Books is Willan, ed., *A Tudor Book of Rates*, which prints and annotates the book for 1582. The valuations given for the imported commodities appear to be based on wholesale prices. See Dietz, ed., *The Port and Trade of Early Elizabethan London*. Fleming, 'Some Points Arising from a Survey of Wills and Inventories', discusses various aspects of these books relevant to the history of musical instruments.

By 1558, the situation has changed. Now the gittern finds a place:

Table 2. Stringed instruments and strings in the Book of Rates of the Custom House (1558) as enrolled in the Patent Rolls 4 and 5 Philip and Mary, Part III, TNA C 66/920, ff. 12d to 22d ('Cullen' = Cologne).

	£	s	d
Claricordes the paire		6	8
Gitternes the dosen		4	4
Harpe stringes the boxe cont[eyning] xij grosse		16	
Harpe stringes the grosse			16
Lewtes with cases *voc[ati]* cullen lutes the dosen	3		
Lewtes with cases *voc[ati]* venis lutes the dosen	12		
Lewte stringes voc. Mynykins the grosse		10	
Vialles the pece		6	8
Virginalles single the paire		16	8
Virginalles doble the paire		33	4

The marked increase relative to 1545 reveals the substantial rise in customs dues, an increase of some 75 per cent overall, that was part of a minor revolution in royal finances during the later 1550s.[3] Some of the new entries are evidently designed to secure higher payments on goods at the luxury end of the market; Venice lutes, for example, now yield more subsidy than the cheaper Cologne variety, a benefit to the Crown that the older and simpler classification did not procure. This explains, in general terms, why the later list is longer than the earlier and more discerning, but it does not clarify why the gittern is the only species of instrument in the 1558 book that is not mentioned in the earlier volume. Lutes, clavichords, harp strings, viols and virginals, but not gitterns, had all appeared before. To be sure, the 1545 inventory was probably inadequate when published, just as the 1558 version cannot have been complete; comprehensiveness in such matters lay beyond the resources of Tudor government. Taken as they stand, however, the two books imply that a new or newly invigorated supply of gitterns was coming into the Port of London by 1558. The revenue from the duty on them had evidently become worth the cost of collection.

If that encourages us to suppose that the gittern swiftly became a 'new fashion' around 1550, we do well to ask what it means to use such an expression in relation to conditions in the later sixteenth century, a period when the call for a return to 'old' rather than one for 'new' fashion in many aspects of life was often heard. Many published works of the later 1500s evoke a vanished but supposedly recoverable England lying somewhere just beyond the bounds of living memory: a land of dutiful

[3] Brenner, *Merchants and Revolution*, 56.

apprentices and country squires dressed in homespun clothes; of men
who did not claim to be gentlemen unless they bore a coat of arms
approved by the heralds; of aristocrats who never employed foreign
cooks.[4] Humanism, by disseminating an understanding of Roman
republican values, added another ideal past that could be used to point
to the vices, and the consequent dangers, of the present. In such a context
as this, many conservative commentators (which means the predominant
printed voices of the period) regarded a change in material things or
social customs as proof of newfangleness, an irresponsible fondness for
imported fashions and an inconstancy made manifest above all in an
appetite for constant change. The mildest manifestation of this newfangleness was a disdain for homely English manufacture; its gravest was
a restive and potentially treasonable dissatisfaction with the political
order. The gittern was one such commodity, for it lacked the long-
established traditions of the lute in England and was mostly imported
from abroad, as we shall see. That is one of the reasons why Nichol
Newfangle, the apprentice in an interlude of 1568, plays the gittern
(emphasis mine).

The vigour of the inward trade in commodities nonetheless brought
many imported goods to London that fostered a sharpened visual and
tactile awareness of new materials or designs; if it had not been so the
moralists would have had no cause for complaint. Tudor writers express
that awareness by using the word 'fashion' in its literal sense of a
particular design, or 'fourme of makynge', derived from its Latin ancestor FACTIONEM formed from FACERE, 'to make'.[5] A 'new fashion' in this
sense meant the novel appearance of a manufactured object.[6] Bowed
instruments with figure-of-eight bodies had been known in medieval
England for centuries, but the renaissance guitar with its incurved sides,
frets, circular sound-hole, fretwork or perforated parchment rose
and plucking technique was very apparent to the eye as a 'new fashion'
in this sense. This is part of what Thomas Whythorne is seeking to
capture when he reports that the gittern appeared 'strange' in the late
1540s (see Chapter 7).

An allusion from 1568 to a costly cradle, made after the 'new fashion'
and described as a commodity that a wealthy or aristocratic family might

[4] See, for example, Braham, *The institucion of a gentleman* (1555); Anon, *Cyuile and uncyuile life*
(1579); and for a survey, Warneke, 'A Taste for Newfangledness'.
[5] *OED*, sv 'fashion', n. See esp. the citation from the *Promptuarium parvulorum*, 'Fascyon or fourme of
makynge'.
[6] In contemporary sources, the items most often spoken of in this way are garments such as various
forms of cut shoes or slashed hose; the root of the modern sense of 'fashion' as something especially
pertaining to the garment industry began under the first Tudors. It is necessary to tread carefully,
however. When the question 'is there any fine apparrell fashionable for the Backe?' is posed in
Averell, *A meruailous combat of contrarieties* (1588), Sig. Aijv, the sense appears to be 'is there any fine
clothing *made* for the body?'.

possess,[7] is one of many sources that might be cited to show how goods made in a 'new fashion' were becoming associated with illustrious persons whom those less distinguished or prosperous might wish to emulate. Continental makers were producing opulent gitterns, sometimes with exotic woods, that were no doubt prized and enviable possessions. When Iberian colonists in the West Indies discovered a tree whose wood was very black and shiny, it was quickly employed 'to make dyuers musicall instrumentes, as Claricymballes, Lutes, Gitterns',[8] and there are a great many references to 'ebony' in the records of Spanish makers.[9] The original parts of the guitar made in Lisbon by Belchior Dias, dated 1581, have been variously identified as African blackwood, Kingwood and ebony.[10] In France, a similar use of rare hardwood explains Maurice de la Porte's 1571 description of the *guiterne/guiterre* as *hebenine*, 'made of ebony' (Appendix G). An Elizabethan eye associated such woods with inlaid decoration, the backs of the finest looking-glasses, miniature chests and comb cases; the sight of them evoked the 'puissant princes of Afrique' who traded in ivory, ginger and dates.[11]

Ronsard's reference to a *guiterre* marked with his name and his lady's *en chifre*, and Edward Courtenay's *ziffre . . . tailée sur une guitarre*, suggest that some of the more luxurious instruments were inlaid with various kinds of ornament: the *enjolivieures* or 'embellishments' of the guitar that impressed Pierre Trichet around 1640, together with the rose, which he regarded as the summit of the guitar maker's art.[12] One Spanish maker, Justo de Aguilera, is known to have been an accomplished worker in marquetry.[13] The atelier of a Parisian luthier in 1589 contained gitterns adorned with marquetry and a carved head (*à teste*), luxury features designed to enhance the pleasure of ownership; instruments without either head or inlay were listed as *guiternes communes* and were evidently of less value.[14] The woodcut traceable to Adrian Le Roy's lost guitar method shows an instrument *à teste* with inlay or a painted design on the ribs and rose; potential purchasers who picked up that book found themselves reaching, in effect, for the elegant possession depicted on the title page (Figures 18 and 20). London supported one of the most

[7] Guevara, *The dial of princes, compiled by the reuerend father in God, Don Antony of Gueuara, Byshop of Guadix* (1568), 148v.

[8] Eden, *The History of Trauayle in the West and East Indies, and other countreys* (1577), ff. 210v–211.

[9] Romanillos Vega and Winspear, *The Vihuela de Mano*, 23; see also 34 (an 'ebony' guitar made for the future King of Spain), 35, 64, 343 (an 'ebony' guitar with a sunken rose), 350 (Brazil wood and 'ebony' plus a white wood), 471 and 480.

[10] London, Royal College of Music Museum, RCM 171. There has been some dispute, which cannot be entered into here, as to whether the Dias instrument should be called a guitar or a vihuela.

[11] Blundeville, *M. Blundevile his exercises containing sixe treatises* (1594), 261.

[12] See Saint-Arroman and Delume, eds., *Méthodes et Traités, Guitare*, vol. I, 16, for a facsimile of Trichet's text.

[13] Romanillos Vega and Winspear, *The Vihuela de Mano*, 23.

[14] Documents in Lesure, 'La Facture instrumentale', 40.

cosmopolitan markets for foreign goods in Europe, to the despair
of conservative commentators. 'Some tyme we followe the fasshyon
of the Frenche men', wrote Thomas Becon in 1542, while 'another
time we wil haue a tricke of the Spanyyardes'.[15] The guitar makers of
France and Spain would have found many customers in England for
their work.

II

The first identifiable owner of the new gittern in England may be Henry
VIII. A spectacular inventory of royal possessions, made after the king's
death in 1547, lists 'foure Gitterons . . . they are caulled Spanishe vialles'.
The document incorporates material provided by the keeper of the royal
instruments, Philip van Wilder, so the term 'Spanishe vialles' is not the
invention of a harassed clerk but the choice of a trained musician.[16] Since
the four items are identified first as 'Gitterons', a term long associated
with plucked fingerboard instruments in England as elsewhere in
Europe, but are also called 'vialles', they were probably deposits from
the especially vigorous period of experiment in Western instrument-
making that took place during the decades on either side of 1500.[17]
The process is revealed with particular clarity by images in manuscripts
and panel paintings from Catalonia across the Western Mediterranean to
Italy; these sources show that makers experimented with many different
kinds of fingerboard instrument, often with incurved sides; they tried
them with or without frets, and created forms to be plucked with the
fingers or swept with a bow. Some instruments had flat bridges – ideal for
playing sequences of chords – others round. The instruments might be
played on the shoulder or held downwards in the lap when bowed; when
plucked, they were held across the chest. Some were perhaps intended for
both plucking and bowing. If there is any means to view Henry's
'Spanish vialles' as one particular constellation of these features, it
probably lies with the only known cognate of their name, recorded
in 1509 when the famous instrument maker Lorenzo da Pavia made a
viola spagnola for Leonora Gonzaga of Urbino. This has been plausibly
interpreted as a vihuela.[18]

---

[15] Becon, *A pleasant newe Nosegaye, full of many godly and swete floures* (1542), Sig. E iij*ͮ*.

[16] For van Wilder, see *ODNB*, sv 'Wilder, Philip van'; *BDECM*, sv 'Wilder, Philip van'; Pearsall,
'Tudor Court Musicians', vol. I, 156–8; Ward, *Music for Elizabethan Lutes*, vol. I, 1–6, to which
should be added Holman, *Four and Twenty Fiddlers*, 71–7 and Dumitrescu, *The Early Tudor Court*,
83–6.

[17] Woodfield, *The Early History of the Viol*, remains an important discussion of this question, notably
for its gallery of pictorial sources. For the need to broaden the scope of the subject beyond the frame
chosen by Woodfield, see Griffiths, 'L'essor et le déclin de la vihuela', 8–15. For various aspects, see
Bryan, '"Verie sweete and artificiall"'; Prizer, 'Isabella d'Este'; and Minamino, 'The Spanish
Plucked Viola'.

[18] Prizer, 'Isabella d'Este', 110–11.

After the execution of Henry Howard, Earl of Surrey, for high treason in 1547, the government swiftly arranged for his chattels to be inventoried. The result includes a 'Gyttorne' listed with various 'necessary Implements' such as hangings, tapestries and cushions. Since the gittern appears near some banners marked with Surrey's arms, and immediately before a set of spears decorated with a pennant, it may not be a musical instrument at all but rather the kind of military banner commonly called a 'guythorne' (spellings vary) from Middle French *guidon* in the same sense (see Appendix A). There is nonetheless something to be said on the other side, and not only because a guitar possibly marked with a monogram or other device would have caught the eye of officials who knew that the charge against Surrey had rested on his supposed abuse of heraldry. In 1532–3, Surrey spent a year at the French court with the bastard son of Henry VIII, Henry Fitzroy; both were accepted within the intimate circle of King Francis I and his sons. The writings of the contemporary poet Mellin de Saint-Gelais contain many references to guitars, including a *guiterre espaignole* given to Charles de Valois (d. 1545), a son of the French king who befriended Surrey during his French sojourn and long remembered him.[19] Late in 1532, and into the next year, Surrey was in Paris and close to the French king's family circle at a time when the lutenist and guitarist Albert de Rippe became a *valet de chambre du roi*.[20] Was Surrey's 'Gyttorne' a gift from those days in France? The earl's most recent biographer takes it to be 'a type of primitive guitar' and a pointer 'towards the kind of social audience before which Surrey read or played and sang his own poems or heard them sung'.[21] Perhaps it is only in the characterisation of the instrument as 'primitive' that we should correct him.

Seven years later, as we have seen, an instrument reported by two imperial ambassadors as a *guiterre* was passing between two high members of the English court, Edward Courtenay and Peter Carew. It was also in 1554 that the court lost Philip van Wilder, the musician who may have shown all courtiers, Courtenay and Carew included, what the gittern could render in accomplished hands. The remains of music more or less securely attributed to van Wilder, who died in 1554, give his name in various forms including Mr Phillipps and Philips. These recall an anonymous elegy for a lutenist named Phillips published in Tottel's 'Miscellany' of 1557, the outstanding mid-century collection of lyric verse in print:[22]

---

[19] Stone, ed., *Mellin de Saint-Gelais*, vol. 1, 94–5.

[20] For the visit and the core documents, see Sessions, *Henry Howard*, 95–107, and for de Rippe, Oxford Music Online, sv 'Ripa, Alberto da', and Nordstrom, 'Albert de Rippe'.

[21] Sessions, *Henry Howard*, 172.   [22] Ward, *Music for Elizabethan Lutes*, vol. 1, 3–6.

Of the death of Phillips
Bewaile with me all ye that haue profest,
Of musicke tharte by touche of coarde or winde:
Lay down your lutes and let your gitterns rest,
Phillips is dead whose like you can not finde.
5   Of musicke much exceadyng all the rest,
Muses therefore of force now must you wrest,
Your pleasant notes into an other sounde,
The string is broke, the lute is dispossest,
The hand is colde, the bodye in the grounde.
10   The lowring lute lamenteth now therfore,
Phillips her frende that can her touche no more.[23]

Although the subject of this poem is a musician, the poet forswears the four-beat line of so much Tudor song and chooses instead the higher style of the spacious pentameter. In decasyllables with a scrupulous 4 + 6 caesura throughout, he wittily makes the words 'an other sounde' introduce a new rhyme in line 7, answered only by the bleak reference to the 'grounde' in which van Wilder is laid. It is also cunning of him to restrict alliteration to the first letter in the name of van Wilder's chief instrument, the lute. The poet has made a series of careful choices, and it is likely that he calls upon musicians to lay their gitterns aside, as well as their lutes, because van Wilder was associated with both instruments.

At the apex of the court, a document of 1559 shows Queen Elizabeth receiving a 'Chest with thre Getternes' as a New Year's gift, subsequently put into the care of a Groom of the Privy Chamber, the lutenist Thomas Litchfield.[24] These were doubtless luxurious instruments, for anything less would have been highly inappropriate; in 1579 Litchfield himself will give the Queen 'a very fayre Lute the backeside and necke of mother of perle the Case of crymsen vellat enbrawdered with flowers and the inside grene vellate'.[25] No such identifying description was necessary for the three gitterns, for there was no mistaking them once they had been inventoried as a boxed assemblage of three. This evidence that gitterns in groups of three were known to the highest in the land is strikingly confirmed by a 1563 inventory of goods at Raby Castle, near Durham, belonging to Henry Neville, the spendthrift Earl of Westmorland whose wooden effigy still lies, not far from the castle, in Staindrop church. Despite the faded and damaged state of the document, one may read that the items found included 'j caise wᵗʰ iij gittrons'.[26] Here therefore is a second trio, kept in a 'caise' by the Nevilles just as the first was presented to Queen Elizabeth

[23] Tottel's 'Miscellany', poem 179.
[24] For Litchfield see Lawson, ed., *The Elizabethan New Year's Gift Exchanges*, 678, and Ward, *Music for Elizabethan Lutes*, vol. 1, 62, n. 164 (references to him in the accounts of John Petre).
[25] Lawson, ed., *The Elizabethan New Year's Gift Exchanges*, 256.
[26] TNA DL 44/96, on the verso of the first leaf devoted to possessions at Raby Castle.

in a 'Chest'. These sound like custom-made containers with sets of gitterns, presumably of different size. We shall return to them.[27]

Two further examples of ownership at the highest level pose a delicate problem. The library of Lambeth Palace in London holds a ledger kept by John Whitgift, future Archbishop of Canterbury, while he was Master of Trinity College, Cambridge; the accounts are mostly devoted to items bought for various pupils at the college and are naturally dominated by essentials such as candles, laundry services and (occasionally) books. One entry, dated 1571, records an expenditure of ten shillings for 'A gitern lute', purchased for George Clifford, Third Earl of Cumberland. This nobleman, painted by Nicholas Hilliard, the owner of a spectacular array of tournament armour that still survives and a poet whose work was set by Anthony Holborne, was a courtier of the highest order, but what was the expensive instrument purchased on his behalf? Although the term 'gitern lute' seems odd, it is not unparalleled; the presents offered to Elizabeth I on New Year's Day in 1584 included 'a spannyssche Gyttorne lute' in a fine velvet case. The grammar of the expression 'gittern lute' in both documents, with its simple apposition of two nouns, might be compared with 'a taffeta hat' in John Whitgift's ledger or indeed with any similar collocation in English formed of a predicate followed immediately by a subject, such as 'silk scarf' or 'ink stand'. The structure is 'gittern' (predicate) 'lute' (subject), and the instrument is therefore essentially a lute that is somehow built or set up 'gittern' fashion. One possibility is that these instruments were strung with six courses like a lute, and therefore had that instrument's musical scope, but were built in gittern fashion, that is to say with a guitar-like waist. If so, we may be dealing once more with a vihuela, which might explain why the record of the royal gift calls the instrument 'spannyssche'.

There are still traces of court interest in the gittern as late as 1574, at least among gentleman servants. In that year a writer with a court position, Edward Hellowes, Groom of the Leash, published a translation of Latin letters by the Spanish prelate Antonio de Guevara. In one of the original letters Guevara advises his correspondent that it is not wise to entrust any business to amorous young men:

I think that you should no longer employ men struck with the dart of Cupid for the discharge of your business. It is not for lovers to transact weighty and difficult matters, but rather to walk hither and thither, peering round all the corners of houses, lingering about the windows and threshold of their sweetheart with sighs, discreet coughs and song by night . . .[28]

---

[27] For the question of sizes, see further below, 102–4.

[28] 'Censeo ne posthac homines Cupidinis telo percussi opera in negocijs tuis expediendis vtaris. Amantium non est seria et ardua negocia tractare, sed interdiu obambulare, et aedicum angulos omnes obscurare, noctu Musico carmine, suspirijs, screatu, fenestras at amicae limen frequentare . . .'. Quoted from the Cologne edition of 1614 (*R. P. D. Antonii de Guevara Episcopi Mondiniensis . . . Epistolae*), 194.

When Hellowes came to translate this passage he decided that this evocation of young men in love needed the addition of a gittern:

If you will credit me, to men inamored you shall neuer commend your busines: For his office is not to be occupied in other affaires, but in writing letters, watching at corners, playing on gitterns, climing on walles, and vewing of windowes.[29]

Hellowes is presumably thinking of young men in England, perhaps including grooms and other gentlemen in court service like himself.

Despite some uncertainties, these sources suggest that the gittern may be assigned a place in court culture. That term conveys more than what took place in the chambers and corridors of the royal residences during long summer afternoons, or the winter revels; the culture of the Tudor court comprised everything in the 'court-centred, elitist and consensual' environment around the monarch with its play as well as its policy, its diversions as well as its deliberations.[30] In such a context there could never be anything entirely trivial about a new court fashion. That is what makes Edward Courtenay's use of an inscribed gittern to subvert the politics of Mary's court so subtly treasonable.

III

Beyond the confines of the court we look first to those who were necessarily drawn to it: the members of the gentry families that served the Crown in some capacity while sustaining a life as landowners, keepers of dependants and employers on their estates. An early owner of this kind was Sir William More, Member of Parliament at various times for Guildford and holder of many public offices including Chamberlain of the Exchequer, Justice of the Peace for Surrey and Commissioner for Recusants and Seminaries. More received the Queen in his Surrey home at Loseley House on several occasions, where his panelled library still survives with a carved overmantel showing the royal arms and initials; there is also a sombre portrait showing him with a white beard of patriarchal proportions and facing a skull as a *memento mori* (inviting an obvious pun upon his name).[31] More's own inventory of his house in 1556 reveals that his parlour contained a portrait of Henry VIII, hangings of green silk, a chessboard, various items of furniture, virginals, a bass lute and 'a gittorne' that he valued at eight shillings, the kind of price perhaps only explicable in terms of the

[29] *The Familiar Epistles of Sir Anthony of Gueuara* (1574), 175.
[30] Lake and Pincus, 'Rethinking the Public Sphere', 271. See also the excellent survey by Mears, 'Courts, Courtiers, and Culture in Tudor England'.
[31] *ODNB*, 'Sir William More', found in 'More, Sir Christopher'.

exotic woods and inlay mentioned above. With his substantial library of classical texts and his collections of verse in English and Italian, More was a mid-Tudor gentleman of some scope, witnessed further by the *all'antica* decorative panels that he possessed, in the best Anglo-Florentine taste.[32]

Another owner in high royal service was Sir Richard Worsley of Appuldurcombe, Captain of the Isle of Wight and therefore responsible for a highly sensitive area of the realm's coastal defences. Upon his decease in 1565, officials came to his mansion on the island to inventory his goods. It was not going to be a quick affair, however, for Worsley had been a person of wealth and consequence, if somewhat overshadowed by the man his widow had chosen for her next husband, Francis Walsingham. Twenty-two membranes of parchment, now in the Record Office of the Isle of Wight, were needed to make a record satisfactory to all parties.[33] A section of the roll entitled 'Aparelle and Stuffe that were in divers places' includes various musical instruments without specifying where in the house they were kept. There was 'an ould paire of Virginalls', a 'Collayne lute with a case locke and kaye', valued at ten shillings, and a 'Gitthorne' worth five. The house has long vanished, but a drawing from the early eighteenth century survives to evoke one grand residence of the 1560s where a gittern could be heard (Figure 10).

Sir William Petre (d. 1572), the son of a Devon tanner who rose to become a senior figure in the government under four monarchs, serving as Senior Secretary to the Privy Council during his later years, is one of the best-documented owners in this high-ranking group. A book of accounts, kept by Petre's London steward John Keyme, now in the Essex County Record Office, records a payment for a viol and some accessories on 11 June 1550, together with a gittern:[34]

June Wednesday the xj day

	s	d
for a small vyall	13	4
for a gyttron	6	
for a canvas bagge to put the viall in		4
for vyall strings		12
for the frenchemans charges		4

---

[32] Sicca and Waldman, eds., *The Anglo-Florentine Renaissance*, 293 and Plate 112. Gunn's essay 'Anglo-Florentine Contacts', in the same volume, provides useful and broader context of More's Italianate reading.

[33] Newport, Isle of Wight Record Office, JER/WA/36/7. For Worsley, see Bindoff, *The House of Commons 1509–1558*, vol. III, sv 'Worsley, Richard'.

[34] Essex County Record Office D/DP/A4. The manuscript is neither foliated nor paginated. For the Petre family as musicians and patrons, see Emmison, 'John Petre's Account Books'; Mateer, 'William Byrd, John Petre'; and Price, *Patrons and Musicians*.

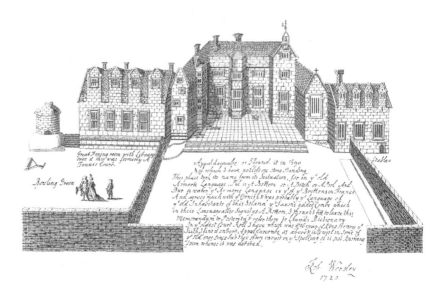

Figure 10.   Old Appuldurcombe House on the Isle of Wight, as Sir Richard Worsley
remembered it in 1720, by which time he had utterly demolished the building,
leaving 'not . . . one stone standing', as he proclaims in his signed and dated note.
Hall, parlour, chapel, staircase, stable, bowling green and great dining room, with a
library, are all indicated. From R. Worsley, *The History of the Isle of Wight*
(London, 1781), 180.

The gittern was considerably less expensive than the viol, but the price
nonetheless amounts to more than half what Petre paid some of his
servants at Ingatestone for an entire quarter. The instrument was perhaps
a present for his second wife, Anne Browne, for one of his daughters or
possibly for one of his wards; he may even have wanted it for himself.
Whatever the case may be, the payment 'for the frenchemans charges' is
arresting. Another book of Petre's accounts, kept by the steward of his
principal seat at Ingatestone, shows that this 'Frenchman' was no mere
courier. A wage list for 18 October 1550 gives the Michaelmas payments
due to a wide range of dependants and servants from a curate to a cartboy,
and here a Frenchman appears again, presumably the same individual.
Now he is named and is clearly a musician:[35]

To John þᵉ frenchman þᵗ playeth on þᵉ instruments 10s

John had resided in Petre's household since at least mid-June, and was
still at Ingatestone in mid-November when the accounts record the
purchase of his new shoes. The possible significance of this emerges
from the gap in Petre's London accounts between 22 April and 19 May
1550, just before the record of the purchase of the gittern. During this

[35] Essex County Record Office D/DP/A10. The manuscript is neither paginated nor foliated.

period Petre was in France to help negotiate the return of Boulogne-sur-Mer to the French king in return for a substantial payment. Petre sailed on 23 April, his second trip that year on this business, and with the other English representatives he met the French court, in circumstances of considerable splendour, at Amiens. He left for home on or about 12 May.[36] It is unlikely to be a coincidence that Petre acquired his gittern so soon after the second and last of his two diplomatic journeys to France in 1550. The year of that embassy is precisely the one that offers our first glimpse of what an elegant and literate art performance on the *guiterne* had become in France, for it was then that Michel Fezandat issued his *Tablature de guiterne où sont chansons, gaillardes, pavanes, bransles, allemandes, fantaisies.*[37]

Although that volume is lost, it was probably a first edition of *Le Premier Livre de Chansons, Gaillardes, Pavannes, Bransles, Almandes, Fantaisies* that Robert Granjon and Michel Fezandat issued in 1552.[38] After two fantaisies, presenting few technical difficulties but of high quality, the collection launches into eight chanson settings, among them pieces by Claudin de Sermisy and Clément Jannequin. These are followed by a large selection of items in dance forms, including branles and allemandes but predominantly galliards. Here was repertoire to show Petre that a guitar would allow him to carry home the music of a continental dance band in a servant's saddlebag (Example 2).

The residences of great men were ideal places for one of the less conspicuous drivers of consumption and fashion in the Elizabethan period to operate: the process whereby the household served to show sons, daughters, wards, secretaries and visitors what the cosmopolitan contacts of wealthy men were newly bringing to notice. Great households, especially, sheltered a shifting population of young men, some in more or less temporary situations as secretaries, others in longer-term accommodation as wards. Petre had various young men living with him at Ingatestone in the kind of familial and affective context, but with the members having different blood, for which modern Western experience offers no close parallel.[39] The interests and enthusiasms of a powerful patron like Petre were not easy to ignore, especially if one were dependent upon him for the chance of a university education, like two of his wards, or even for a period of attendance at court, like another. It had long been the custom for the

---

[36] For this episode see Emmison, *Tudor Secretary*, 88–9; the dates are established by *Calendar of State Papers (Spain)*, 1550–2, at 87–8.

[37] Brown, *Instrumental Music*, [1550]₂.

[38] *Ibid.*, 1552₅. For a facsimile see Tyler, *Simon Gorlier and Guillaume Morlaye*.

[39] A gittern coming into Petre's residences at London or Ingatestone would have arrived among women and wards whose names we know. In addition to Petre's son John there were the four daughters of his wife's first and second marriages, together with Edward Sulyard, John Eiston, Thomas Leigh and John Gostwick. Emmison, *Tudor Secretary*, and *ODNB*, sv 'Petre, Sir William'.

Example 2.   Guillaume Morlaye, Gaillarde, from *Le Premier Livre de Chansons, Gaillardes, Pavannes, Bransles, Almandes, Fantaisies, reduictz en tabulature de Guiterne par Maistre Guillaume Morlaye ioueur de Lut* (Paris, Robert Granjon and Michel Fezandat, 1552), ff. 16v–17.

young men in a household to learn a musical instrument, if they were capable, as part of their service and hope for preferment. *The Boke of Nurtur for men seruauntes and children*, by Hugh Rhodes, a member 'of the Kinges Chappell', published in six editions from (?) 1545 to 1577, leaves no doubt that young men should 'use honest pastime, talke or singe or some instrument use', for their masters will not decline to listen to them even though they be of superior station.[40] Petre, whose interest in music is well attested, would surely not have refused.

IV

Inventories of property *post mortem*, drawn up for probate, reveal the gittern in more modest contexts than the mansions of knights such as William More, Richard Worsley or William Petre.[41] University men,

[40] Rhodes, *The boke of nurtur for men seruauntes and children*, Sig. Ai.
[41] The more prosperous yeomen, craftsmen, shopkeepers and artisans, wealthier merchants and gentry dominate these records, while members of the nobility are rarely represented (for their inventories it is generally necessary to consult what remains of their household archives in private or public repositories). This means that the records omit a substantial proportion of the population, comprising the cottagers, labourers, husbandmen and others who were too poor to merit a listing of their goods. Regrettable though this may be, it probably represents no grave distortion of the historical picture, for the majority of Tudor labourers, husbandmen and yeomen may never have aspired to possess a stringed instrument of any kind, unless it were homemade. This was not necessarily because instruments were expensive; even some of the poorer artisans could have purchased a modest gittern outright with the ready money in their purses, to judge by what their executors found; it was rather because money could not be spared from more urgent needs. The use

students and Fellows of colleges, provide the richest lode of material, for Oxford and Cambridge were proving increasingly attractive to young men of gentry background during the later sixteenth century; lodged in colleges of brick or stone – country houses, in effect, set down in a city – they prepared themselves for entering what was still predominantly a patron-client society by cultivating the gentlemanly arts. Cambridge documents make the remarkable extent of instrument ownership among such persons especially clear. Between 1535/6 and 1605 there are Cambridge inventories, readily accessible and calendared in a recent edition, for 179 individuals, most of them Fellows of colleges but also a few domestics;[42] 32 of these men owned a musical instrument, meaning (in descending order of frequency) a lute, a pair of virginals, a clavichord or a gittern. By adding those who possessed 'a luting book' or something similar, but who are not otherwise on the list, we raise the number to 36.[43] This represents just over 20 per cent of the total – a spectacularly high level of ownership relative to non-university men. Four individuals were found to possess instruments the executors chose to identify as gitterns – none of them before 1559/60.

One is a college domestic named John Walker, the butler of Peterhouse College (inventory of 1559/60). Responsible for the food and wine of the buttery, he represents a class of respectable and professionally successful townsmen flourishing as servants in the colleges of the universities who

of a musical instrument required a measure of release from the daily struggle to keep hunger and cold at bay. Even among the records of the more prosperous individuals there are many inventories listing fine textiles, hangings and elaborate furniture, arranged in a dozen rooms or more, but no instruments. In general, this is probably because the makers of the inventories were concerned above all with objects that helped to constitute a household and could therefore be sold on; a musical instrument was a more personal and specialised possession than fire tongs, a truckle bed or a spit, and it cannot always have been easy to find a buyer, not least because some instruments were no longer in a playable condition when they were inventoried. (Virginals, we may suspect, were rarely missed, even when they were dilapidated, for they were significant pieces of cabinetwork.) Some instruments were passed on to members of the deceased's family, or to friends, before the inventory was made (to judge by the way they are sometimes mentioned in wills but not in the accompanying inventories). We may also be sure that many executors did their work in a cursory and even a dishonest manner; phrases such as 'thinges unseene and unknown' or 'certayne other stuffe' are not rare, and there are even cases where a comprehensive valuation is offered for everything in a particular room, without the goods being itemised or even viewed. Some of the instruments that occur in the inventories are listed as old or damaged, while some were stored with arrows, old mattresses and other such goods, suggesting objects that are on their way to becoming lumber or already there. See, for example, Crossley, 'A Templenewsam Inventory', 99, for a 'Chappel Chambre' containing a lute, a crossbow, arrows and old mattresses. For probate inventories and their use, see Arkell, 'Interpreting Probate Inventories'; Shephard and Spicksley, 'Worth, Age, and Social Status in Early Modern England'; Spufford, 'The Limitations of the Probate Inventory'. For specific uses see Garrard, 'English Probate Inventories'; Foister, 'Paintings and Other Works of Art in Sixteenth-Century English Inventories'; and Howard, 'Inventories, Surveys and the History of Great Houses 1480–1640'. For the importance of some of these sources, notably testaments and lists of possessions, for the historian of musical instruments, see Fleming, 'Some Points', and 'An "Old Violl"'.

[42] Leedham-Green, *Books in Cambridge Inventories*. List of instruments at vol. II, 826, but unaccountably omitting Edward Lively (d. 1605), who owned a gittern. I have included Lively in my account.

[43] *Ibid.*, 563–4.

might themselves be men of some learnèd interests (we shall return to his small library of books). The Fellows of colleges include George Allsope of Queens', a curate, whose possessions, in addition to a substantial library with some medical but otherwise mostly standard works, encompassed a 'gyttourne' valued at 20*d*. The most remarkable Cambridge example, however, is Thomas Lorkin, Regius Professor of Physic. His effects after his death in 1591 included his arms engraved on glass, a very extensive library of 631 volumes and a small collection of stringed instruments comprising 'a lute with a case and 2 Gittornes' which he kept in Trinity Hall where he had rooms.

We gain some sense of what these instruments meant to Lorkin through references to music and the scholar's life in his *Recta Regula et victus ratio pro studiosis et literatis* (1562), a compilation of dietary and other advice compiled from ancient authorities, such as Galen, but with an eye to the conditions of Tudor Cambridge, surrounded by undrained fens, pestilential in the summer and with a perennially damp atmosphere in winter. By the time Lorkin wrote this work, practical books on health and regimen formed one of the best-established streams of self-help books among the Tudor prints, having begun handsomely with Sir Thomas Elyot's *The Castel of helth* (1539), and Lorkin preserves Elyot's interest in the proper nurture of men who must spend long hours in study. His principal concern in the relevant passage is melancholy, the scholar's disease, and the deleterious effects of this phlegmatic condition upon health. Mental diseases are often more dangerous than physical ones, he argues, so those weighed down with study should lighten their spirits with *lyra* and *cithara*, perhaps meaning lute and gittern if precise identifications are intended, as they may well be.[44]

The Oxford owners include Ralph Allen, Fellow of Balliol College and a curate at the church of St Giles (inventory dated 1561–2). His possessions included a standard teaching collection of theological books showing signs of the new interest in Greek, and his other reading was not exclusively in Latin for he also owned 'a french boke'. Allen's gittern had lost its bridge, but it is exceptional for the instruments of university men to be listed as either old or damaged in this way. For the students perhaps never intending to remain in the university very long, we have the

---

[44] *Recta Regula et victus ratio pro studiosis et literatis*, 14. See Sayle, *The Library of Thomas Lorkin*. The heroic couplet quoted by Lorkin, 'Tange liram digitis animi dolor omnis abibit/Dulcisonum reficit tristia corda melos' is from *De tuenda bona valetudine libellus* by Helius Eobanus Hessus, 17. Cf Timothie Bright, *A Treatise of Melancholie* (1586), 247–8: ' . . . not onely cheerefull musicke in a generalitie, but such of that kinde as most reioyceth is to be sounded in the melancholicke care: of which kinde for the most part is such as carieth an odde measure, and easie to be discerned, except the melancholicke haue skill in musicke, and require a deeper harmonie. That contrarilie, which is solemne, and still: as dumpes, and fancies, and sette musicke, are hurtfull in this case, and serve rather for a disordered rage, and intemperate mirth, to reclaime within mediocritie, then to allowe the spirites, to stirre the bloud, and to attenuate the humours, which is (if the harmony be wisely applyed) effectually wrought by musicke'.

Oxford letter of 1562 from Thomas Madock, servant to one John Somerford.[45] The text reveals that Somerford was 'verye desirous' to have 'a gitterne and bowe and arrows', which Madock considered necessary for his young charge, presumably because they were important if Somerford were to cut a proper figure in Oxford. The longbow was increasingly regarded, with a measure of nostalgia, as the source of England's military victories in an age before gunpowder. The ethos of the gittern was the opposite, for even though music and shooting were both pastimes for gentlemen – Roger Ascham weighs their competing claims in his *Toxophilvs* of 1545 – the gittern thrived on peace, was new and was foreign. Read in this way, John Somerford's request for a bow and arrows and a gittern implies a surprisingly wide range of means to project an image of gentlemanly accomplishment.

Beyond the confines of the universities, a gentleman who owned both a lute and gittern appears in the person of William Calley of Hatherden in Hampshire. Calley belonged to a gentry family whose fortunes had flourished in the cloth trade under his grandfather and namesake (d. 1515), twice a Member of Parliament, Warden of the Drapers' company, a Merchant Adventurer and Master of Blackwell Hall in London where cloth was gathered for sending to the finishing markets in Bruges, Ghent and Antwerp. Hatherden was one of the family estates.[46] Our William Calley's will of 1558, now in the Hampshire Record Office in Winchester and written a few days before his death, is markedly Catholic in emphasis, for it bequeaths his soul 'to Allmyghty God and to oure blessyd Lady the vyrgyne and to all the holy company in heaven'. There are some small donations to the maintenance of Andover parish church, where he asks to be buried, and to the Mother Church of Winchester, together with various gifts to family and the provision that a quart of wheat should be baked for the poor. The will also shows that he owned a lute and a gittern with the former on loan to a certain Mr Alford who might conceivably be the J. Alford who translated *A briefe and easye instru[c]tion to learne the tableture to conducte and dispose thy hande vnto the lute* (1568).[47] Calley refers in the

---

[45] I am grateful to Dr Michael Fleming for a personal communication about Madock, from which I extract the following: 'I wonder if he could be connected with the Thomas Maddockes who applied for an alehouse licence in Oxford in 1601? Supporting the application were two musicians and a joiner, and having an alehouse licence was very common among musicians in Oxford. He would have been pretty old then, which may make it less likely, though perhaps alehouse keeping was felt to be easier than performing, for an old man. On the other hand, a Thomas Maddoxe/Maddockes took apprentices as a joiner in Oxford in 1588, 1590, 1593, 1594, 1601, 1606 and 1609 so perhaps he is a more likely candidate.'

[46] Bindoff, *The House of Commons 1509–1558*, vol. I, sv 'Calley, William'. For the family pedigree and arms, see Metcalfe, *Visitation of Wiltshire 1565*, 11. For Hatherden, see Wiltshire and Swindon History Centre, Archives 1178/245, an undated rental of the estates of John Calley of Hatherden, Hampshire, lying at Highway and Clevancy in the parish of Hilmarton, Wilts., at Orsett in Essex, and at Knights Enham, Andover, Hatherden and Winchester in Hampshire.

[47] Price, *Patrons and Musicians*, 23, identifies John Alford with the member of Pembroke College, Cambridge of that name in 1545 (Venn, *Alumni Cantabrigienses*, sv 'Alford, John').

testament to 'my lute and my gyttorne', the note of possessiveness leaving little doubt that he was (or had been at one time) a player of both instruments.

The gentleman who has most to say about himself and the gittern, however, is Robert Langham, author of a letter describing the 1575 celebrations staged at Kenilworth Castle by Robert Dudley for Queen Elizabeth. According to his own account, and in the spelling that he invented for himself:

> In afternoons and a nights, sumtime am I with the right woorshipfull Syr George Howard, az good a Gentlman az ony lyuez: And sumtime at my good Lady Sydneys chamber, a Noblwooman, that I am az mooch boound vntoo, az ony poor man may be vntoo so gracioous a Lady: And sumtyme in sum oother place: But allweyz amoong the Gentlwemen by my good wyll (O, ye kno that cumz allweyz of a gentle spirit) and when I see cumpany according, than can I be az lyuely too: sumtime I foot it with daunsyng: noow with my Gyttern, and els with my Cyttern, then at the Uirginallz: Ye kno nothing cums amiss to me: then carroll I vp a song withall, that by and by they cum flocking aboout me lyke beez too hunny: and euer they cry, anoother good Langham another.[48]

Langham was a mercer who became Keeper of the Privy Council Chamber from 1572 until his death in late 1579 or early 1580, a position that required him to provide 'flowers, cushions, fire shovels, tongs, bellows, and the like' for the Council meetings.[49] Despite this relatively modest position, he claims some distinguished company for himself in this passage, including Robert Dudley's sister, Mary Sidney; even when Langham was not moving in such exalted circles as these he passed some evenings with gentlewomen where his dancing, singing and performances on the gittern, cittern and virginals had them crowding round him and calling for more ('another, good Langham, another'). Here, therefore, is a gentleman and minor court official cultivating the gittern as a particularly companionable form of social aspiration, and the English sources of music for the instrument do not lack pieces for an occasion where there was a general desire to 'foot it with daunsyng' (Example 3).

A curious case of gittern ownership among gentlemen emerges with Francis Saunders. In 1562, this person was allowed to take a gittern into the Tower of London while a prisoner there and to play it during his

---

[48] *A Letter: whearin. part of the entertainment vntoo the Queenz Maiesty, at Killingwoorth Castl, in warwik Sheer in this soomerz Progress 1575. is signified: from a freend officer attendant in Coourt vntoo hiz freend a Citizen, and Merchaunt of London* (1575), 84. Modern edition in Goldring, *et al.*, eds., *John Nichols's The Progresses and public Processions of Queen Elizabeth I*, vol. ii, 239–87, at 284.

[49] *A Letter*, 84. For an edited text see Kuin, ed., *Robert Langham*, 39. There has been much discussion about the authenticity of this text. See now Goldring, '"A mercer ye wot az we be"', where it is argued that 'the Letter began life as a bona fide missive from Langham to his fellow mercer Humphrey Martin, which, though envisioned for circulation in manuscript, was almost certainly not – in the first instance at least – intended for publication'. See also Goldring, *et al.*, eds., *John Nichols's The Progresses and public Processions of Queen Elizabeth I*, 233–9.

Example 3.   'Gallia[rd]'. Osborn Commonplace Book (Beinecke Rare Book and Manuscript Library of Yale University, Osborn Music MS 13), f. 45 (old foliation), f. 41 (new foliation). Barring as in the original. The original can be viewed in the Digital Library of the Beinecke at http://beinecke.library.yale.edu.

captivity. This is revealed by a letter from the Warden of the Tower to the Queen's Secretary, Sir William Cecil, in which the Warden jokes that the Tower Lieutenant 'shal be fayne to take the sound' of Saunders' gittern for payment of his 'dyete', meaning his food and fuel (Figure 11). This may be humour of a kind, but it is no more light-hearted than we would expect from a man who administered the most ominous of all the Tudor fortresses; the Warden's point is that Saunders' money will eventually run out, if he is kept in prison for very long, and that the cost of food and a fire will then have to be charged to the Tower.

Who was this Francis Saunders? The Inns of Court reveal a promising candidate: a Francis Saunders who entered the Middle Temple on 7 February 1561 as a 'special' admission, meaning that he paid more than the usual fee to be exempted from both learning exercises and residential requirements. The record describes him as the son and heir of Robert Saunders esquire of Quiddenham in Norfolk.[50] It was in the next village to

[50] Sturgess, ed., *Register of Admisisons to the Honourable Society of the Middle Temple*, vol. 1, 26; Hopwood, ed., *Calendar of Middle Temple Records*, 130. Robert Saunders is traceable in two further documents: Norfolk Record Office NCC Administration Act Book 1563–70, ff. 199 and 205; in both instances, from the year 1566, he is granted Administration. There is no trace of the family arms in the Norfolk Visitations of 1563 and 1589, so perhaps the Quiddenham Saunders had only recently entered the ranks of the gentry whence the great majority of students at the Inns were drawn (Rye, ed., *The Visitacion of Norfolk (1563, 1589 and 1613*); Howard and Armytage, eds., *The Visitation of London in the Year 1568*, 34, has the Northamptonshire pedigree). Alternatively, since the 'Innes of court in these days are so furnished with shomakers sonnes, taylers sonnes, Inholders sonnes [and] farmers sonnes', as Barnabe Rich observed in 1578 (*Allarme to England*, Sig. Hij), voicing a familiar complaint, the clerks who compiled the Middle Temple record may simply have

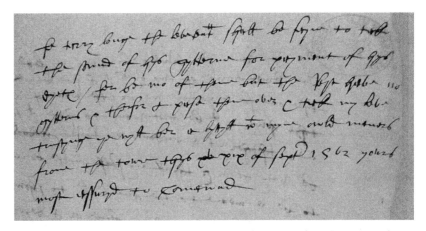

Figure 11.   Playing the gittern while imprisoned in the Tower of London. Extract from a
letter of 19 September 1562, where Edward Warner, Knight Lieutenant of the Tower
of London, writes to Sir William Cecil, Secretary of State, concerning the prisoners in
his care. TNA SP 12/24/39. Reproduced by permission.

Quiddenham, namely Kenninghall, that the Catholic Mary Tudor had
settled on her right to succeed her brother Edward VI in July 1553; this
would seem a merely incidental detail were it not for the fact that
Quiddenham was dominated by a Catholic gentry family of considerable
wealth and influence, the Bedingfields, who had been prominent suppor-
ters of Mary and remained unshakeably of the old faith into the reign of
Elizabeth. Such was the leading family of the village where the Middle
Temple Saunders was raised: the clan upon whom his own family would
inevitably have been in some measure dependent. The Tower records do
not specify the nature of Saunders' offence – which the Warden thought
serious – but if he is indeed the namesake admitted to the Middle Temple
then there is reason to suppose he was a victim of the government's early
attempts to move against the Catholics whom they believed to be keeping a
low profile in the various Inns of Court.[51] The Tower was well stocked
with Catholics at the time of Saunders' imprisonment, including the
majority of the Marian bishops deemed guilty of active protest against
the Elizabethan settlement and suspected of clandestine contact with
Rome. Other known Catholics imprisoned with him, and men closer to
his own station in life, included Thomas Valence and Francis Yaxley.
Imprisonment for owning forbidden books, for speaking against the

disguised Saunders' background if they knew it to be humble, a common practice. For context for
the Middle Temple record, see Prest, 'Conflict, Change and Continuity'. Since Saunders was
admitted in 1560/1, he cannot be the much better documented namesake who was already
admitted to the Middle Temple by 1559 when he was fined for failing to be Autumn reader
(Bindoff, *The House of Commons 1509–1558*, vol. III, sv 'Saunders, Francis ... of Welford.
Northants'). He was almost certainly a relative of that individual, however.
[51]   See Fisher, 'Privy Council Coercion', and McGrath and Rowe, 'The Imprisonment of Catholics'.

monarch's right to be head of the Church or indeed for any offence deemed seditious would explain how Saunders came to enjoy the privilege of taking a musical instrument into the Tower. This was the kind of concession only possible, for the most part, when prisoners were 'close and severallie kept' in their own chamber to prevent them passing messages, celebrating clandestine masses or framing conspiracies.

The studies of students at the Inns of Court, insofar as their curriculum can be determined, were restricted to the law and to disputations, but already by *c.* 1470 their appetite for learning to dance, fence and study music had inspired Sir John Fortescue to describe the Inns as 'a kind of academy of all the manners which teach the noble. There they learn to sing and also to exercise themselves in every kind of harmony.'[52] Today, this famous passage is rarely taken to imply an actual curriculum, which is surely wise, but many sons of gentry, lodging at one of the Inns, had principally come to widen their horizons and to experience the virtues (and the vices) of London life rather than to become barristers. They could also make a range of contacts: the royal ushers, knights, Members of Parliament, senior churchmen, judges and even the Lord Chancellors of the future. Saunders, as mentioned above, was not committed to follow any course of study. In such cases, ambition may often have gone no further than the basic law necessary to run an estate without excessive dependence upon inferiors, if indeed it extended so far. With much time on their hands, and an allowance to spend, some pursued a vigorous round of extra-curricular pursuits, making full use of the dancing and fencing schools of London. As Humfrey Braham observed in *The institucion of a gentleman* (1555), there were 'manye cunnyng Scholemasters' in London ready to teach young men how to be 'rude Roysters'.[53]

The Tower document, collated with the Middle Temple record, places Francis Saunders and the gittern in a rich context of verse and song with links to the royal court.[54] The printer Richard Tottel, printer of the

---

[52] Chrimes, ed. and trans., *Sir John Fortescue: De Laudibus Legum Anglie*, 1467–71. See the essays in Archer, Goldring and Knight, eds., *The Intellectual and Cultural World of the Early Modern Inns of Court*, esp. Baker, 'The Third University', and Prest, *The Inns of Court*.

[53] Sig. Bv. Cf. Shepard, *Meanings of Manhood*, 28–9.

[54] John Petre's accounts from October 1567 to Michaelmas 1570 show just how much time a young man at one of the Inns might devote to string playing. We have already met the household of his father, Sir William Petre, above. The accounts abound in references to lutes, such as the 'Brugges lute' which was brought to his chamber, together with two more from a family house in Aldersgate Street, carried to his rooms in the Temple. There are frequent references to the purchase of lute strings and to the services of a certain master Petro, evidently a player/teacher/dealer who, at various times, provided copies of lute pieces and accompanied airs, supplied bundles of strings and provided at least one lute in exchange for another. Petre also learned to dance; in April 1567 he paid twelve shillings in all to the 'Vssher and musitians' in order to join Currance's dancing school while in March 1568 he enrolled with the somewhat better known Richard Frith and paid another twelve shillings 'for my admyttaunce into his dauncyng schole'. He also joined a fencing school, to judge by his purchase of 'fopyles and daggers' from a certain William Napper. The extracts given here are cited from the original, Essex County Record Office, D/DPA17. See also Emmison, 'John Petre's Account Books'.

'Miscellany' mentioned above as the outstanding lyric collection of the early Elizabethan years, made most of his money from printing 'bokes of oure temporall lawe called the Common lawe'; it would be fanciful to imagine his printing house thronged with students from the Inns of Court pressing their poetic effusions into his hands for publication in what became the 'Miscellany', but some of the anonymous poems in that book may be the work of poets from the Inns of Court whose names have left some trace 'In Lyncolnes Inne and Temples twayne,/Grayes Inne and other mo'.[55] (It is no surprise to find that the earliest Tudor treatise on vernacular poetry, *Certayne Notes of Instruction*, not published until 1575, is the work of a Gray's Inn student, George Gascoigne, admitted in 1555.) Nobody has ever seriously doubted that a great deal of the strophic poetry in Tottel's 'Miscellany' was associated with musical settings, not least because well over a dozen have been traced, and it is reasonable to suppose that much poetry that was once sung to the gittern and other instruments, during the 1550s, has come to rest in its pages.[56]

The traces are not entirely lost. The prince of that collection, in every sense, is Henry Howard, Earl of Surrey, and two items for gittern in the Osborn Commonplace Book bear titles taken from the first lines of Surrey's verse (Examples 16 and 19). There are also several 'carriers' in that manuscript: items that could have borne a number of poems by Surrey (or those of any other poet) cast in the right metrical forms. One untitled piece, for example, evidently carries both the melody and the accompaniment for a lyric: the balanced phrases of the melody, stepping evenly in minims, cry out for a text in the long-established syllabic manner of the courtly ballad. Example 4 presents the piece on the lower stave, while the melody appears on the higher stave underlaid, for the purposes of illustration, with the first couplet of Surrey's 'Such waiwarde waies hath love'. This is the fourth poem in Tottel's anthology and the first to which the music can be accommodated.

v

The gittern was often to be found in the hands of apprentices. There were sons of gentlemen in the apprentice population, notably among the Merchant Adventurers who barred artisans, bastards, bankrupts, criminals and persons of a disreputable manner of life, but many were the sons of craftsmen, husbandmen and smaller traders. Taken together, this is a constituency so diverse that it would be misleading to evoke an apprentice

---

[55] *The seconde tragedie of Seneca entituled Thyestes faithfully Englished by Iasper Heywood* (1560), The Preface. See Warner, *The Making and Marketing of Tottel's Miscellany*, 14–24; Winston, 'Lyric Poetry'.

[56] See Ward, *Music for Elizabethan Lutes*, vol. i, 81–3, on poems in the 'Miscellany' for which musical settings have been found.

Example 4.   On the lower stave: untitled piece in the Osborn Commonplace
Book (Beinecke Rare Book and Manuscript Library of Yale University, Osborn Music
MS 13), f. 48 (old foliation), f. 44 (new foliation). On the upper stave: the melody
underlaid with the first couplet of Surrey's 'Such waiwarde waies hath love'.
In measure 12, the MS incorrectly gives the tablature letter on the chanterelle as
'h' in place of 'f'. The dot of augmentation added to the very first tablature flag
belongs with the second. The value of the last four notes in the penultimate measure
has here been halved. Text from Jones, ed., *Surrey Poems*, 8.

'class' or an apprentice 'culture'.[57] What apprentices undoubtedly did
share, however, and whatever their background, was the severe regard of
their elders and the weight of stern parental expectations. Young urban
males who had not yet assumed the adult responsibilities of marriage and
trading on their own account were a target for the rarely mitigated censure
of magistrates, constables, parents and guildsmen concerned with social
order. In November 1554, for example, the Masters of the Merchant
Adventurers at Newcastle issued 'An Act for the Apperell of Appryntyses'
to counter what they saw as a decline in moral standards among the rising
generation. Although the document was compiled to address the current
sins of the young, it succeeds best in exposing the eternal vices of the old.
Witheringly censorious, the Masters of the Company charge their juniors

---

[57] Ben-Amos, 'Failure to Become Freemen', 159; see further Smith, 'The London Apprentices as
Seventeenth-Century Adolescents', 150. For the issue of apprentice culture see Griffiths, *Youth and
Authority*, 165ff.

with excessive attention to their youthful pleasures and to fine clothing or 'Apperell', but their criticisms extend much further than the ornamented coats, silk-lined hose and cut shoes that are listed in the document with an accusatory precision. The apprentices are also charged with wearing beards, playing at cards and going to mummings, with drinking and dancing, with embracing loose women and with playing 'gitterns by nyght'.[58]

No other instrument is mentioned in the Newcastle document save the gittern, which appears again when the text runs through the malefactions of the apprentices a second time, in much the same order, to make a series of individual prohibitions that are henceforth to be observed. We could scarcely ask for a clearer sign of the gittern's place in a certain construction of youthful manhood during the second half of the sixteenth century. These apprentices evidently wished to appear as gallants with money in their pockets for gambling (of which they stand accused), with a dagger at hand to avenge any offence to their honour (the Masters mention the weapon) and with clothes of the newest manner. They had no desire to appear in garments made from the 'coarse clothe . . . of housewifes making' they were required to wear, marking them as servants not yet worthy of a man's respect or a woman's interest. By the same token, they did not wish to appear with smooth chins like mere boys or adolescents, but with beards as a sign of man's estate. Such aspirations came easily to young men who knew that the 'slowe thrifte' of the mercantile life was widely regarded as unfit 'for a gentleman's exercise' whereas clothes of the newest variety certainly were a fitting complement to it, especially if they seemed foreign (to George Gascoigne in 1573 it seemed that 'sylke hose', which the Newcastle apprentices wore, were an affectation that English gentlemen had caught 'abroade in forayne lande'). Nonetheless, those same Newcastle apprentices had no inclination to accept the constraints that came with settled adulthood, or with mature years, for they did not forego the pleasures of the night hours. To be about in the streets when decent people were at home or abed was to skirt the edges of criminality and vice that sought the cover of darkness, just as it was to damage the chances of doing an honest day's work in the master's shop and to flout the natural order. If gitterns seemed bad to the Newcastle Merchant Adventurers, 'gitterns by nyght' were worse.

The gittern appears again among apprentices with the letters that members of the 'Candelwick Crew' exchanged in 1561 with counterparts overseas, in Deventer. The members of this group were perhaps indentured to merchants in the cloth trade, since Candlewick Street, running east-west from Walbrook in the west to the beginning of Eastcheap, and now Cannon Street, was inhabited by 'rich Drapers, sellers of woollen cloth', as John Stow

---

[58] For a comparable document, issued in London in 1582, see Goldring, *et al.*, eds., *John Nichols's The Progresses and public Processions of Queen Elizabeth I*, vol. III, 159–60.

relates. Deventer, like some other towns in the Overijssel province, was famous for its linen market. One of the Candlewick Crew, John Graves, was evidently an accomplished player, for 'on the gyttourne he playes verye well', in addition to virginals and 'fyddel'. These men were still serving out their time, as far as we know, even if they were often unruly, but wandering apprentices who had forsaken their trade also have a place in the history of the Tudor guitar. John Felde, indentured to the Norwich cordwainer Robart Crispe, 'went runnyng aboute the contry wth a gitterne' in 1561; caught and committed to prison for three days, he was returned to his master. Such errant apprentices were prominent among those whom the public authorities regarded as loose livers and vagabonds, since the dropout rate for London apprentices during the sixteenth century was high, despite the legality of severe corporal punishment for those who abandoned their masters.[59] Felde's flight with a gittern looks like an attempt to embark on the minstrel life with a relatively cheap instrument: a snatch at a profession scarcely distinguished from vagabondage in the minds of the authorities.

The probate inventory of an otherwise unknown Dennys Bucke introduces a yeoman. Bucke lived at Great Walsingham, in Norfolk, set amidst some of the richest arable land in England. The inventory, dated 9 September 1584 and now in the Norfolk County Record Office, offers a perambulation of the house he shared with his wife Alice from the main parlour to the inner chamber, passing to the 'hall or parlor' that led to the kitchen and finally reaching the 'corn chamber' with barley, wheat and rye; the back door then gave onto the barn and the yard with the livestock. The parlour chamber was the principal living and sleeping space, with four featherbeds, blankets and pillows, a warming pan, chairs, a table and a chest or desk. It was there that the executors found a 'gitterne' valued at just 12*d*. (For the full text of the inventory see Appendix C.)

Bucke is not styled a gentleman in his inventory, and nor are any of his executors. He was probably one of the yeomen farmers – free tenants working arable land – whose fortunes were in the ascendant during the second half of the sixteenth century.[60] The spread of pewter vessels among such men, and the increasing incidence of silver objects, mostly saltcellars and spoons, in the inventories of their property give a material trace of their increasing worth; Bucke, for his part, owned four ounces of 'broken' silver, a silver spoon and eight pewter dishes. This was a modest hoard, but it shows the kind of creeping gentrification that inspired many yeomen to restyle themselves as gentlemen. A certain Robert Buck of Great Walsingham, presumably a relative, is named on a monumental brass of 1632 in the parish church and

[59] Ben-Amos, 'Failure to Become Freemen', 155.
[60] On the marked increase in yeoman wealth during the later sixteenth and earlier seventeenth centuries, see Shephard and Spicksley, 'Worth, Age, and Social Status'. Older studies, still of value, include Campbell, *The English Yeoman*, esp. 21–63 and 229–61, and Schmidt, *The Yeoman*, esp. 21–6.

styled GENT,[61] so perhaps the family rose to gentry status on the back of their agricultural prosperity. This was a common pattern in the period, notably among yeomen farmers who prospered, by careful husbandry and investment, on lands released by the dissolution of the monasteries. Dennys Bucke's inventory shows that he leased some land from the 'late prior' of Walsingham; since the Priory of (Little) Walsingham was dissolved long before 1584, the land in question was perhaps a parcel granted to one of Bucke's forebears on an extended lease by the Prior of the house, as far back as the later 1530s, to keep the land out of government hands. This was a common monastic ploy. The inventory leaves no doubt that Bucke dwelled in a working farmhouse on the land that he leased, but the thin line separating such men from the gentry was easily crossed; the yeoman of the later Elizabethan years was not prepared to leave himself 'fallow and untilled' but, in the words of Thomas Wilson in 1600, might wish to 'skipp into his velvett breeches and silken dublett ... getting to be admitted into some Inn of Court or Chancery'.[62] Dennys Bucke had no velvet breeches, or none that his executors chose to list, but it is tempting to suppose that his gittern, like his warming pan, silver and pewter, was a sign of a yeoman's ambition to the gentlemanly status that his family seems to have achieved within little more than a generation.

Finally, there is one who must be placed last because he had no place in Tudor society. More of a vagabond even than the fleeing or wandering apprentice with a gittern was the itinerant rogue and chancer.[63] A passage in William Bullein's *A Dialogve bothe pleasaunte and pietifull wherein is a goodly regimente against the feuer Pestilence* (1564) shows how elaborate the figure of the rootless reprobate, skilled with the gittern, could become in a fictionalised presentation offered by 'one of the many eccentric yet brilliant experiments in literary prose during the mid-Tudor period that never inspired an imitation'.[64] Written by a provincial physician in response to an outbreak of plague in 1563, Bullein's book combines advice on how to avoid the pestilence with a diagnosis of the many social ills that bring down such divine judgement. The dialogues announced in the title are in effect miniature plays; one introduces the figure of Mendax, or 'Liar', who arrives at an inn and is invited to join a married couple at their table. The guests find themselves in 'a comlie parlour, verie netlie and trimlie apparelled, London like', when a servant announces:

---

[61] Stephenson, *A List of Monumental Brasses in the British Isles*, 372.

[62] Fisher, ed., *The State of England Anno Dom. 1600 by Thomas Wilson*, 19.

[63] For vagrancy, see Beier, 'Social Problems in Elizabethan London'; Roberts, 'Elizabethan Players and Minstrels'. For the legislation, see Hartley, ed., *Proceedings in the Parliaments of Elizabeth I*, vol. I, 366–7 ('The bill of vagabondes' from the Lords first read 20 May 1572, with record of the debate) and 384 ('The bill for vagabondes the third tyme read. Much argument pro et contra was made aboute minstrels, and the bill commytted').

[64] Maslen, 'The Healing Dialogues of Doctor Bullein', 119.

Sir, there is one lately come into this hall, in a grene Kendale cote, with yellow hose a bearde of the same colour, onely vpon the vpper lippe a russette hatte, with a greate plume of straunge Feathers, and a braue scarfe aboute his necke, in cut buskins. He is plaiyng at the trea trippe with our host sonne: he plaieth tricke vpon the gittarne, and daunce Tre[n]chmore, and Heie de Gie, and telleth newes from *Tera Florida*. He loketh a squinte, I did see him geue the good man, a pece of a Unicornes horne, good against poison: he semeth a pretie Scholer. But I heard him praie the chamberlain in his eare, to lende him vj d vpon a pressing yron, whiche chamberlain refused the gage.[65]

Mendax wears the ostentatiously feathered hat of the gallant, a scarf that looks 'braue', meaning showy, grand or handsome, and he pretends to be an adventurer who has travelled far. He is clearly no pauper, or is not impoverished all the time, and he chooses well to speak of Florida; travelogues such as *A true and perfect description, of the last voyage or Nauigation ... into Terra Florida, this yeare past* (1565), by Nicolas le Challeux, reveal that the new land was a subject of lively interest in the 1560s. Mendax has an air of decayed gentility, matching his claim to be a gentleman, 'linially descended of an auncient house', and he performs 'tricke' on the gittern, probably to be understood in the sense 'A feat of dexterity or skill, intended to surprise or amuse; a piece of jugglery or legerdemain'.[66] Bullein takes it for granted that all the roles combined by Mendax consort well enough with the gittern, whose true home here seems to be the tavern, with familiar grounds such as 'Trenchmore', which Bullein names, and other dance music never far away. The 'Heie de Gie' of Mendax is probably a version of the gittern piece entitled 'The hedgynge hay', in the Osborn Commonplace Book of *c.* 1560 (Example 5).

Mendax seems appealingly roguish, and Bullein cannot help but describe him with verve, so that the damaging implications of his name, meaning 'Liar', are liable to be forgotten or read as a residue from the allegorical procedures of the Tudor interludes; viewed through the eyes of a contemporary magistrate, however, Mendax is a dangerous man. Masterless and rootless, he has no intention of living honestly in settled employment or quietly as a respecter of the king's peace. Perhaps to be envisaged as a discharged seaman without the proper paperwork – such men loomed large among the 'sturdie beggers' that so vexed the authorities – he is a swindler, card sharp and vagrant whose claim to the title of gentleman is as false as his bogus coat of arms. Living in the shadow of Tyburn tree, he seems to be the epitome of Shakespeare's 'needy Nothing trimm'd in jollity'.

* * *

[65] F. 67. [66] *OED*, sv 'trick', n., sense 5.

Example 5.   'The hedgynge hay'. Osborn Commonplace Book (Beinecke Rare
Book and Manuscript Library of Yale University, Osborn Music MS 13), f. 40r
(old foliation), f. 44r (new foliation). The original can be viewed in the Digital Library
of the Beinecke at http://beinecke.library.yale.edu. The chords with the seventh
against the bass have been questioned on the curious grounds that the instrument
lacks the ability to lower the D in the bass to C (Ward, *Sprightly and Cheerful
Musick*, 49). This would have to mean that the scribe has made do with the seventh
because he or she lacked the wit to raise the D on the fourth course to an E, thereby
producing a standard chord. An interpretation both more plausible and
attractive is that this item of dance music records a drone-based technique of
strummed play where the seventh ceases to be of any account because it arises
from the necessary and continuous sounding of the 'fourth under' drone, that is to
say the lowest course (with an octave string on that course the drone would also have
sounded at the higher octave, not shown in the transcription).

Taken together, the documents gathered for this chapter place the
ownership of gitterns in a wide range of social contexts from the apex
of the royal court to the yeoman class.

I   THE COURT

Monarch and nobility

? Henry VIII
Elizabeth I (as a gift)
Edward Courtenay/Peter Carew
?Henry Howard, Earl of Surrey
The Nevilles

Gentlemen with a court office

Sir William More (Privy Council)
Sir William Petre (Privy Council)
Sir Richard Worsley (Captain of the Isle of Wight)
?Philip van Wilder (Privy Chamber)

Domestics

Richard Langham (Keeper of the Privy Council Chamber)

II   GENTRY

William Calley
Francis Saunders (Middle Temple)
Thomas Whythorne

III   THE UNIVERSITIES

Fellows of colleges (F) and students (S)

John Somerford (S) (Oxford)
Thomas Lorkin (F) (Cambridge)
Ralph Allen (F) (Oxford)

College servants

John Walker (Cambridge)

IV   APPRENTICES

John Graves (London)
Merchant Adventurers (Newcastle)
John Felde (Norwich)

V   YEOMAN-FRANKLIN

Dennys Bucke (Norfolk)

CHAPTER 3

The gittern trade

I

A roll listing the presents offered to Elizabeth I on New Year's Day in 1559
may reveal a professional maker of gitterns in Tudor England. We have
already encountered the gift – a case of three gitterns – but not the name of
the giver, who appears towards the end of the strictly hierarchical list. Long
hidden from view by the slip of a nineteenth-century editor, he is the
celebrated instrument maker of London, John Rose senior.[1] Rose was
already at work in 1552 when he repaired lutes, made viols and provided
strings for Sir Thomas Chaloner the elder, but when he offered his present
to Elizabeth he was rapidly approaching the height of his fame (not that it
counted for much to the clerks of the Jewel House who inventoried his gift
in 1559). Two years later, he is handsomely praised in the Court Book of
Bridewell Hospital for a most notable talent 'geven of God in the makyng
of instruments even soche a gift as his fame is spred through a great part of
christendome . . . '.[2] In recognition of this ability, Rose was granted rooms
in the former Presence Chamber of the original Bridewell Palace, on the
banks of the Fleet, with accommodation above the Great Chamber; the
order for his tenancy was signed by leading lights of the city, all members of
the most illustrious companies.

The gifts offered by other gentlemen on the same occasion reflected the
best productions of their professions, but not necessarily their own

[1] The name appears in the roll of gifts as John Roose. For the spelling 'roose' for 'rose', common
between the fifteenth and seventeenth centuries, see *OED*, 'rose', n. 1 and adj. 1. For John Rose, see
Fleming, 'John Rose'; Pringle, 'The Founder of English Viol-Making'; and for the Rose 'orpharion',
Harwood, *Wire Strings at Helmingham Hall*. Rose would not have presented the instruments to
Elizabeth in person; the chest would have been sent with a servant to be registered, in the appointed
gift chamber, by officials of the Jewel House.

[2] Bethlem Royal Hospital Archives and Museum, Item bcb-01, f. 249r. Rose was an advantageous
tenant for a hospital just emerging from a decade of religious turmoil, and which occupied the
lowest position in the hierarchy of London hospitals at this date. For the Bridewell hospital, the
principal prison at this date for vagrants and those convicted of sexual misdemeanours, see
Griffiths, *Lost Londons*. The quality of the surviving orpharion (or small bandora) dated 27 July
1580, probably the work of John Rose junior, fully justifies the reputation of the family workshop.
See Pringle, 'The Founder of English Viol-Making', with illustrations of the label and the
orpharion (or bandoret?), and Nordstrom, *The Bandora*. Further discussion in Harwood, *Wire
Strings at Helmingham Hall*.

handiwork. William Treasurer, maker of keyboard instruments, presented a pair of virginals, while the printer Richard Jugge offered a Ptolemaic map with text in Italian.[3] Rose may either have given the fruit of his own labours, which was probably the case with William Treasurer's offering, or some especially fine wares in his own line obtained from abroad, probably the case with Richard Jugge's map. One might imagine that the Queen bestowed no more or less attention upon the gitterns than upon any other present she received that day, but that was not the case; the entry on the roll records that the instruments were currently 'with the Quene by Mr. Lichfild', which means that one of the royal lutenists, well known from court and other records, had conveyed the case of gitterns to the Queen's presence so that she could examine them, and perhaps even play them.

If John Rose senior did indeed make these three gitterns then they were probably an isolated venture by a craftsman who practised a trade that appears to have been rare in Tudor England.[4] This is not to deny that a great many stringed instruments were being manufactured, ranging from homemade examples to more accomplished work by those with the necessary woodworking skills; it is rather to maintain that this kind of cottage manufacture was far removed from any formal structure of indentured apprenticeship serving a trade with an established economic base. Tudor England can offer nothing in that regard to match the abundant guild records of the Spanish *violeros*, for example, and no parallel to the situation in contemporary France where an enterprising writer could publish a method for fretting the gittern so that professional makers might create a template for use in their shops. The great majority of gitterns played in Tudor England were apparently imported.

This was part of a much broader pattern in English economic life. For the most part, foreign merchants did not seek any finished or fine commodities from London, but only raw materials such as lead, alabaster and pitch, together with many varieties of cloth, in every way the principal export. This was not only a mark of English inability to bring goods of an appropriate quality and price to foreign notice; it also exposed an inability to compete with overseas manufacturers even in the domain of essential goods required for home markets. When John Hales, sometime before 1571, asked a stationer why there were no Englishmen manufacturing paper, for example,

---

[3] For Treasurer, appointed tuner of the royal instruments in 1551 and often mentioned in court records thereafter, see *RECM*, vol. VI, 3, 8, 15 *et passim*, and vol. VII, 118, 120 *et passim*.

[4] Only recently has the tally of instrument makers in Tudor records been extended beyond a mere handful. I am grateful to Dr Michael Fleming for sharing the results of his researches in this domain. For two lute makers of 1433–4, see Page, *Music and Instruments*, Essay III, 44. The significance of the two documents is well brought out in Spring, *The Lute in Britain*, 19. For later-sixteenth-century instances, see again Spring, 41 and 69, and Ward, *Music for Elizabethan Lutes*, vol. I, 25.

he was told that no native artisan could make it 'as good cheape' as the foreign product. One recent attempt to do so had collapsed.[5]

The scale of continental (and especially French) operations had defeated the merchant concerned, whose identity remains unknown.[6] A craftsman in England, pondering whether to divert spare capacity towards the manufacture of gitterns in the 1550s and 60s, could expect to be squeezed in the same way, for continental workshops were already achieving impressive economies of scale. By 1559, Gaspard Tieffenbrucker was producing enough instruments to be styled 'maître faiseur de guiternes' in a Lyon document of that year,[7] and other French makers were active in Lyon and Paris on a smaller but still impressive scale. The workshop of one Parisian craftsman, Claude Denis, contained 250 boards of pine 'to make gitterns' in 1587; there were also 24 gitterns, presumably finished and ready for sale, together with 7 more and 7 separate necks (*collets*), betraying systematic division of work whereby 1 or more workers manufactured a single component in quantity to streamline operations.[8] A comparable situation can be traced in Spain where the *violero* Mateo de Arratía purchased 88 'tops with roses' from Venice in 1575, and while these were perhaps for vihuelas, he also made guitars.[9] His fellow Toledan, Francisco de Haro, bought 98 guitar soundboards from a Milanese merchant in 1585.[10] There may be signs here of a commerce in ready-made or part-finished guitar components operating throughout the Western Mediterranean, enhancing rates of production still further. Makers abroad evidently had the means to saturate the English market with reasonably priced instruments; a carpenter in Bristol, Oxford or even London, with spare capacity in his workshop, was well advised not to compete with them.

II

The official record of imported musical instruments in the Tudor period alternates between long periods of silence when no records survive and sudden screeds of information for years when a Port Book is available. These books were compiled in response to an Exchequer Order of November 1564 requiring all customs officials, in the various ports of

[5] Hales, *A compendious or briefe examination*, f. 26.   [6] Reynard, 'Unreliable Mills', 242–4.
[7] Lesure, 'La Guitare en France', 189.
[8] Lesure, 'La Facture instrumentale', 36–7. For further information on instrument makers in England, as revealed by documentary sources, see Fleming, 'Some Points'.
[9] By my count, Romanillos Vega and Winspear, *The Vihuela de Mano*, lists 139 Spanish makers of plucked instruments whose periods of activity lie either entirely in the sixteenth century or in a significant part thereof. Of these, there are sixteen cases where guitar making is explicitly mentioned, the makers being located in Lorca (1), Madrid (7), Mallorca (2), Murcia (1), Toledo (4) and Zaragoza (1), but the genuine total is undoubtedly much higher.
[10] *Ibid.*, 480–2 and 179.

England and Wales, to make their entries in large, blank volumes of parchment specially prepared and issued to them by the Exchequer. They do not give a complete picture of inward commerce during the period they cover, for the imports by native and alien merchants were often kept in different books, many of them lost, while the number of smuggled instruments (if there were any) is beyond discovery. These volumes nonetheless provide an unprecedented opportunity to trace merchants who had put money into the instrument trade, and to view their consignments.[11]

That does not mean, however, that all the port records are equally informative. Port Books survive from Bristol, Southampton, Chichester, Deal, Dover, Colchester and other ports as far north as Hull, but the volume of trade – any trade – coming into these ports was sometimes low.[12] The officials at Hastings, Romney, Winchelsea, Arundel and Colchester, for example, came nowhere near filling the books sent to them from the Exchequer in 1591.[13] Other ports, notably Sandwich in 1584, and Dover and Deal in 1590–1, were more active, with Dover and Deal receiving ships from Dunkirk, Flushing, Ostende, Rotterdam and other ports abroad; yet even for these centres, which were undeniably important, there appears to be no trace of imported musical instruments or strings arriving at the wharves. Nothing relevant has so far appeared in documents for the ports of Bristol, Sandwich, Southampton, Dover or Ipswich,[14] so it seems that the commerce in imported instruments was a

[11] TNA E 190/4/2. The extreme dates of the entries are 24 September 1568 and 30 September 1576. This document, now lavishly rebound using the technology of the period, is difficult to use, owing to the fact that the leaves, foliated with a stamp in the nineteenth century, are in many places out of order. Hitherto, discussion of this material by historians of instruments appears to have been exclusively based upon the edition of Dietz, *The Port and Trade of Early Elizabethan London*, as in Ward, 'A Dowland Miscellany', 116, and Spring, *The Lute in Britain*, 68–9, citing Ward. For basic bibliography on the books, which were long neglected and are often in a poor state, see www.nationalarchives.gov.uk/records/research-guides/port-books.htm. The edition by Dietz rearranges the material so that the contents of each ship are gathered together, giving a complete conspectus of the hold. This is valuable, but it somewhat weakens the sense, so keenly conveyed by the much damaged original, of crowded wharves where the cargo of any one ship might be unloaded, case by case, or sack by sack, taking as long as a week to be processed since each merchant's goods had to join the queue with consignments from other ships being unloaded in the same way. During the course of a single day, the officers might therefore have to deal with a great many individual chests, sacks and boxes brought in from half a dozen vessels, so that the name of the ship at issue, the home port, master, and so on changed with each entry and had to be written out each time.

[12] Harbours lying further north such as Hull were served from London via the coastal trade; a licence was made out on a slip of parchment – in effect, a pocket charter – serving as a receipt for duties paid and a proclamation that the merchant was authorised to ship his goods on to the stated port, and nowhere else. Some of these licences or 'cockets' survive for the Boston coastal trade up to Hull (for example TNA E 122/225/96).

[13] TNA E 190/747/26 (Hastings, three entries), E 190/747/18 (Romney, entirely blank), E 190/747/20 (Winchelsea, entirely blank), E 190/747/5 (Arundel, single page) and E 190/594/2 (Colchester, a page and a half).

[14] E 190/643/18 (Dover, 1590–1) and E 190/642/10 (Sandwich and Deal). See Vanes, ed., *Documents Illustrating the Overseas Trade of Bristol*, 5–11, on the poor state of Bristol's trade in the sixteenth century as it lost out to London; for the extent of under-recording, see Jones, *Inside the Illicit Economy*. I am grateful to Dr Jones for advice.

distinctively metropolitan trade. Commodities so far removed from the daily
business of keeping hunger and cold at bay as a lute or gittern necessarily had
an aura of plenty about them, even cosmopolitanism, which distilled the
sense of surplus wealth, and of wide prospects, proper to the luxury imports of
a metropolitan centre. The situation throughout England in the Tudor
period was probably much as it remained in the Jacobean years when the
Shuttleworths of Gawthorpe Hall in Lancashire sent to London, or to the
capital's satellite fair at Stourbridge, near Cambridge, for commodities such as
hops, fish, books, a lute and a bandora.[15]

Among the London Port Books the volume covering the twelvemonth
from Michaelmas to Michaelmas 1567/8 is of special value as a fortunate
survival from a key moment (Box 1). Although it only lists imports by
native merchants and some Hanse traders, it records the important
Antwerp to London trade on the verge of the temporary (but finally
lasting) closure of that market for political reasons, to which we shall
return. The lute dominated the trade during the period covered by the
book, with eighty examples arriving in five different varieties ('Antwerp',
'Venice', 'Cologne', 'coarse', 'small').[16] Next come the eighteen citterns,
six of them described as 'slight', and finally fourteen gitterns. There are no
viols; John Rose and others were active by now, with results that were to
make English viol making famous.

During the period covered by the book, this commerce rested with just
five men. The gittern trade, however, was in the hands of only one: John
White. He must have known all his competitors, and indeed all these men
would have been acquainted with one another; the Port Book reveals that a
single ship might bring in miscellaneous goods for as many as five of the
merchants represented in Box 1.[17] It is also clear that John White must
have planned his enterprise in consultation with his fellow merchants. His
activities, taken together with theirs, seem to encompass the full range of
available products, from Venice lutes at the high end, through more
modest 'cullen' lutes in the middle, to 'coarse' lutes at the bottom, and
yet there is remarkably little overlap.[18] A measure of discussion and

[15] Harland, ed., *The House and Farm Accounts of the Shuttleworths of Gawthorpe Hall*, vol. II, 252. A poem in Francis Davison's collection *A Poetical Rapsody Containing Diuerse Sonnets, Odes, Elegies, Madrigalls, and other Poesies both in Rime, and Measured Verse* (1602), 125–6, is entitled 'Vpon his Ladies buying strings for her Lute' and seems to refer to a purchase at a 'wishèd Fayre'.
[16] By my reckoning, Ward, 'A Dowland Miscellany', 116, counts six more Venice lutes than are actually there in the record, giving a total of eighty-six lutes all told whereas I make it eighty. Not surprisingly, the costly Venice lutes always came in cases of their own that the buyer would certainly require, while the cheaper 'Cologne' lutes, perhaps primarily for the amateur market where players might not expect to travel so much, were not always so equipped. The six citterns for the haberdasher William Cooper came packed in a single chest.
[17] Dietz, ed., *The Port and Trade of Early Elizabethan London*, no. 157.
[18] Imported lutes were evidently graded by quality using much the same terminology as traders used for pouches or razors, the latter sorted into those of 'fyne prys', the 'medyll sortt' and 'course' (Archer, *The History of the Haberdashers' Company*, 25). A 'coarse' lute was presumably one that was cheaply made, with the minimum of decoration.

BOX 1

Names and occupations of importers bringing in legal cargoes of musical instruments or strings to the Port of London between Michaelmas 1567 and Michaelmas 1568. From TNA E 190/4/2, a record of overseas inward trade by native and Hanse merchants. The numbers assigned to each cargo correspond to the entries in the edition of Dietz, *Port and Trade*, but all entries have been checked against the original. The occupations given for the individuals named are those provided in the document. Valuations are only given here in cases where the consignment of instruments or strings is not mixed with other commodities. 'Cullen' is Cologne.

JOHN ALDEN *grocer*

703　*Mary George* of London, Antwerp, '12 Andwarp lutes'

- In the same consignment: liquorice, saltpetre, alum.

HENRY BILLINGSLEY *haberdasher*

339　*Jesus* of London, Antwerp, '20 grs harpe stringes'

- In the same consignment: pins, thread.

RICHARD BILLINGSLEY *haberdasher* **(brother of the above)**

435　*Swallow* of London, '30 grs harpe stringes'
465　*Primrose* of Lee, Antwerp, '30 grs harpe stringes and 3 grs minikins'
523　*Trinity* of Erith, Antwerp, '40 grs harpe stringes'
540　*Marygold* of Lee, Antwerp, unspecified number of 'harpe stringes'
574　*Primrose* of Lee, '40 grs harpe stringes'
702　*Sacre* of Lee, Antwerp, '30 grs harpe stringes'
729　*Swepstake* of Lee, Antwerp, '20 grs harpe stringes'
787　*John Baptist*, Antwerp, '30 grs harpe stringes'

- All mixed consignments, including packthread, pins, white latten, Bruges thread . . .

JOHN BOORNE *leatherseller*

45　*Prym Rose* of Milton, Antwerp, '20 grs harpe stringes, 20 grs lute stringes and 12 lbs claricorde wier'
298　*Ellen* of London, Antwerp, '18 lbs claricorde wier'
388　*Falcon* of Lee, Antwerp, '12 lbs claricorde wier'

- All mixed consignments, including thread, thimbles, needles, awl blades . . .

JOHN BROOKE *draper*

409　*Christofer* of Antwerp, Antwerp, '6 Venis lutes £6'

- No other goods in this consignment.

BOX 1 (*cont.*)

ROBERT BROUNE *goldsmith*

45 *Prym Rose* of Milton, Antwerp, '20 grs harpe stringes, 20 grs lute stringes and 12 lbs claricorde wier'

• In the same consignment: pins, thread, awl blades, compasses, hourglasses . . .

EDMUND BURTON *clothworker, Freeman of the Company of Clothworkers in 1575*

18 *Lion* of Lee, Antwerp, '60 lbs claricorde wier'
211 *Owl* of Antwerp, Antwerp, '20 lbs claricorde wier'
259 *Anne* of Antwerp, Antwerp, '60 lbs claricorde wier'

• All mixed consignments, including nails, frying pans, sword blades, saws, curtain rings, horse bells . . .

GEORGE COLLIMER *draper*

154 *Peter* of Lee, Antwerp, '30 grs harpe stringes'
234 *Barsaby* of Lee, Antwerp, '20 grs harpe stringes'
463 *Beniamin* of Lee, Antwerp, '50 doz lute stringes'

• All mixed consignments, including pins, gartering threads, Bruges thread, packthread . . .

WILLIAM COOPER *haberdasher*

53 *Santa Maria de Gracia* of Venice, '6 Venis lutes £6'

• No other goods in this consignment.

572 *Swan* of Antwerp, Antwerp, 'chest with 6 sitternes'

• In the same consignment: coarse gloves, 'garding' velvet, hooks, tinsel, halberd heads, a bugle.

THOMAS EATON *grocer*

212 *James* of Antwerp, Antwerp, '6 grs minikins'
340 *Primrose* of Milton, Antwerp, '30 lbs claricorde wier'
433 *Mary Fortune* of Lee, Antwerp, '6 grs minikins'
465 *Primrose* of Lee, Antwerp, '3 grs minikins and 20 lbs claricorde wier'
627 *Barthelemew* of London, Antwerp, '6 grs minikins and 12 lbs claricorde wier'
729 *Swepstake* of Lee, Antwerp, '20lbs claricorde wier'
787 *John Baptist* of London, Antwerp, '12 lbs claricorde wier'
808 *Lyon* of Lee, Antwerp, '12 lbs claricorde wier'

• All mixed consignments, including pins, halfpennyware glasses, needles, wooden dials, thimbles, hatbands, tacks, cotton . . .

BOX 1 (*cont.*)

JOHN ELIOTS *leatherseller*

   45 *Prym Rose* of Milton, Antwerp, '8 grs minikins'
   46 *John* of Lee, Antwerp, '20 lbs claricord wier' as two consignments of
          10 + 10
 210 *Sampson* of Antwerp, '8 grs minikins and 16 lbs claricorde wier'
 576 *Ellen* of London, Antwerp, '4 doz minikins'

- All mixed consignments, including thread, pins, coarse looking-glasses, awl blades, ribbon . . .

ROLAND ERLINGTON *haberdasher*

 522 *John Bonadventure* of London, Antwerp, '24 grs harpe stringes'

- In the same consignment: Oudenaarde thread, bottom thread.

WILLIAM HOBSON *citizen and haberdasher*

 750 *Cock* Adrianson (no other details), '20 grs harpe stringes'

- In the same consignment: curtain rings, looking-glasses, Lyons thread, knives . . .

ANTHONY SCOLOKER *milliner*

 298 *Ellen* of London, Antwerp, '2 grs lute stringes'

- In the same consignment: wooden writing pens and needles.

 339 *Jesus* of London, Antwerp, '48 grs minikins, boxes and pipes'

- These are the only goods in this consignment.

NICHOLAS SPERING *goldsmith*

 435 *Swallow* of London, '3 grs cours catlins . . . 24 cours lutes with cases'
 466 *Hound* of Lee, Antwerp, '8 cullen lutes and 3 grs harpe stringes'

- Both mixed consignments, including coarse knives, brazen gold weights, small writing tables, steel buttons, packthread . . .

JOHN WHITE *draper*

 305 *Spledegle* of Antwerp, Antwerp, '12 chests with 6 sytternes, 6 git-tornes, 4 *parv.* lutes and 6 lutes in cases £6'

- No other goods in this consignment.

 402 *Falcon* of Antwerp, Antwerp, '6 Venis lutes with cases £6'

- No other goods in this consignment.

BOX 1 (*cont.*)

461 *Sea Rider* of Antwerp, Antwerp, '1 case with 6 slight citerns, 8 giterns
      and 2 *parv.* lutes £5 3s 4d'

• No other goods in this consignment.

572 *Swan* of Antwerp, Antwerp, '6 cullen lutes £1 10s'

• No other goods in this consignment.

agreement between these merchants seems the best way to explain why
Richard Billingsley imported many strings but no instruments, why John
White and Nicholas Spering imported large numbers of instruments but
relatively few strings (in John White's case, none at all), and why Spering
imported 'coarse' lutes but none from Venice while John White purchased
Venice lutes but no 'coarse' ones.

John White was a draper. Like all of the importers on the list, he was a
member of a London livery company. There are five haberdashers, three
drapers, two grocers, two goldsmiths, two leathersellers, a milliner and a
clothworker. These trades may seem surprising in this context, but in
terms of contemporary trade there is nothing strange about their appearance here; if a Tudor merchant had the necessary capital, and could bear
the risk of loss, he was ready to diversify. John Alden, who imported
twelve Antwerp lutes, appears elsewhere in this same Port Book buying
pepper, ginger, rice and onion seed, among other commodities, so he was
presumably a grocer as described; another grocer, Thomas Eaton,
imported pincushions and awl blades as well as top strings or minikins.
Nicholas Spering was a goldsmith who bought thimbles, needles, looking-
glasses and knives as well as lutes. At the time when Anthony Scoloker,
formerly an Ipswich printer, imported a large consignment of minikins he
was trading as a milliner, one of those who sold 'Shirts, Bands, Bracelets,
Iewels, and such pretty toies for Gentle women', in the words of Robert
Greene.[19]

This is where the unique nature of John White's commerce becomes
clear. Whereas the other importers named in the book combined their
musical instruments with various other commodities, in mixed consignments, White never did so, or not in any period for which we have record.
He certainly imported other goods including dye, Gascony wine and skins,
but these never came in the same shipments as his instruments. His range
of contacts, his ability to command credit overseas or to raise a loan at
home, and the quality of his foreign agents, were clearly exceptional. He is

---

[19] *A Quip for an Vpstart Courtier* (1592), Sig. Fij^{r-v}.

the closest approximation to a dealer in musical instruments that any document of sixteenth-century England has so far disclosed.

Among the various John Whites that can be traced in contemporary documents, following the trade of draper, there is one of special interest in the archives of the Rochester Bridge Trust.[20] The medieval bridge over the Medway, which survived long enough, with modifications, to be admired by Charles Dickens and written into *The Pickwick Papers*, was partly supported by rents from various London properties in the care of the Wardens of the bridge trust. Their records show that a draper named John White rented a property from the Wardens in Leadenhall Street; the lease is dated 12 June 1577, but White was probably in residence before that for he appears in the property survey made for the Wardens between 1575 and 1577.[21] He can still be traced in the rental for 1583/4. The next rental is lost, but the book for 1585/6 survives and shows that White's widow Livia was now paying the rent. In all probability, therefore, this John White is the individual of that name whose burial is noted in the register of the parish of St Andrew Undershaft, where his Leadenhall property lay, in an entry for 21 December 1585.[22]

The reason for connecting this John White with the draper of our Port Book is that the Rochester documents show he had a close neighbour of particular interest. That person's name was Nicholas Sperynge, and he was a goldsmith: precisely the name and trade of the only other merchant importing stringed instruments, on a scale comparable to John White's enterprise, in 1567/8. This means that the names and trades of the two men who dominated the commerce in imported musical instruments, including gitterns, during 1567/8, and who show signs of collaborating to the extent of dividing the market between them, can be found about a decade later when the Rochester documents identify two individuals living in the same row of tenements and sharing the same landlords; indeed, both men were called to Rochester on 12 June 1577 to renew and to sign their leases.[23] There is therefore a strong chance that this John White and Nicholas Sperynge, both of Leadenhall Street, are the same as the importers of instruments in 1567/8. Perhaps they were even working together and

[20] Boyd, ed., *Roll of the Drapers' Company*, 198–9, lists the following John Whites who come into consideration: (1) apprenticed in 1541, no further details; (2) apprenticed in 1546, approximate date of death 1589; (3) apprenticed 1547, no further details; (4) freedom by patrimony, 1584.

[21] A copy of the fifty-year lease is to be found in RBT: E 01/01/001, ff. 46 and 47, dated 12 June, 19 Eliz. The property survey is RBT: E 01/02/008; White appears on f. 17r.

[22] For White paying the rent in 1583/4, see RBT: F 01/102, f. 89, and for the rental that shows the payment by his widow Livia, RBT: F 01/103, f. 108.

[23] For Sperynge's leases see RBT: E 01/01/001, ff. 52–3 (first lease, twenty-one years) and ff. 99v–101 (second lease, 11 June 1590, for fifty years, in consideration of his having done substantial rebuilding of the tenement). The tenancy passed to his daughter and son-in-law in 1608/9 (RBT: F 01/105, f. 295v), showing that he is the individual of that name whose burial is recorded in the register of the parish of St Andrew Undershaft, where the Leadenhall properties lay, under the date 3 December 1608. LMA P69/AND4/A/001/MS04107/001.

Figure 12. 'The uprights of the houses belonging to Rochester Bridg that front Leaden hall Street in London.' From the 1719 estate plan drawn by George Russell for the Wardens of Rochester Bridge (RBT: E01/02/014). These tenements survived the Great Fire of 1666. The property leased by John White is the substantial building (commanding a high rent) which appears on the far right. In addition to the main door 'K', there was an entrance on Leadenhall Street under the archway 'L'. It also therefore in part bordered on Shaft Alley 'L'. The door to Nicholas Sperynge's property is marked 'D'. Published by permission of the Wardens and Assistants of the Rochester Bridge Trust.

selling imported instruments from their rented tenements; John White's renewed lease of 1577 shows that his high annual rent of £6. 6s. 8d. secured him a large tenement comprising 'shoppis, sellers, sollers and all and singuler the casements comodities and appurtenances to the same belonging . . . '.[24] An elevation drawn by George Russell for the Wardens in 1719 shows the White and Sperynge properties as they then appeared, no doubt after much reconfiguration of the interior and external modification (Figure 12).[25]

There may be another trace of this John White. In 1559, a certain 'John White citizen of London, draiper' was in Bristol, endeavouring to obtain payment for a bill of exchange made out in Bilbao. The debtor's widow refused to pay at first, but White eventually recovered the money and produced a handwritten receipt for it.[26] He was acting on behalf of a London merchant named John Jakes. This is the individual of that name who was Master of the Merchant Tailors' Company in 1552–3 and whose will of 1565 records a bequest of three pounds (or mourning clothes of the same value) to a brother-in-law named John Whyte.[27]

---

[24] The rent was to be paid annually at the Crown Inn in Rochester, whose descendant still stands, by Rochester bridge chapel.

[25] The advice of Dr James Gibson, archivist of the Rochester Bridge Trust, has been of immense assistance in establishing these details.

[26] Bristol Record Office, P.St JB/ChW/7/b, no. 233. See Vanes, ed., *Documents Illustrating the Overseas Trade of Bristol in the Sixteenth Century*, 126–7.

[27] TNA PROB/11/48/191.

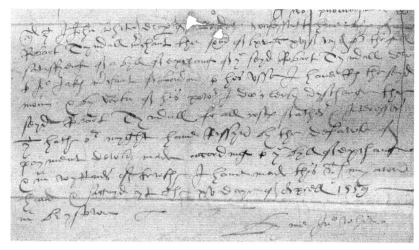

Figure 13.   Receipt in the hand of 'John White draper of London'. Bristol Record Office, P.St JB/ChW/7/b, no. 233. Dated 15 April 1559. Reproduced by permission.

In the same will, Jakes refers several times to his father-in-law, the draper John Brooke. This is the name and trade of a merchant who imported six Venice lutes in 1568; furthermore, the ship that brought that cargo of instruments for John Brooke also carried skins for a certain John White, draper. This is either an unusually dense network of coincidences or an indication that we have found our John White again and have also stumbled upon a document both written in his hand and bearing his signature (Figure 13).

In the 'relatively intimate society' of Tudor England, a lack of institutional support for business activity, investment and credit meant that 'family and kinship support structures were vital'.[28] Bills of exchange passed between men who trusted one another and invested in one another's schemes, their capital and credit enhanced by loans, gifts and bequests. So it was with the commerce in instruments. Much of it lay in the hands of men closely acquainted or even related by marriage.

III

John White dealt with nowhere but Antwerp, and no London merchant of 1567/8 imported instruments or strings, in a legal manner, from anywhere else save one consignment from Venice. Some of these instruments and strings were manufactured locally – the grocer John Alden imported twelve 'Antwerp lutes' – but for the most part we may suspect that Antwerp served as a redistribution centre for instruments built elsewhere. This was

[28]   Raven, *The Business of Books*, 42.

essentially a matter of commercial geopolitics. For most English travellers who were not envoys to the French royal court, continental travel predominantly meant going eastwards once the Channel was crossed. When one English voyager of the early 1550s put to sea he went to 'low Duchland', meaning Flanders and Brabant, and then passed six months in Antwerp before heading down to Italy; even though he was a musician, not a merchant, his horizons were set by voyages to the staple market for woollen broadcloths that had worn a rut in the sea, so to speak, as surely as any cartwheel on the land, stretching from the English ports to Antwerp.[29] It was especially in Antwerp that Protestant and other controversialists published their polemics for an English readership with impunity, exploiting the same well-worn route, and there also that the Merchant Adventurers, the most powerful financial interest group in Tudor England, kept a headquarters to control the trade in unfinished cloth that was the basis of their wealth and influence. In 1567/8 it was therefore inevitable that English merchants would source instruments in Antwerp because of its vital importance – for the time being at least – to the English textile trade; any London merchant could count on a regular supply of hold-space in ships that had gone out with cloth for the continental finishing centres and were ready to make the return journey.

This was not destined to last. At the end of 1568, sensing themselves threatened on all sides by Catholic powers, the English authorities impounded a cargo of coin in a Spanish ship bound for the Netherlands but compelled, by stormy weather, to put in at Southampton. The Spanish swiftly took reprisals against English merchants; ships at Dunkirk and Antwerp were seized and merchants were arrested.[30] From the end of 1568, when the money was taken, until the summer of 1573, when an attempt was made to address the question of Spanish losses, the authorities in the Spanish Netherlands imposed a block on maritime movement that prevented English commerce with the Low Countries; the English government, in turn, forbade trading with the Spanish royal dominions in the Netherlands and repeatedly sequestered ships passing from Spain to Flanders. The Merchant Adventurers made arrangements to trade elsewhere, notably in Hamburg and Emden, the former more apt to their purposes than the latter. Antwerp was sacked by a mutinous Spanish army in 1576, and in October 1582 English merchants abandoned the city altogether.

[29] This musician is Thomas Whythorne, the subject of Chapter 7 below.
[30] *Calendar of State Papers (Domestic), 1547–80*, 325–7; *Calendar of State Papers (Spain), 1568–79*, 89ff, and 100–2 for the official English account of the seizure of the Spanish money. The major study of these events and their long-term implications for the Antwerp trade is Blanchard, *The International Economy in the 'Age of Discoveries'*; Ramsay, *The City of London*, and *The Queen's Merchants*.

For the importation of gitterns, and indeed most stringed instruments, the effects of the rupture with Antwerp were surely profound. To compare the entries in the Port Book of 1567/8 with the records of overseas inward trade for 1574 (Box 2), a year for which a book also survives, albeit recording the alien trade, is to discover the commerce in imported instruments much reduced from what it was a decade earlier, and that Antwerp has vanished.[31]

BOX 2

Names of importers bringing in cargoes of musical instruments or strings to the Port of London between Michaelmas 1574 and Easter 1575. From TNA E 190/6/3.

f. 3r, 20 October 1574, *Le Sigoma*, Calais, Rouen
Lewis Cassaris 'allien j paier virginals j vyoll'

f. 4, 5 November 1574, *Elizabeth*, Burnam, Dunkirk
Handburt Vasner 'allien j cheste with aparell et iiij coverlite v yardes baies liiij yardes grogram ij yeardes borato ij deske for a womman j harquebut j crowsbowe j sitterne'

Many of the London Port Books have perished, so the surviving volumes can only give isolated glimpses of imports in a volatile trading environment where the cost of credit could vary sharply in a comparatively short time. The decline measured here from the 1567/8 levels is so severe, however, that it seems reasonable to assume a major change has overtaken the structure – and the vigour – of the market for these commodities. Now there is only a pair of virginals, a viol (the only one I have encountered anywhere in the London Port Books) and a cittern. There is no trace of the gittern. Advancing further to the book for 1588 (Box 3), we find that trade in musical instruments appears to have collapsed altogether, although there is still a ready market for strings.

BOX 3

Names and occupations of importers bringing in cargoes of musical instruments or strings to the Port of London between 1 January and 31 December 1588. From TNA E 190/8/1, a record of overseas inward trade conducted by native and Hanse merchants. The numbers in parentheses are those assigned to each consignment in the original.

---

[31] For this section, E 190/8/2, imports by aliens from 1 January 1589 to 31 December 1589, was also checked.

BOX 3 (*cont.*)

f. 3r   10 April (18)   *Le Greyhound*, Hamburg, Hamburg
William Barnabe *haberdasher* 'half a groce lut stringes'
f. 8v   9 May (8)   *Le Mereman*, Hamburg, Hamburg
Richard Osborne *haberdasher* 'j chest wᵗ xxx boxes lut strings'
f. 34v   23 July (3)   *Le Fortune*, Amsterdam, Middleburg
Jerome Gossens *mercer* 'j chest wᵗ iij groce wooden pypes, j groce of Ffiddles for
    children'
f. 35   24 July (6)   *Le Fortune*, Amsterdam, Middleburg
Peter Jacobbes 'iiij c. small Lightwod boardes to make virgynalles cost xls'
f. 40v   26 July (189)   *Le Adonias*, London, Stade
Richard Foxe 'lxx lb virginall wyer'
f. 41r   26 July (193)   *Le Tobie*, London, Stade
Richard Foxe *leatherseller* 'iij boxes lut stringes'
f. 41r   26 July (195)   *Le Dolphin*, Lee, Stade
Richard Foxe *leatherseller* 'ciiij ix lbs virginall wyer'
f. 41r   26 July (201)   *Le Pinnace*, Lee, Stade
Richard Foxe *leatherseller* 'cxlviij [lbs] virginall wyer'
f. 43v   26 July (276)   *Le Salamander*, Lee, Stade
Luke Lane *grocer* 'x boxes lut stringes'
f. 44v   26 July (303)   *Le Talbot*, Lee, Stade
John Passfild *armourer* '30 lbs weight claricord wyer'
f. 44v   26 July (305)   *Le Ant. Bonaventure*, London, Stade
John Passfild *armourer* 'xx gr[oce] lut stringes'
f. 46r   26 July (354)   *Le Pinnace*, Lee, Stade
Thomas Webbe *haberdasher* 'xxvij boxes minikins'
f. 46v   26 July (355)   *Le Salamander*, Lee, Stade
Christopher Willoughbie *mercer* 'j Iron chest wᵗ viij boxes lut stringes'
f. 51v   26 July (533)   *Le Salamander*, Lee, Stade
Randall Symes *clothworker* 'v bundles Jewes trumpes'
f. 60r   27 July (44)   *Le Marie Gallant*, Lee, Stade
Jon Clietts *leatherseller* 'xiiij boxes lutt stringes'

There are some surprises here, notably the 'Jewes trumpes' and 'Ffiddles for children'. The former were set to become one of the toys, in the Tudor sense of 'trifles', that Elizabethan mariners used to beguile (as they supposed) the native populations that they encountered, while the 'Ffiddles for children' were toys in the modern sense, slowly developing into an important part of the haberdasher's stock-in-trade during the later Elizabethan period. The only evocation of a serious instrument appears with the load of 'iiij c. small Lightwod boardes to make virgynalles'. The home ports of the shipmasters now include the Hanse port of Stade on the Elbe, Middleburg in Zeeland and Hamburg. Without knowing it, John

White imported his gitterns in the nick of time when he dispatched his various orders to Antwerp in 1568.

IV

What of the trade in strings? In 1541, a musical-instrument maker of Barcelona named Melcior Gallard signed a receipt to meet half the cost of the entrails that a local butcher, Pedro Salino, would supply on a contractual basis.[32] The viscera were to be taken from slaughtered rams, but similar contracts from sixteenth-century Spain also mention the intestines of pigs. Such arrangements are not often documented, and yet they must have been common in many parts of Europe. The manufacture of a stringed instrument in the sixteenth century (and long after) was not just a matter of craftsmanship with fragrant timber; it also required a material as unmusical, in its raw state, and as unappealing, as anything in Creation. The string maker, using bundles of entrails that began to slither towards putrefaction as soon as they were obtained from the abattoir, worked quickly to clean, stabilise and twist the filaments that gave each instrument its voice.

The paradoxical process of drawing sweet music from such a noxious material struck Shakespeare while he was writing *Much Ado About Nothing* ('Is it not strange that sheeps' guts should hale souls out of men's bodies?'), but there is little reason to suppose that the process of string making was very familiar to anyone in Tudor England. Musicians in London and elsewhere chiefly depended upon the imported work of craftsmen in foreign cities with established traditions of expertise in the craft.[33] The distribution centre of outstanding importance, until the late 1560s, was Antwerp. The London Port Book of 1567/8 provides an unparalleled record of the strings imported into the English capital, and all consignments came from there. The book distinguishes harp strings, lute strings and minikins (treble strings), all listed in the Rate Book of 1558, but also the basses and middle-range strings called catlins,

---

[32] For sixteenth-century references to strings of pig and ram gut, see Romanillos Vega and Winspear, *The Vihuela de Mano*, 134, 256 and 311.

[33] John Dowland offers a conspectus of these centres in *Varietie of Lute-Lessons* (1610), D1^r–v. There were strings from 'Rome and other parts of Italy', including Livorno in Tuscany, that arrived 'bound vp by certain Dozens in bundels'; others came packed in boxes from Germany, notably 'Monnekin and Mildorpe' (presumably Munich and Meldorf), together with 'the greater sorts or Base strings, some . . . made at Nurenburge, and also at Straesburge, and bound vp onely in knots like other strings'. Dowland reports that Bologna also produced good bass strings, sent on to Venice and therefore called 'Venice Catlines' (see n. 34). From there they were shipped to the marts at Frankfurt and Leipzig, where the wise merchant was careful to buy strings at the Michaelmas fair, made the previous summer, for the winter-made strings on sale at the Easter marts were of inferior quality (the difference presumably arose from the quality of the summer as opposed to winter feed).

meaning 'kittens' (the full list of musical items listed in the book is given in Box 1 above).[34]

Tudor merchants had good reason to add musical strings to the commodities they imported, despite the impossibility of guaranteeing either quality control or customer satisfaction in a market where no maker, and therefore no middleman, could guarantee that every string in a bundle would be equally true. Strings fetched a good price relative to their weight and bulk, both of which were negligible, especially if they were the expensive trebles or 'minikins' associated with Munich but not exclusively from there. This is evident from the work of the merchant who dominates the string trade in the Port Book mentioned above, the haberdasher Richard Billingsley. He belonged to a well-known family whose most conspicuous member in contemporary records is Henry Billingsley, Lord Mayor of London in 1596 and an important collector of music books printed on the continent, including a series of motet and chanson anthologies published by Phalèse in 1554–60; Henry also imported at least one substantial consignment of strings, as Box 1 above shows.[35] His brother Richard, however, was a much more prolific importer, for he brought in eight different shipments during a twelve-month, together with the more obvious stock-in-trade for a haberdasher, such as packthread and pins. Box 1 shows that *The Swallow* of London brought him thirty gross of harp strings while soon after *The Primrose* of Lee came with thirty gross more and three gross of minikins. The same ship brought him another forty gross of harp strings (we begin to suspect that 'harp strings' was used by the officials as a general term). This by no

---

[34] The origin of the term 'Catlin', which appears in various spellings, is unknown, but the word is presumably identical to Early Modern English 'catling' (spellings vary) meaning 'kitten' (*OED*, 'catling'; *LEME*, 'cat'; the form 'catling' is used in a musical context in *Romeo and Juliet* (Act IV, Scene 5). If so, then the '-lin' element is not a form of the noun 'line' but the diminutive suffix 'ling' to be pronounced as in 'earthling'. In *Varietie of Lute-Lessons* (1610), Sig. Di[v], as mentioned in n. 33, John Dowland reports that Bologna produced good bass strings which were sent on to Venice and were therefore called '*Venice* Catlines'; this plainly means that the strings were called '*Venice* Catlines' because they were sent to Venice and distributed from there, but it may also imply that they were called 'Venice *Catlines*' for the same reason. A possible explanation is suggested by the figurative use of Early Modern English 'cat', which in canting speech meant a prostitute (*OED*, 'cat', sense 2b, with examples from 1401; cf. the more recent 'cat house', for 'brothel'). Venice was famous for its prostitutes, whence George Baker, trans., *The newe iewell of health* (1576), 211, 'a famous curtisan in Venice'; George Gylpen, trans., *The bee hiue of the Romishe Church* (1579), 194, 'the Courtesans of Rome and Venice'; and Laurence Ramsay, *The practice of the diuell* (1577), Sig. Bi[v], 'Curtizans of Venice'. Cf. also (1) John Webster, *The White Devil* (1612) recounting 'The Life and Death of Vittoria Corombona the famous Venetian Curtizan'; (2) Iago's exploitation of the reputation of Venetian whores in Shakespeare's *Othello* (Act IV, Scene 2, 'I took you for that cunning whore of Venice'); and (3) Thomas Coryat's account of Venetian whores in his *Crudities* (1611), 264ff. The association became proverbial, as recorded by James Howell in his *Paroimiographia Proverbs* of 1659: 'Treviso tripes Padua bread, and Venice whores ... '. For Venetian prostitutes and the lute, see again Coryat, *Crudities*, 267. The term 'Venice catline' may therefore mean, in the literal sense 'Venetian kittens', figuratively Venetian whores.

[35] Milsom, 'Sacred Songs in the Chamber', 178–9, n.

means accounts for all Richard's imports, which never included musical instruments and mark him as a determined importer of strings for the English market.

As a result of such imports, strings were easy to find, at least in London. John Petre, at the Inns of Court, had no difficulty securing a dozen lute strings in February 1567, and when he needed more in May he obtained them from a certain Bartlett at Fleet Bridge, evidently a middleman.[36] Those far from the capital could also be quite well served. It was an easy and potentially profitable undertaking to transfer strings at London to another vessel for the coastal trade to regional ports, to load them up along with other goods for internal carriage by wagon, or even perhaps to sell them at wholesale price to a peddler. In the 1580s, a merchant named William Wray was supplying clients in Ripon, North Yorkshire, with a wide range of general goods, including knots of minikins, small quantities of cloth, buttons and silks that he sold to a certain William Meres of Leeds. Meres was an unusually distant client for Wray, most of whose customers dwelled within six miles of Ripon, so it is possible he was a peddler.[37] Other documents, notably inventories, show sellers of haberdashery or general goods stocking strings in other provincial towns. In 1564, the stock of John Lughting, a Southampton mercer, included 'a boxe of lute stringes xijd'.[38] There was a similar shop in Norwich; the shelves in 1584 carried ginger, playing cards, spectacles, needles and 'a boxe with old lute stringes'.[39] An especially striking inventory lists the vast number of goods that a shopkeeper named James Backhouse kept in the small town of Kirby Lonsdale (Cumbria) in 1578; haberdasher, draper and stationer combined, Backhouse evidently kept a significant stock of strings, for his executors found 'A gros of kettlins' valued at three shillings and 'iij dos. of mynykens' valued at three shillings and sixpence.[40] These records do not necessarily show that provincial mercers were diversifying their general wares beyond what a London merchant would consider usual, and indeed the situation in the capital was probably much the same, though a buyer surely had a better chance of acquiring more specialised items there. It is certain that 'dedicated' strings for the gittern, for example, could be bought in London, at least by 1578; in that year a certain John Whithall wrote

---

[36] Essex County Record Office, D/DPA17.
[37] Fowler, 'The Account Book of William Wray', 81 (18 June, 'ij knotes of menykinges, iiijd'; 29 June, 'ij knots of menykings iiijd'; and 2 September, 'iij knots of menyking vjd'). Wray also paid a minstrel 4s. 7d. for unspecified 'wares' (*ibid.*, 56). This would have bought him an instrument. There is an illuminating analysis of Wray's accounts in Willan, *The Inland Trade*, 63–70. See also 53–6 and 77–8 on peddlers.
[38] Roberts and Parker, *Southampton Probate Inventories*, vol. 1, 201–23, inventory of John Lughting, merchant, 1564.
[39] Norfolk County Records Office, DN/INV 2/134.
[40] Raine, ed., *Wills and Inventories . . . Richmond*, 280. Further on this shopkeeper, see Willan, *The Inland Trade*, 60–1.

from Santos in Brazil to the London shipping magnate Richard Staper with an order for many small goods, most of which he would have expected his contacts to find in a haberdasher's shop, such as scissors, knives, and locks for doors and chests; his order also included 'Foure mases of gitterne strings'.[41]

[41] The letter is quoted in Hakluyt, *The Principal Nauigations*, 703.

CHAPTER 4

'An instruction to the Gitterne'

I

Sir Thomas Elyot's *The boke named the Gouernour* is a work that Surrey, the most exalted poet of Elyot's generation, might have called a 'guide to bring/Our English youth, by travail, unto fame'. First published in 1531, and dedicated to Henry VIII, the book counsels all tutors of the young – the future servants of the common weal – to be temperate. The more severe parts of the curriculum should alternate with some pleasant learning, including music, so that pupils do not become exhausted or disgusted with their studies. To this end, Elyot offers a chapter to explain 'in what wise musike may be to a noble man necessarie', but without neglecting 'what modestie ought to be therin'. Such allusions to 'noble' men reflect the decorum customarily observed by Tudor authors, obliged to write as if only the patron class need be addressed; they do not define the only audience Elyot wished to reach, and the 'modestie' that he commends in musical study, implying restraint and temperance, was not traditionally regarded as a noble virtue.[1] (Although the virtue of keeping to 'the meane' in all things was a favourite topic of contemporary poets, one did not commission a portrait from Nicholas Hilliard, or pay a fortune for tournament armour, in order to appear temperate.) Moderation, however, could mean a great deal to those who aspired to become respected persons in their livery company, or in their parish, without the benefit of an inherited title or estate. Furthermore, Elyot recommends that a young man should learn to play instruments 'for the refresshynge of his witte', a counsel well suited to lawyers, merchants compiling their ledgers and all self-made men in Tudor England with a career to pursue.[2]

Such men and their wives were increasingly becoming members of what might be called the portrait class: those whose ambitions ran to commissioning a panel portrait in oils. The sitters in such pictures almost

---

[1] *OED*, sv 'modesty', 1.i.
[2] *The boke named the Gouernour* (1st edn, 1531), ff. 21v–24. For the political dimension of Elyot's writing as advice to a prince, see Walker, *Writing Under Tyranny*.

invariably appear with bare hands – holding their gloves, not wearing them – for hands that were well groomed, not roughened or soiled by work, were a source of pride. To play a musical instrument like the gittern or lute was therefore to display an indisputably elite form of hygiene. When players of the gittern were finally offered a printed tutor for their instrument, very late in the 1560s, they were not taught how to 'play' but to 'conduct and dispose the hand', while in 1603 Thomas Robinson advised the players of various stringed instruments 'to keepe your hands cleane'. This is evidently more than merely practical advice, as witness the vast number of blacksmiths, husbandmen, yeoman farmers and pressmen that it excludes.[3] Several generations later, the counsel of Mary Burwell in her lute book is similar to Robinson's, save that the social register of well-groomed hands is more sharply conveyed; they must be kept spotless because that is 'the marke of a Gentleman and a Lady'.[4] Like a panel portrait in oils, at first an aristocratic fashion, the gittern lay at the point where the refinement, ostentation and profligacy of the nobility met the aspirations, the moderation and the thrift of the middling sort.[5] Much more accommodating to those of modest ability than the lute, it offered a courtier the chance to display a nonchalant ease just as it gave the professional man a quick return on his investment.

In Sir Thomas Elyot's day, amateur musicians studied their instruments with a friend, a member of their own family or a professional such as a minstrel, a singing man in a major church or a musical factotum like John Heywood. Some manuscript materials, including sets of instructions for tuning harp and lute, passed from hand to hand, and some of them may have been quite substantial, but there is no sign of anything reaching print before the 1560s.[6] Unlike the craft of tending to horses, or grafting and planting, the rudiments of musical instruments seem never to have formed an antecedent stream of material in manuscript that printers could use and adapt; during the first half of the sixteenth century, even a royal lutenist like Giles Duwes only ventured into print as a teacher of his native tongue, which

---

[3] *The Schoole of Musicke: Wherein is Tavght, the Perfect Method, of Trve Fingering of the* Lute, Pandora, Orpharion, *and* Viol de Gamba, Sig. Cij.

[4] Spencer, ed., *The Burwell Lute Tutor*, f. 16v. The history of touch on renaissance instruments is an unwritten chapter in the history of grooming and hygiene. In the modern West, prosperity and plumbing together have literally washed away the idea that the state of an individual's hands may be a guide to their social position, and bathing is sufficiently widespread that washing is no longer 'an act of seemliness confined to the visible parts of the skin', primarily the hands and the face (Vigarello, *Concepts of Cleanliness*, 48).

[5] For examples, extending into the seventeenth century, see Cooper, *Citizen Portrait*, Plates 1, 23, 26, 39, 55, 78, 80, 82, 86, 87, 105, 108, 114, 123, 124 *et passim*.

[6] See the instructions for tuning a harp in Cambridge, Trinity College MS O.2.53 (edited in Handschin, 'Aus der alten Musiktheorie', 3) and the diagram of a harp, with tuning instructions, in Youngs, *Humphrey Newton*, Plate 8. See also Hanham, 'The Musical Studies of a Fifteenth-Century Wool Merchant', 271–2, and cf. Page, 'The Fifteenth-Century Lute', 18–19, and Plate 5 (instructions for the lute, *c*. 1500).

was French, not as a master of the lute.[7] Yet it would not be correct to say that print was generally divorced from practice in England before 1550; books were primarily used to guide readers 'within particular fields of practice or knowledge, toward some more or less practical end',[8] and the advent of printing allowed some forms of knowledge that had once been the exclusive property of court musicians, masters of hawking, physicians and members of literary coteries to become a commodity in the marketplace. As Richard Tottel observes in the preface to his 'Miscellany' of 1557, with specific reference to courtly poetry, 'ungentle' people had long hoarded such treasure; now it could be disseminated through the medium of print.[9] The Elizabethan book trade therefore developed a healthy innovative sector where publishers hazarded works on such matters as hawking, board games and medicine, hoping to sell out the first edition with some speed and then reprint.[10]

It was probably in 1569 that Tudor players of the four-course guitar were offered the only tutor for that instrument published in England, and the only one to survive from sixteenth-century Europe.[11] To say that the book was 'published' is something of an exaggeration, since the surviving leaves of the book represent a series of test-pulls, not pages from the volume as it was printed for sale. Even to maintain that the book 'survives' is somewhat to overstate the case, since only eight pages have so far been found, all of them by chance. Yet the book did appear, showing that the demand for such instruction in England now exceeded what personal networks, or the employment of professional teachers, could provide. Not everyone could afford to keep a French instrumentalist in the way that Sir William Petre retained John the Frenchman, and some were accordingly prepared to use an impersonal and commercial alternative to supplement or even replace the personal instruction long regarded as a mark of leisure and gentility amongst men of Petre's class.

To meet this demand, various tutors for stringed instruments were printed in London, or were at least licensed, in a sudden burst of activity that extended for just under a decade, beginning in 1565/6. These books are listed in Box 4, with the tutor for the four-course guitar forming the entry for 1568/9.

[7] *An introductorie for to lerne to rede, to pronounce, and to speake Frenche trewely* (1533?). For Duwes see *ODNB*, sv 'Duwes ... Giles'; *BDECM*, sv 'Duwes, Giles'; Pearsall, 'Tudor Court Musicians', vol. 1, 146–8, and Dumitrescu, *The Early Tudor Court*, 82.

[8] Cormack and Mazzio, *Book Use, Book Theory*, 4. See also Weiss, 'Didactic Sources of Musical Learning'; Sherman, *Used Books*; and Keiser, 'Practical Books for the Gentleman'.

[9] Tottel's 'Miscellany', 3. Tottel's book has inspired a great deal of recent work on the changing status of English in the mid-sixteenth century and the political, confessional and cultural discourses surrounding it. See Warner, *The Making and Marketing of Tottel's Miscellany*, and the essays in Hamrick, ed., *Tottel's* Songes and Sonettes *in Context*.

[10] On the 'innovative' sector in the Elizabethan book trade, see Farmer and Lesser, 'What is Print Popularity?', 42ff.

[11] I leave out of account the Latin instructions in *Selectissima elegantissimaque gallica italica et latina in guiterna ludenda carmina*, published by Pierre Phalèse in 1570, since these appear to have been hybridised with instructions for cittern. See Appendix D.

BOX 4

Sets of instructions for musical instruments, either (a) represented by extant copies, or (b) attested by entries in the register of the Stationers' Company, from the first traces of such works to 1603. Note that (1) all titles in Arber's transcript known only from the Stationers' Register have been checked against a microfilm of the original, and (2) the dates assigned to titles known only from the Register represent the financial year (running from 22 July to 22 July) in which the printer's payment for permission to publish was entered in the fair copy of the Warden's accounts for audit; they do not indicate the year in which the book was actually published, which remains unknown, confirm that the book was eventually published or imply any oversight or censorship of the contents by the Stationers.

1565/6

John Alde pays 4d. for a licence to print *The Scyence of lutynge*. This publication is known only from an entry in the Stationers' Register. Alde was a well-known printer with a flourishing line in broadsheet ballads; his decision to venture this book or pamphlet shows a versatile printer trying his hand at material for amateur instrumentalists and then moving on without apparently returning. (Arber, ed., *Transcript*, vol. 1, f. 133v, where 'Scyence' is mistranscribed as 'Sequence', followed by Brown, *Instrumental Music*, [1565]$_6$.)

1567

Edward Sutton, stationer and bookbinder, pays 6d. for a licence to print *An exortation to all kynde of men how thay shulde lerne to playe of the lute by Roberte Ballarde*. This publication is known only from an entry in the Stationers' Register. The fee of 6d. is a step above the standard minimum and may indicate a book of some substance, but it remains unknown how the fee charged was affected not only by the number of sheets required to print the book but also by the presence of tablature.[12] (Arber, ed., *Transcript*, vol. 1, f. 156. Brown, *Instrumental Music*, [1567]$_1$.)

1568

James Rowbothum, bookseller and Freeman of the Drapers' Company, publishes his first lute book, *A Briefe and easye instru[c]tion to learne the tableture to conducte and dispose thy hande vnto the lute*, translated from a lost

---

[12] See Jackson, 'Variant Entry Fees'. I am grateful to Peter W. M. Blayney for an informative letter on this point.

BOX 4 (*cont.*)

French original by Adrian Le Roy and printed by John Kyngston. (Brown, *Instrumental Music*, 1568₃. Available on *EEBO*; facsimile also in Saint-Arroman and Dugot, *Méthodes et Traités, Luth*, vol. I, 55–93).

1568/9

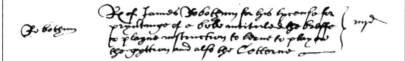

James Rowbothum pays 4*d.* for a licence to print *The breffe and playne instruction to lerne to play on the gyttron and also the Cetterne.*[13] Only eight pages (four leaves) are known to survive, reproduced below as Figures 14–17. The title page is lost, but something very close to the full title of the published work can be recovered from Andrew Maunsell's 1595 *Catalogue of English Printed Bookes* (vol. II, 18), where it appears as *A briefe and plaine instruction for to learne the Tablature, to Conduct and dispose the hand vnto the Gitterne* (i.e. with no reference to the cittern). For a reconstruction of the title page, see Figure 20 below. The book was almost certainly printed by John Kyngston. For convenience, this work is referred to in this chapter by the short title on most of the surviving pages: 'An instruction to the Gitterne'. (Arber, ed., *Transcript*, vol. I, f. 174; Brown, *Instrumental Music*, [1568]₉.)

1574

James Rowbothum completes his series of methods (to judge by what survives) with a second lute book translated from a lost original of Adrian Le Roy. The English version is entitled *A briefe and plaine Instruction to set all Musicke of eight diuers tunes in Tableture for the Lute* and incorporates another edition of the 1568 book, with the text reset. Printed by John Kyngston.[14] (Brown, *Instrumental Music*, 1574₂. Available on *EEBO*; facsimile also in Saint-Arroman and Dugot, *Méthodes et Traités, Luth*, vol. I, 95–185.)

Given that Box 4 spans a period of nearly forty years, from 1565/6 to 1603, it reveals a relatively meagre and derivative set of publications,

---

[13] Arber, ed., *Transcript*, vol. I, 174v. Brown, *Instrumental Music*, 1568₉. *ESTC* S96083 incorrectly describes the notation as 'French cittern tablature'.

[14] For editions and the textual history of the Le Roy lute books, as published in English translations, see Jacquot, *et al.*, eds., *Œuvres d'Adrian Le Roy*, vol. I.

BOX 4 *(cont.)*

1593

William Barley issues *A new booke of Citterne Lessons*. This publication is known only from the listing in Andrew Maunsell, *Catalogue of English Printed Bookes* (1595), vol. II, 18. (Brown, *Instrumental Music*, [1593]$_1$.)

1596

William Barley issues *A new Booke of Tabliture, Containing sundrie easie and familiar Instructions, showing howe to attaine to the knowledge, to guide and dispose thy hand to play on sundry Instruments, as the* Lute, Orpharion, *and* Bandora. (Brown, *Instrumental Music*, 1596$_{4-6}$, listing the three elements of the book, which have separate title pages, as separate items. Available on *EEBO*; facsimile published by Cornetto-Verlag (Stuttgart, 2000).)

1603

Thomas Robinson issues *The Schoole of Musicke: Wherein is Tavght, the Perfect Method, of Trve Fingering of the* Lute, Pandora, Orpharion, *and* Viol de Gamba*; with most Infallible Generall Rules, both Easie and Delightfull.* (Brown, *Instrumental Music*, [1593]$_1$. Available on *EEBO*; facsimile published by Da Capo Press (New York, 1973).)

massively outclassed by the output of continental printers, and until the end of the sixteenth century there is no sign of original English work. It seems that manuals for instrumentalists only emerged in England when a work was published abroad that a native printer or bookseller saw an opportunity to translate. (Much the same may be said for books on the kindred accomplishments of dancing and fencing.[15]) The earlier methods listed in Box 4 are all translations of Parisian originals by Adrian Le Roy, and one not yet found was registered as the work of his business partner, Robert Ballard. What is more, the actual tally of published methods for the

---

[15] The art of dancing had reached the printing house as early as 1521 with Robert Coplande's treatise *The maner of dauncynge of bace dances after the vse of fraunce and other places*, but that was because the book had been '*translated out of french in englysshe*'. See Ward, 'The Maner of Dauncying'. The art of fencing – the means to slay an opponent in a personal quarrel arising from a slight to one's honour – did not acquire a substantial literature in England until the 1590s when suitable models became available. See Jackson, ed., *Three Elizabethan Fencing Manuals*. More broadly see Boffey, 'Wynkyn de Worde, Richard Pynson, and the English Printing of Texts translated from French'. On the general poverty of sixteenth-century English printed materials relating to 'theory, description or comment' in the musical domain see Bray, 'Music and the Quadrivium'.

whole period may be even smaller than the table suggests, for two are known only from entries in the Stationers' Register (including the Ballard example) and it is possible that they were never printed.

Has a great deal of material perhaps been lost, without trace? We have reason to doubt it. Andrew Maunsell's *Catalogue* of 1595 records printed works on music from as far back as 1560, but lists only one instrumental tutor that we no longer possess, namely William Barley's cittern book of 1593. Apart from that volume, Maunsell knows of just two published methods for musical instruments, and they are both listed in Box 4.[16] Early readers of his catalogue sometimes accepted his invitation to annotate and update his work; there is no census of these annotations, but a preliminary survey of copies in Britain, Ireland and the United States has yielded no evidence that Maunsell's readers found method books for instruments 'buried in some few studies' (his words) that we do not know.[17] Needless to say, Maunsell's catalogue has its limits; he only recorded books that he had seen, and he knew that many publications were 'quite forgotten'. As it stands, however, the record he provides, and the evidence of the annotated copies, do not suggest that many Tudor instrument method books in English have vanished.[18]

II

Until the end of the century and the work of William Barley, the key figure in the publication of method books was evidently James Rowbothum. All the tutors that he published survive, either whole or in part. An apprentice draper in 1556 and then 'very yonge' (but not too youthful to be granted the Freedom of the Company that he received on 1 September 1557), Rowbothum appears several times in the Stationers' records, in addition to

---

[16] Maunsell, *Catalogue*, vol. II, 18. For the cittern volume, see Brown, *Instrumental Music*, [1593]₁.

[17] I have personally inspected, or have gathered information about, the following: (1) Cambridge, Trinity College, VI.3.60; though annotated, this adds nothing to the page listing tutors for instruments. (2) Cambridge, University Library, Adv.b.52.1, with MS additions taken from a copy owned by Samuel Harsnett, Archbishop of York (d. 1631), and with some additions by the antiquary Thomas Baker (d. 1740); it adds only William Barley's *A new Booke of Tabliture* (1596) which Maunsell could not list. (3) A heavily annotated copy in the Henry E. Huntington Library and Art Gallery, available on *EEBO*, adds only Barley (1596). (4) The annotated copy in London, Lambeth Palace Library, 1595.5, adds only Barley (1596). The following were found to be without annotations either entirely or on the relevant page: (a) Trinity College, Dublin, Department of Early Printed Books, OL 015.42 MAU. (b) British Library, 618.i.17, reproduced in the 1965 Gregg Press facsimile. (c) Lambeth Palace Library, 1595.5. (d) University of Michigan, SPEC\Z\2002\451. (e) Harvard, Houghton Library, B. 2076.1*. (f) Cambridge University Library, Syn.4.59.16 lacks the section on music.

[18] The gap in publications revealed by Box 4 coincides suspiciously well with the period of the Tallis and Byrd monopoly, ceded by royal patent for twenty-one years from 1575 to 1596, but it is not clear whether the terms of that patent extended to tutor books, mostly using tablature with some staff notation. The monopoly governed the publication of 'set songe or songes in partes' in various languages which might be 'plaid or soonge' in church, chamber or elsewhere. The terms are quoted in Milsom and Fenlon, '"Ruled Paper Imprinted"', 139–40.

the entries recording what he paid for licences to print.[19] In 1563 he was
fined for binding 200 primers in wooden boards or 'skabertes', which may
indicate that he operated a bindery (though the work could have been put
out), while in 1577 he appears among those who 'do lyve by bookselling'
and were hindered by various royal privileges, including one granted to
'Byrde, a Singingman'. Making his living from books alone, Rowbothum
was quite prepared to pirate material, and even to defy a bishop of London
by doing so, which resulted in him being called 'a man of notable impudens' (see below).

In that regard, Rowbothum did not differ from most of his fellow
booksellers. He was exceptional, however, for the attention he gave to
pastimes. In 1562 he published a manual of chess with a fulsome preface
addressed to Robert Dudley; this was followed in 1563 by a book on
another board game, also dedicated to Dudley and stoutly defended by
Rowbothum against any possible detractors on the grounds that it is better
for men to play in honest fashion than to 'passe the tyme in idlenes'.[20]
(It would be easy to miss the weight of that assurance now that the value of
leisure is not contested.) When Rowbothum finally turned his attention to
the lute and gittern he did so with such enthusiasm that by 1574 his
address in the heart of the London printing district was 'Paternoster row at
the signe of the Lute'.[21]

In his musical ventures, Rowbothum kept one step ahead of his customers, as a good bookseller should. When he issued his first translation of
Adrian Le Roy's pedagogy for the lute in 1568 he wished all potential
buyers to know that the original was Parisian, and he included an English
version of Le Roy's preface which makes that clear, but without acknowl-
edgment of its author. Apparently the name of Adrian Le Roy meant little
in London, at least for the time being. In 1574, however, when interest had
clearly mounted, in part due to his own efforts, Rowbothum was careful to
assure the readers on the title page that the lute material he published that
year was 'first written in French by Adrian Le Roy'. Taken together,
Rowbothum's three tutors teach the reader how to use French lute

[19] One of the books published by James Rowbothum closes with a device that includes the three tiaras
    of the Drapers' Company (Ralph Lever, *The most noble, auncient, and learned playe, called the
    Phi[l]osophers game* (1563)). See McKerrow, *Printers' and Publishers' Devices*, 48–9, and Aldis, *et al.*,
    A Dictionary of Printers and Booksellers, sv 'Rowbotham (James)'. In the preface to the 1569 edition of
    The Pleasaunt and vwittie Plaie of the Cheastes renewed Rowbothum refers to himself as 'citisin of
    London', indicating that he is a freeman of a livery company. For the date of Rowbothum's freedom,
    and further details of his apprenticeships, see Blayney, *The Stationers' Company*, vol. II, 817.
[20] *The most noble, auncient, and learned playe, called the Phi[l]osophers game*, 'To the reader'.
[21] *A briefe and plaine Instruction to set all Musicke of eight diuers tunes in Tableture for the Lute*, title
    page. Merchants did not generally announce their premises with signs that related directly to their
    trade, to avoid confusion in a street where there might be several traders or merchants pursuing the
    same profession. For similar examples among printers, cf. Rycharde Jugge's shop 'at the signe of
    the Byble' or John Day's 'at the signe of the Resurrection', both designed to further a reputation for
    the authoritative issue of Protestant works and vernacular Scripture. Perhaps Rowbothum was
    envious of Pierre Attaingnant, who published in the 'Rue de la harpe'.

tablature, including the pointing system that guides the fingering of the right or plucking hand, while the musical examples range from simple chord sequences to render basic grounds (as in the gittern tutor), through elaborate fantasies (again in the gittern tutor) to sophisticated, even quasi-professional intabulations of French polyphonic vocal originals in the lute book of 1574. For an Elizabethan printer this was a commercial and typographical odyssey indeed.

It was also a metropolitan journey. The sense of London as the major centre of pedagogy for musical instruments, and as the heartland of the language for imparting it, was evidently of some account to Rowbothum, notably in the first of his lute books where the translator, J. Alford, is styled 'Londenor' on the title page. There are other cases of such usage in books issued during the second half of the sixteenth century and a surprisingly large number of them identify translators.[22] Potential buyers were apparently being assured by all these title pages, including Rowbothum's, that they were buying the work of a metropolitan gentleman at a time when there was a developing sense of 'our Southerne English . . . the vsuall speach of the Court, and that of London and the shires lying about London within lx. myles, and not much aboue'.[23]

In a translator's note to Rowbothum's lute book of 1568, J. Alford supplies a note declaring that 'If I doo perceaue this mi doings to be thankfully taken, it shal moue me to deale farther hereafter . . .'.[24] So it was perhaps to Alford that Rowbothum turned for the translation of a second tutor by Adrian Le Roy, this time devoted to the gittern. Rowbothum's payment of 4*d.* for a licence to print the book was entered in the Stationers' Register, between 22 July 1568 and the same day in 1569

---

[22] See, for example, *A worke of the predestinacion of saints wrytten by the famous doctor S. Augustine byshop of Carthage, and translated out of Latin into Englysshe, by Nycolas Lesse, Londoner* (1550); *A verye fruitful Exposicion vpon the syxte Chapter of Saynte Iohn . . . translated into English by Richard Shirrye, Londoner* (1550); *A most excellent Hystorie Of the Institution and firste beginning of Christian Princes and the Originall of Kingdomes . . . First written in Latin by Chelidonius Tigurinus . . . and now englished by Iames Chillester, Londoner* (1571); *A briefe and pleasaunt treatise, entituled, Naturall and Artificiall conclusions: Written first by sundrie scholers of the Uniuersitie of Padua in Italie . . . And now Englished by Thomas Hyll Londoner* (1584).

[23] George Puttenham, *The Arte of English Poesie* (1589), Sig. Riij. On the emergence of a standard, and the concept of one, see Blank, '"niu ureiting"'. By the late 1560s, a book like Rowbothum's tutor for the gittern could circulate widely, for a list of stationers traceable outside London in 1571 mentions shops in Winchester, Lincoln, Salisbury, Exeter, Worcester and Canterbury, and 'there is good reason to think the list incomplete' (Levy, 'How Information Spread Among the Gentry'). None of these places was exactly provincial, but a London method, in metropolitan English, would have had some interest for those who lived at a distance from the capital.

[24] *A Briefe and easye instru[c]tion*, 'The Translatour to the Reader'. For the possibility that John Alford is the 'Mr Alford' (first name unknown) mentioned in the will of William Calley, gentleman of Hatherden in Andover parish (1557–8), and said there to have Calley's lute in his keeping, see above, p. 47. Ward (*Music for Elizabethan Lutes*, vol. I, 1, n.) has another candidate, a John Alford of Pembroke College [Cambridge] in 1544. See further his comments in 'A Dowland Miscellany', 124–6. Rowbothum's 1574 lute book was translated by 'F. Ke', whom Casey (*English Lute Instruction Books*, 3) identifies as the poet Francis Kinwelmersh(e) or Kindlemarsh. The identification, not strong, is mentioned in *ODNB*, sv 'Kinwelmersh . . . Francis' and in *ESTC* (15487).

(the actual date of publication is unknown) with the title *The breffe and playne instruction to lerne to play on the gyttron and also the Cetterne*.[25] Eight pages of a book whose pages mostly bear the running heading 'An instruction to the Gitterne' have so far come to light (reproduced below as Figures 14–17) and there is no other known work from which they might derive. Two of these leaves are now in the library of the University of Pennsylvania; two more are held in the Robert Spencer Collection in the library of the Royal Academy of Music in London (these may fittingly be called the Duckers leaves after Peter Duckers who discovered one of them by chance, and the other by design, in 1986) (Box 5).

BOX 5

The recovered leaves of 'An instruction to the Gitterne':

The Duckers Leaves: London, Royal Academy of Music, Robert Spencer Collection, 161921–1001, four pages of 'An instruction to the Gitterne'. Used as flyleaves for a copy of *Certayn Godly Sermons* by Hugh Latimer, printed by John Day in 1562, they were already separated from the volume when found, and the volume dismembered, but not entirely dispersed, since Duckers was able to buy a few pages of it. They are now kept with the leaves in the Spencer Collection at the Royal Academy of Music. **The Pennsylvania Leaves**: Pennsylvania, University Library, Rare Book and Manuscript Library, Folio MT654.C58.L47 B7 1568. (*ESTC*, S96083.) Used as flyleaves in a copy of W. Lambarde's edition of *Archaionomia* printed by John Day in 1568. The page size is approximately 125 mm by 185 mm and the longest of the full-page staves measure approximately 160 mm across. All leaves are printed on both sides, and may use the same paper stock with chain lines approximately 26 mm apart. The paper was almost certainly French; one of the Pennsylvania leaves, carrying ff. 13r and 15v, has a watermark of a single-handled pot with a

---

[25] For the witness to the 1551 edition of Le Roy's book see Lesure and Thibault, *Bibliographie des éditions*, 32–3, transcribing the note of de La Caille which records a *Méthode de tablature de la guitarre, in 4°, 1551*. Brown, *Instrumental Music*, [1551]$_4$ refers to the note and mentions the reference to the treatise by Pierre Trichet, *c.* 1640, who gives no date. See Saint-Arroman and Delume, eds., *Méthodes et Traités, Guitare*, vol. 1, 16, for a facsimile of Trichet's text. The French original probably bore the title *Briefve et facile instruction pour apprendre la tabulature a bien accorder, conduire, et disposer la main sur la Guiterne*, the form given in Du Verdier and La Croix du Maine (*Les bibliothèques françoises*, vol. III, sv 'Adrian Le Roy'; I cite the *nouvelle édition* of 1772) and very close to the English as recorded by Andrew Maunsell in 1595, namely *A briefe and plaine instruction for to learne the Tablature, to Conduct and dispose the hand vnto the Gitterne* (*Catalogue of English Printed Bookes*, vol. II, 18). There is good evidence for an edition in 1567 (Vanhulst, 'Les éditions de musique polyphonique'), the one that was probably both the inspiration for Rowbothum's initiative in 1568/9 and the volume that his translator had open before him. Brown raises the possibility of a translation of Le Roy's guitar method into Latin (in 1570$_4$), as argued by Heartz, 'An Elizabethan Tutor for the Guitar', but the argument has been disposed of by Jacquot and others (*Œuvres d'Adrian Le Roy*, vol. I, xxiv), supported with detailed discussion by Vanhulst ('Édition comparative', 82–3, *et passim*). See also Vanhulst's 'A Fragment of a Lost Lutebook', and Dobson, Segerman and Tyler, 'The Tunings of the Four-Course French Cittern'.

BOX 5 (*cont.*)

supported crescent moon and letters that may be UV. The closest analogues are all French (Briquet, *Les Filigranes*, 12784 (Clermont-en-Beauvoisis, 1579) and 12876 (Rouen, 1561)).

Since the preliminary pages of the book are lost, together with much else, the name of the printer is not recorded, but there can be little doubt that it was John Kyngston, the member of the Grocers' Company who printed the translations of Adrian Le Roy's lute pedagogy that Rowbothum published in 1568 and 1574.[26] Comparison of the tablature letters used in the two volumes shows that the same type was used for both. The tablature seems to be without fault, and there are no signs of proof correction.

F. 13R (FIGURE 14)

= Pennsylvania Leaves Z recto. **Tablature grids 1 and 2**: Rising and falling major scale exercise, pointed throughout for right-hand fingering, with the second course stopped at the second fret. Read against the clef on the **staff with white notation**, this note is b durum, or b natural. The exercise runs from the fourth course open to fret 'h' on the *chanterelle*, the complete resources of the first position, and ends with a brief passage of two-part counterpoint creating a cadential movement common in the French guitar books of the 1550s. The sign for covered play appears in the penultimate measure and the final, four-note chord is marked with a fermata. Since the **staff with white notation** and **tablature grid 3** are headed *Accorde by b. mol.*, **Tablature grids 1 and 2** should presumably have been headed *Accorde by b. durum*. The heading may have been on the previous leaf, which is absent, or was never given. The **staff with white notation**, printed from woodblock and therefore presumably a London addition, shows the open strings, with intervening diatonic stops, from the fourth course open to the first course open, with a five-line stave and C4 clef. **Tablature grid 3** gives the same in tablature, ending with a scalar passage without pointing for the right-hand fingering. The second course is now stopped at the first fret which, read against the clef, is to be solmised as *b fa* or b flat, hence the heading *Accorde by b. mol.*

F. 13V (FIGURE 14)

= Duckers Leaves 1. **Tablature grids 1–3**. A rising and falling scalar exercise, pointed for right-hand fingering, identical to the one on the previous page save that the second course is now stopped at the first fret (whence the heading 'Petit

---

[26] John Ward recognised this (*Sprightly and Cheerful Musick*, 16). On Kyngston, see McKitterick, *A History of Cambridge University Press*, vol. I, 58–64, and Blayney, *The Stationers' Company*, vol. II, *passim*.

BOX 5 (*cont.*)

prelude per b. mol') and the same cadential counterpoint leads to a brief passage mostly lost through tearing. A heading 'Petitte fantasie dessus l'accord' introduces a free composition of high quality, beginning imperfectly in **tablature grid 4**, designed to sound as if it is emerging from a tuning check. The piece is transcribed here as Example 6. There are numerous pen trials, some solmisation syllables with no direct relation to the tablature, and fragments of text, including the beginning of a legal document ('The condicyon of this . . . ') and seemingly a scrap of the Athanasian Creed ('Here what . . . [illegible] *salvus esse*').

F. 14R (FIGURE 15)

= Duckers Leaves 2. 'Petitte fantasie dessus l'accord' continued. The sign for covered play appears frequently. There are more fragments of text, in hands of various dates, including the bottom line of an account (*Summae totales*, xs viij d / xxs), a row of pen trials with the figure 2, the name 'Margot More' in a sixteenth-century hand but written upside down relative to the tablature, and in a (?) seventeenth-century hand the characters N.10–2 written twice at a right-angle to the tablature, probably a library class mark. At the top of this leaf, the running heading 'An Instruction to the Gitterne' appears both in its correct position and, above, upside down, showing that these pages have been poorly cut down from a larger sheet.

F. 14V (FIGURE 15)

= Pennsylvania Leaves Y verso. 'Petitte fantasie dessus l'accord' continued. The page is remarkably clean, save for lines taken from John Heywood, *An hundred epigrammes* (1550), Sig Aiiij, in a late-sixteenth-century hand at the bottom of the page.

F. 15R (FIGURE 16)

= Duckers Leaves 3. **Tablature grid 1**. 'Petitte fantasie dessus l'accord' concluded with signs for covered play. **Tablature grids 2–4**. Graded ways to render 'Passamezzo moderno' and 'Romanesca' begin. A substantial part of the folio is lost, but the simplicity and repetitiveness of the music, here entitled 'Les buffons', allow a complete reconstruction, confirmed by the appearance of the same music in the 1570 guitar book of Pierre Phalèse and Jean Bellère (Brown, *Instrumental Music*, 1570$_4$, 59v). Transcription here as Example 9.

F. 15V (FIGURE 16)

= Pennsylvania Leaves Z verso. Graded ways to render the 'Passamezzo moderno' and 'Romanesca' grounds continue, now at the 'Plus diminués'

BOX 5 (*cont.*)

level with signs for covered play. The tablature for the fourth course has been
lost at the base of the leaf, but once again the simplicity and repetitiveness of
the piece allow a confident reconstruction, confirmed by the appearance of
the same piece as it appears in the 1570 guitar book of Phalèse and Bellère
(Brown, *Instrumental Music*, 1570$_4$, ff. 59v–60). Transcription here in
Example 10. The current shelfmark appears in pencil, and the name
'Adrian Le Roy' in a modern hand.

F. 16R (FIGURE 17)

= Pennsylvania Leaves Y recto. Graded ways to render 'Passamezzo
moderno' and 'Romanesca' grounds continue, now at the 'Plus fre-
donnes' [*sic*] level. This folio has an elaborated setting of the
'Passamezzo moderno'. At the bottom of the page a sixteenth-century
hand has added lines taken from John Heywood, *An hundred epigrammes* (1550), Sig Aiiij.

F. 16V (FIGURE 17)

= Duckers Leaves 4. Graded ways to render 'Passamezzo moderno' and
'Romanesca' grounds concluded. This folio has an elaborated setting of
'Romanesca'. As the leaf is now mounted the running heading 'An
instruction to the Gitt[erne]' appears, on a separate strip of the original, detached from the main leaf, in the position it would occupy if it
were originally the remnant of a page cut down from a larger sheet,
like f. 14r above.

The recovered pages of 'An instruction to the Gitterne' do not show
what Elizabethan guitarists saw during their first steps on the instrument
but rather what James Rowbothum inspected when some test sheets came
off John Kyngston's press.[27] By taking into account the printed folio
numbers (when they appear), the syntax of the music and the material
on either side of each individual leaf, it is possible to establish that all the
surviving pages descend from a preliminary arrangement of the material
necessary for one gathering; the recto of each folio faced its verso on
the same side of the sheet, with two complete folios per side (the numbers
of the Pennsylvania leaves are underlined, those of the Duckers leaves
left plain):

---

[27] Rowbothum may well have wished to be present, not merely to check on the quality of the results,
given that very little tablature had been printed in London before this, but also to ensure that the
pressmen were dealing fairly with him and not pulling off sheets to make illicit copies for sale on
their own behalf. See Johnson, 'Printers' "Copy Books"'.

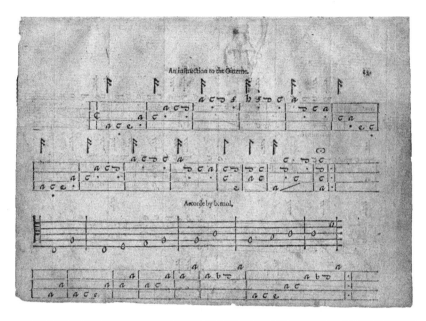

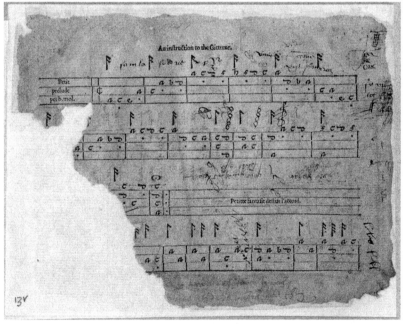

Figure 14.   'An instruction to the Gitterne', f. 13 r–v.

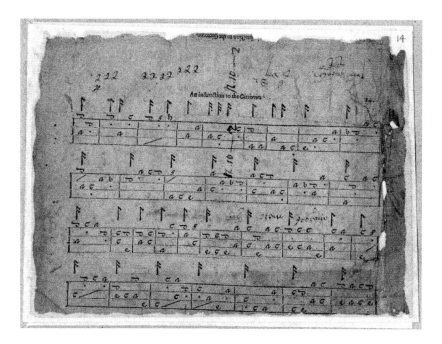

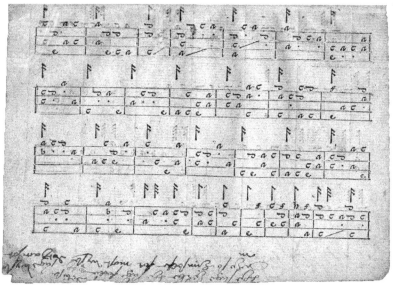

Figure 15.   'An instruction to the Gitterne', f. 14 r–v.

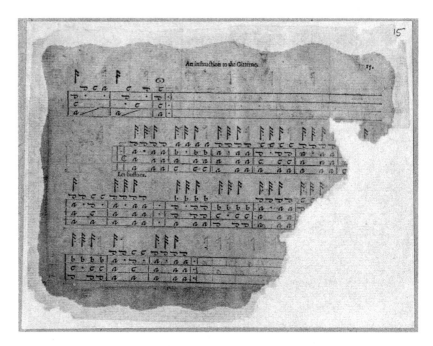

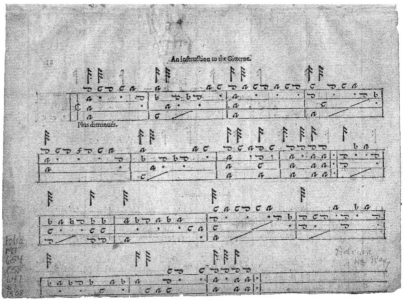

Figure 16.   'An instruction to the Gitterne', f. 15 r–v.

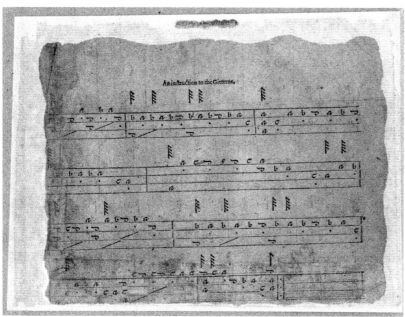

Figure 17. 'An instruction to the Gitterne', f. 16 r–v.

Side A		Side B	
<u>13r</u>	13v	15r	<u>15v</u>
<u>14r</u>	<u>14v</u>	<u>16r</u>	16v

This arrangement could not have served for the final book since the recto and verso of each folio are both on the same side of the sheet, but it was ideal for checking that the tablature ran correctly from one page to the next. Once printed in this way, the separate pages were roughly cut from the sheet; f. 14r (Figure 15) has the running heading 'An instruction to the Gitterne' cut through and upside down, showing that the page was imperfectly cropped, and the same was apparently true of f. 16v (Figure 17). Once this was done, and everything verified, the paper was deemed too valuable to be discarded and was passed as waste to a binder. (Some other leaves from this phase of testing may even have been put into long-vanished drawers or boxes to serve as linings or patterned 'damask' paper.)[28] Given that the surviving leaves cannot by themselves prove the book was ever issued, it is fortunate that Andrew Maunsell lists what is surely this volume in his *Catalogue* of 1595 (*A briefe and plaine instruction for to learne the Tablature, to Conduct and dispose the hand vnto the Gitterne*) and that John Playford refers to 'a Book Printed in English of instructions and Lessons' for the 'Gittar' which appeared 'about the beginning of Qu. Elizabeth's reign'.[29] This sounds like a copy of Rowbothum's tutor with the title page missing, since Playford cannot give a precise date. There is no other known candidate to be the book Maunsell had seen or the 'Book . . . of instructions and Lessons' known to Playford.

The title page of the volume may not be entirely lost, as it apparently was for Playford. Marin Mersenne's *Harmonie universelle* of 1636 shows a four-course guitar marked with tablature letters; comparison with the cut of a cittern from the *Breve et facile instrvction povr apprendre la tablatvre, a bien accorder, condvire et disposer la main svr le cistre* (1565), the only one of Adrian Le Roy's tutor books to survive in its original state, shows the same carved head of a lion, very similar fonts for the tablature letters and an identical *fleur-de-lis* design around the rose (Figures 18 and 19). Mersenne's immediate source is Pierre Phalèse (*Selectissima . . . in guiterna ludenda carmina*, 1570), who almost certainly took it from the lost Parisian tutor for the gittern by Adrian Le Roy, translated to make 'An instruction to the Gitterne'. Rowbothum would have used this cut. So within the limits of what can be surmised, the image of a four-course guitar that English players saw when they used the English version may be said to survive. Since that book followed so hard upon the heels of Rowbothum's

---

[28] Fleming, 'Damask Papers'.   [29] *Musick's delight on the Cithren* (1666), preface.

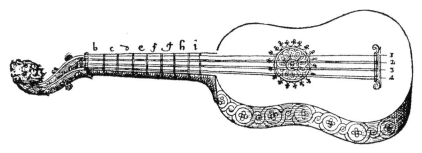

Figure 18.   Woodcut of a four-course guitar printed by Marin Mersenne (*Harmonie universelle*, 1636) and virtually identical to another given by Pierre Phalèse (*Selectissima . . . in guiterna ludenda carmina*, 1570).

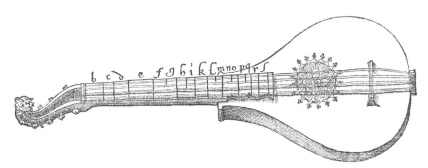

Figure 19.   Woodcut of a cittern from the only one of Adrian Le Roy's tutors to survive in the original edition, the *Breve et facile instrvction povr apprendre la tablatvre, a bien accorder, condvire, et disposer la main svr le cistre* of 1565 (Brown, 1565₃). From the unique copy in the Stadtbibliothek/Stadtarchiv, Trier, 1/1428°. Reproduced by permission.

1568 lute book, had a very similar title, was produced by the same printer, had the same quarto format and may even have had the same translator, we may venture a hypothetical reconstruction of the full title page using the 1568 lute book as a template (Figure 20).

This title page was probably the principal means that Rowbothum used to advertise the book. Printers often produced multiple copies of title pages and attached them to the many kinds of pillar found in London: posts for tethering horses outside taverns or theatres, the doorposts of houses, the markers that separated pedestrian areas from the roadway and the columns inside St Paul's.[30] Such bills could reach the entire literate constituency of the city from 'every dull Mechanicke', scorned by Ben Jonson in precisely this context, to the more prosperous men and women who might send their servants out to gather up the bills (especially the playbills) for perusal

[30]   Stern, '"On each Wall/And Corner Post"'. Even books of theology might be advertised in this way. See also Voss, 'Books for Sale'.

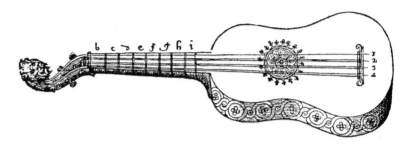

Figure 20.   Hypothetical reconstruction of the title page of *A Briefe and plaine instruction for to learne the tableture to conducte and dispose the hande vnto the Gitterne* (?1569), as printed for James Rowbothum by John Kyngston, using their 1568 lute book as a template.

at home. Viewed in this light, Figure 20 shows a flyer for the public streets, with an image to catch the eye and the announcement that copies are sold at Rowbothum's shop, complete with the address.

III

The remains of Adrian Le Roy's pedagogy for musical instruments are imperfect. As mentioned above, only the cittern tutor survives in its original form; the two lute books are only known from English translations and the *mandore* material has vanished without trace. Enough survives, however, to gain some sense of Le Roy's intentions as a teacher. His purpose, as presented in relation to the lute and rendered by an Elizabethan translator, was to provide some guidance for complete beginners: those with 'no entraunce in this arte'. These novices are principally 'younglings', meaning children but also persons old enough to be servants and (if male) to enter into apprenticeships. They do not live in Paris, 'or such lyke flowrishing citties', and may therefore find themselves beset by a 'lacke of perfit instructors'. The book will help them avoid the spiral of disappointment and disillusion that leads many such beginners to abandon their studies.[31]

---

[31] *A briefe and easye instru[c]tion to learne the tableture to conducte and dispose the hande vnto the Lute*, 'The Author to the Reader'.

To lack a 'perfit' instructor was not necessarily to be without instruction at all, and Le Roy concedes that a student will still require the help of a teacher, though it be 'very small'. In fact, however, the advice of a teacher would still have been vital, for there are some important matters that Le Roy seems never to have discussed in print. The question of how one should place the tied frets, for example, to yield an acceptable result was almost certainly never broached in any of Le Roy's books. The author of *La maniere de bien et iustement entoucher les Lucz et Guiternes* (1556) had seen even the best guitarists blush at the results of poorly placed frets, and a great many times.[32] To avoid such embarrassment, the purchasers of a Le Roy method had no option but to put the book down and seek help, and even if they could lay hands on a copy of *La maniere* they would still need an experienced player to show them how the Pythagorean fretting advocated there might be empirically tempered for some chords but not others. How was a novice to obtain good strings? Which strings were best to use? Perhaps understandably, Le Roy left such large matters to the 'very small' help of a teacher.

Maybe the most fundamental omission, however, is the matter of touch. It is the nature of touch on a musical instrument, paradoxically enough, to be intangible: 'not a fixed commodity [but] a sensitivity' that requires 'constant cultivation and renewal to retain its presence and dynamism'.[33] It is especially here that a teaching text will most noticeably fail to counterfeit a teacher's presence, and Le Roy did not try. 'An instruction to the Gitterne' may even have ignored the issue of whether the player should strike the strings with the flesh or the nails of the right hand; Le Roy probably assumed that players would sound the instrument in some adapted form of lute technique, as the texture of the music he published, with the accompanying pointing, invited them to do. This would generally have meant plucking the courses with the flesh, the nails kept short,[34] but there seems to be no explicit guidance in any English source relating to the guitar before 1666 when John Playford counselled players of the cittern to 'rest only your little finger on the belly . . . and so with your Thumb and first finger and sometimes the second strike your strings, as is used on the *Gittar* . . . and be sure you keep your Nails short on the right hand'.[35]

Although little of Le Roy's teaching survives in its authentic form, there remains enough to show that he followed much the same structure in his manuals and even used the same wording in some instances, though it was sometimes necessary to adapt the text according to the instrument in hand.[36]

---

[32] *La maniere de bien et iustement entoucher les Lucz et Guiternes*, 98 and 106.
[33] Smith, '"Whose heavenly Touch doth ravish human Sense"', 295.
[34] Thomas Robinson advises lutenists to keep their fingernails short (*The Schoole of Musicke*, Sig. Cij).
[35] John Playford, *Musick's delight on the Cithren*, 'Instructions for playing on the Cithren'.
[36] Thus in the cittern tutor Le Roy explains that the tuning of the *cistre* is 'quasi contraire a tous autres Instruments' (f. 7v). Nonetheless, Le Roy's use of a consistent pedagogical frame, and even identical wording, is well established. See Jacquot, *et al.*, eds., *Œuvres d'Adrian Le Roy*, vol. I, xxi–xxvi, and esp. Vanhulst, 'Édition comparative'. The extent to which material might be shared between

By collating the various witnesses to his pedagogy it therefore becomes possible to gather what 'An instruction to the Gitterne' probably contained from the title page to f. 13r where the surviving leaves take up the story. The book would have begun with rules for interpreting the form of notation used, thus fulfilling the claim of the title to offer guidance 'to learne the Tablature'. Then there would be instructions to 'Conduct and dispose' the hand, also promised in the title, and a discussion of the pointing system that directed the use of the thumb and fingers of the right hand. When a single letter appeared with a dot (in contemporary terminology a 'prick' or 'point') below it, the string was to be struck upwards with one of the fingers, not necessarily the index but rather with the finger 'as shall best fit it'.[37] If there were none, the player used the thumb. When a single dot appeared beneath two or three letters, the strings were to be plucked with the fingers alone; absence of a dot in that context indicated a 'grip', meaning that the thumb struck the lowest course to be sounded by moving downwards and the first two or three fingers struck upwards.[38] Some of this teaching can be read in Rowbothum's 1568 lute book, perhaps in language that is often very close to the text set for the gittern method, since the same matters had to be discussed in both:

different tutors emerges with particular clarity from a comparison of the cittern manual with the corresponding matter in the 1568 Alford translation of Le Roy's lost book of instructions for the lute, concerning the technique of covered play. The English renders the surviving French rules for the *cittern* remarkably well, even though the English text is actually translating material from Le Roy's lost method for the *lute*:

Breve et facile instrvction povr apprendre la tablatvre, a bien accorder, condvire et disposer la main svr le cistre (Paris, 1565), f. 6:

Reste maintenant te faire entendre, que sert la barre qui trauerse en biez dessoubz les lettres ou passages, et pour mieux l'entendre je t'ay mis cy dessoubs vn exemple dedans lequel ne trouueras vne seulle mesure, qui ne se puise jouer sans leuer quelq'vn des doigts durant ladite mesure, la congnoisance de laditte barre est si necessaire, que la trouuant, il ne te faut leuer sinon les doig[t]s que seras forcé de leuer, ce qui nous appellons jeu couuert.

A Briefe and easye instru[c]tion to learne the tableture to conducte and dispose thy hande vnto the lute (1568), Sig. Cij^v–Ciij:

It is also necessarie to giue thee to vnderstande, to what purpose the barres that be drawen bias, vnder the letters or passages doe serue for, and for thy better vnderstandyng, I haue here vnder drawen thee an example at large, and very familier, in the whiche thou shalte not finde one example, trimmed or measured, that thou shalte nede to remoue any of thy fingers from the saied measure: the knowledge of the saied barre is so necessarie, that hauyng founde out, and exercised the same, thou shalte not neede to remoue, but those fingers, whiche thou shalt be forced, whiche wee call close, or couerte plaie . . .

[37] *A Briefe and easye instru[c]tion*, Sig. Bi–Bij. An edition of this text, as it was drawn into *A briefe and plaine Instruction to set all Musicke of eight diuers tunes in Tableture for the Lute* (1574), is available in Jacquot, *et al.*, eds., *Œuvres d'Adrian Le Roy*, vol. 1, 51–3.

[38] In effect, the pointing distils the verbal recommendations in Rowbothum's 1568 printing and translation of Adrian Le Roy's teaching: 'For to plaie .iiij. partes, it is easely to be vnderstand, that the thombe and the.iij. fingers together, serue easely to strike the fower strynges or partes, eche doyng his parte, strikyng vpward and dounward . . . For to plaie three partes onely, the thombe will serue, as wee have alreadie taught thee in the rules aforesaied, to strike the counter base dounwardes, the first and the seconde finger, to strike vpwardes the twoo other, whiche make the three partes . . . (Sig. Biij^r): For to plaie twoo partes, the thombe, as of custome shall strike dounwarde the base stryng, and the first, or other finger, the other stryng' (Sig. Biv^r).

... you muste also note, that although there be but one pointe or pricke, vnder one, twoo, or thre letters, thei must bee all striken with the fingers without the thombe, as if euery letter were marked seuerally with his pricke or pointe.[39]

Many renaissance players of the gittern, including Adrian Le Roy himself, were also lutenists and the techniques of the two instruments were probably quite similar (which is not to say that they were identical).[40] These instructions nonetheless cause no difficulty when transferred to the four-course guitar, with such adaptations as the player may find necessary, and in notational terms the pointing system provides a typographically elegant and economical means to guide the novice in the choice of right-hand fingering.

After the material designed to explain the principles of the tablature, including the signs for note values, the reader of 'An instruction to the Gitterne' would have encountered the account of the strings and their disposition in three double courses and a single *chanterelle*. (Around 1640, Pierre Trichet reported having seen this part of Le Roy's original.)[41] Next would come the advice for tuning the open strings. This is where the surviving leaves begin. The expected tuning of rising fourth/major third/ fourth appears in three different forms (Figure 14). There is first a scalar exercise from the lowest course open to fret 'h' on the *chanterelle*, the complete resources of the first position, ending with a brief passage of counterpoint creating a cadence that is very common in the French guitar books of the 1550s and which leads to a final chord marked with a fermata. Since the exercise is pointed throughout, it may be designed for practicing thumb and forefinger alternation while strengthening the weak fourth finger on the left hand, required for the highest note. Next, the notes of the open strings, with intervening diatonic stops, appear on a five-line stave with C4 clef. Finally, the same information appears in tablature, followed by a scalar exercise running from the fourth course open to the open *chanterelle*. One should not underestimate the time required for a novice to perform these exercises cleanly and to develop 'the presence and dynamism' of touch on the strings after a day pulling at a bridle or wielding a pen in the counting house.

---

[39] *A Briefe and easye instru[c]tion*, Sig. Bi[v].

[40] It is likely that, for the kind of music published by Adrian Le Roy, many guitarists used the 'thumb under' method where, in the words of the Capirola Lute Book of *c.* 1517, 'the thumb of the right hand should be placed under the index finger and in this action one finger should not encounter the other while playing'. Compare the advice in the Capirola Lute Book: 'il deo groso de la mana destra fa che stia sotto al secondo et questo azio non se scontri uno deo con laltro . . .'. Chicago, Newberry Library, Case MS VM C.25: 'Compositione di meser Vincenzo Capirola, gentil homo bresano' (copied in Venice by Capirola's student Vidal, *c.* 1517), f. 2. See Beier, 'Right-Hand Position in Renaissance Lute Technique'. Spring, *The Lute in Britain*, 496, succinctly describes the background to the recovery of this technique; Eastwell, 'Twenty-First Century Lute Technique', offers some important reflections.

[41] See Saint-Arroman and Delume, *Méthodes et Traités, Guitare*, vol. 1, 16, for a facsimile of Trichet's text: 'Adrian Le Roi en son instruction pour en iouer escrit que de son temps l'on n'y mettoit que quatre chordes, dont les trois estoint doubles, et la chanterelle simple'.

In the matter of tessitura, the chart in Rowbothum's tutor is both explicit and unexpected. The strings, and the diatonic stops between them, are represented on a five-line staff printed from woodblock, probably an English addition to the original for the sake of those feeling their way with tablature. In contemporary sources of English vocal polyphony the C4 clef is generally associated with the tenor part,[42] and since 'An instruction to the Gitterne' was published in the later 1560s, when clefs were beginning to be associated (albeit later in England than elsewhere) with relative tessitura, there are grounds for supposing that the C4 clef was selected to give the general impression of relatively low pitch. The staff labelled 'Accorde by b. mol.', when collated with the tablature below, shows that the note produced by the second course stopped on the second fret is construed as b *fa*; taken together with the clef, this means that the same course when open is to be solmised as a *la mi re*. Expressed in sixteenth-century terms, and omitting octave strings as well as unison pairs, this establishes a tuning of C *fa ut*|F *fa ut*|a *la mi re*|d *la sol re* for the gittern. However surprising it may seem, the lowest course of this guitar is only four degrees away from the very bottom of the gamut.[43]

If this seems low – and the implied instrument unexpectedly large – we do well to remember that references to guitars of differentiated size appear in scattered European sources, including some from England, and that the tuning in our method is not, in terms of tessitura, without parallel for the four-course guitar.[44] In England, as we have seen, there are several traces of gitterns built in boxed assemblages of three, one of which was given to the Queen in 1559; in the entire record of New Year gifts to Elizabeth throughout her reign, the only directly comparable present is 'a Case of siluer guilt with thre hower glasses' (1563), and these were undoubtedly of different sizes to mark different stretches of time (the naval hourglasses, for example, were commonly built in one-hour and four-hour sizes).[45]

---

[42] On these matters, with specific reference to England, see Bowers, 'To Chorus from Quartet'.

[43] No mention is made of any other setting such as *corde avallée* with the fourth course lowered a tone, used in some of the French guitar books of the 1550s, or the rare tuning with the major third moved so that it lies between the third and fourth courses. The notation does not reveal whether the fourth course is to comprise two strings set an octave apart, like its counterpart on the guitars known to Bermudo, or the guitar that is explicitly called for in the 1546 tablatures of Alonso de Mudarra. Nothing is said or shown about the possibility of a higher octave string on the third course. See Appendix D.

[44] In 1553 the Toleden *violero* Francsico Tofiño made one guitar and nine *discantes* for a client named Alonso Ruiz; the latter have been plausibly identified as small guitars (Romanillos Vega and Winspear, *The Vihuela de Mano*, 401). The inventory of instruments in the Parisian workshop of the late Philippe de la Canessière, dated 23 March 1551, lists an eleven-string gittern together with two more 'small' examples; the former was presumably a larger and deeper instrument with five double courses and a single *chanterelle*. These are almost certainly gitterns of two different sizes, as they are assuredly of different tessituras. Lesure, 'La Facture instrumentale', 22: 'troys guiternes dont une à unze cordes et les deux aultres petites'.

[45] Lawson, ed., *The Elizabethan New Year's Gift Exchanges*, 78.

Something similar may be proposed for the three gitterns since the great majority of renaissance instruments built in families were distinguished by size and tessitura. It is reasonable to suppose that the boxes of three gitterns held instruments of at least two, and perhaps three different sizes and ranges to form a *set*. (If there had only been two gitterns in the container, we might have assumed that the chest contained two identical instruments for professional use, one to serve as spare; the presence of three rules that out.) We have seen that two guitars of different sizes are shown on the painted overmantel in the Summer Parlour, now the Dining Room, at Hengrave Hall in Suffolk (Figure 7), and we may wonder about the 'great gyterne' mentioned in the 1608 will of Francis Fitton of Gawsworth.[46]

In terms of solmisation and an implied position in the gamut, the tuning given in 'An instruction to the Gitterne' corresponds to the lower of the two four-course guitars inventoried in staff notation by Michael Praetorius.[47] Hence it may be possible that Rowbothum's book teaches the lower instrument in a standardised set of two, or even perhaps the lowest in a set of three. At the risk of carrying speculation too far, the 'Tudor ukulele' shown in the Eglantine Table might be the soprano in such a set, for if modern gut is any guide to the properties of Tudor viscera taken from animals raised before the industrialised production of feeds based on biochemical research – which, in the normal run of events, are those available today – then the limit for the top string of the Hardwick instrument may be cautiously placed a ninth above middle C. This allows the following reconstruction of a three-gittern set (once more octave strings and unisons are omitted):

Soprano

dd	*la sol*
aa	*la mi re*
f	*fa ut*
c	*sol fa ut*

Alto

g	*sol re ut*
d	*la sol re*
b	*fa*
F	*fa ut*

---

[46] Earwaker, ed., *Lancashire and Cheshire Wills and Inventories*, vol. II, 172.

[47] Michael Praetorius, *De Organographia*, 28 (staff-notation table). This is not the place to become embroiled in the fraught debate about Praetorius and pitch standards; I go no further here than to weigh the wise comments of Segerman ('Pitch Relativity'): 'For most of the sixteenth century, when music was usually performed either solo or with sets of instruments that had previously been tuned to one another, the pitch level was quite arbitrary. The important thing was a correspondence between the notes in the music and the fingerings on the instrument'.

Tenor

d   *la sol re*
a   *la mi re*
F   *fa ut*
C   *fa ut*

Perhaps nothing in 'An instruction to the Gitterne' better confounds modern expectations of a tutor than the way these tuning preliminaries give way immediately to an elaborate composition, the most demanding piece for gittern known to have circulated in England. The first Duckers leaf has the damaged beginning (only two measures are lost, perhaps three) of a 'Petitte fantasie dessus l'accord' which skilfully emerges from a tuning exercise to become a piece of some sophistication. As James Tyler recognised long ago, this composition can be reconstructed as it passes seamlessly back and forth between leaves on different sides of the Atlantic. It is cast in Adrian Le Roy's most accomplished manner and includes a quotation from the first fantasie in his *Premier livre de tabulature de guiterre* of 1551 (Example 6; the quoted sections are boxed).

From here the surviving leaves follow the same pattern as the cittern tutor by exploring ways of rendering or decorating the 'passamezzo moderno' and 'romanesca' grounds. The historical importance of this material is out of all proportion to its musical value, since some of these tablatures count among the earliest traces of music for the guitar proceeding almost entirely in block chords that set all the strings in motion at once. It is possible to imagine a great many uses for the simplest of these grounds, including a harmonic support for extemporised settings of verse declaimed in a syllabic manner, a chord of the guitar per syllable in a manner destined to be of considerable importance later and already found, as we shall see, in the Osborn Commonplace Book of *c.* 1560.[48] 'An instruction to the Gitterne' then treats both the 'passamezzo moderno' and the 'romanesca' grounds as a sequence of chords elaborated at the 'Plus diminués' level (Example 10, in Chapter 5 below). Next comes a yet more ornate or 'Plus fredonnés' version, and with an equally elaborate setting of the expected 'romanesca' ground, the testimony of the surviving leaves ends.

What came next? Given Le Roy's characteristic way of working, re-using material where possible, it seems reasonable to look in the cittern tutor for material that may have had a counterpart in the gittern method. After settings of the 'passamezzo moderno' and 'romanesca' grounds, just as in 'An instruction to the Gitterne', the cittern manual gives nine 'branles de Bourgongne' followed by 'La muniere de Vernon'. The material occupies one gathering. Precisely the same module of music occupies the final gathering of Le Roy's *Premier livre de tabulature de guiterre*, which

---

[48] Griffiths, 'Strategies for the Recovery of Guitar Music'; Hill, 'L'accompagnamento *rasgueado*'.

Example 6.   'Petitte fantasie dessus l'accord', from 'An instruction to the Gitterne'.

Figure 21.   The first 'Branle de Bourgongne' from *Premier livre de tabulature de guiterre*,
Adrian Le Roy and Robert Ballard (Paris, 1551). From the copy in the British
Library. Reproduced by permission. © British Library Board.

obligingly provides nine 'Branle[s] de Bourgongne' and 'La muniere de
Vernon' on ff. 21–4 (Figure 21). There is therefore some likelihood that all
these pieces formed part of Le Roy's French gittern tutor. If so, this
recuperates ten pieces from 'An instruction to the Gitterne'.

IV

In his introduction to the manual of chess that he published in 1569, *The
Pleasaunt and vwittie Plaie of the Cheastes renewed*, Rowbothum observed that

IT may peraduenture seeme straunge vnto some that anye man should bestow his
labour and tyme in setting out such kynd of bookes as this is, whereby men may
learne to playe, when in dede most men are geuen rather to play then to studye.

A book about a mere pastime, even one as cerebral and martial as chess, was
bound to attract criticism and therefore needed a protector. The manual
for the gittern was even more vulnerable. Rowbothum dedicated his books
on chess and a pastime commonly called 'the philosopher's game' to the
royal favourite Robert Dudley. Rowbothum was determined to gain
Dudley's favour, even to the point of piracy, for the material in the manual
for the philosopher's game was stolen from William Fulke who responded

with an attack on 'Iames Rowbothum, a man of notable impudens'.[49] Fulke had intended to dedicate the material to Dudley himself, and even though Rowbothum received a warning from the Bishop of London not to use the material he nonetheless went ahead. He was still courting Dudley's favour as late as 1569 when his chess manual went into a second edition with the dedication retained.[50] Was this great Elizabethan courtier the dedicatee of Rowbothum's method for the renaissance guitar? It is hard to think of someone more appropriate, since one of the very few images of a guitar from Tudor England adorns a portrait of Dudley (Figure 2), and there may be some reason, beyond mere favouritism, why the Earl received a fourteenth-century plucked instrument, a citole, from the Queen as a present.[51]

In conclusion, there follows an outline reconstruction of the entire volume.

Note: The cittern method has twenty-four leaves, the same structure as all but one of Le Roy's five books of music for the guitar. If his guitar method were constructed in the same way, and the English version followed suit (both volumes were certainly in quarto), then about a sixth of 'An instruction to the Gitterne' has survived and the pages that remain, comprising ff. 13–16, very neatly represent the complete material of the fourth gathering. **Surviving material is in bold.**

ff. 1–12, gatherings A^4–C^4

Title page (reconstructed as Figure 20) and preliminaries, possibly including a dedication to a patron. Tablature lines explained; how letters are assigned to frets; meaning of letters ('a' = an open string etc.); how the layout of tablature guides the plucking hand; the points below tablature letters and their implication for finger/thumb alternation; the left hand; names of the fingers; covered play; explanation of repeat signs, and fermata; note-value signs explained. Number of strings and coursing.

ff. 13–16, gathering D^4

13r   **[Pennsylvania Leaves Z recto. Here Figure 14] tuning instructions**

13v   **[Duckers Leaves 1. Here Figure 14] scalar exercise, beginning of a fantasie**

---

[49] *A Goodly Gallerye with a Most Pleasaunt Prospect, into the garden of naturall contemplation, to behold the naturall causes of all kynde of Meteors* (1563), 'The Epistle'.
[50] *The Pleasaunt and vwittie Plaie of the Cheastes renewed* (1569), Sig. ‡ ii.
[51] See most recently Kevin, *et al.*, 'A Musical Instrument Fit for a Queen'.

14r   [Duckers Leaves 2. Here Figure 15] fantasie continued
14v   [Pennsylvania Leaves Y verso. Here Figure 15] fantasie continued
15r   [Duckers Leaves 3. Here Figure 16] fantasie concluded; basic grounds
15v   [Pennsylvania Leaves Z verso. Here Figure 16] the grounds elaborated
16r   [Pennsylvania Leaves Y recto. Here Figure 17] the grounds elaborated further
16v   [Duckers Leaves 4. Here Figure 17] the above continued and concluded

ff. 17–20, gathering E⁴

Nine 'Branle[s] de Bourgongne' and 'La muniere de Vernon' (= *Premier livre de tabulature de guiterre*, ff. 21–4).

ff. 21–4, gathering F⁴

(If present, contents unknown.)

CHAPTER 5

Sounding strings

I

Much of the music performed on the guitar in Tudor England was probably spontaneous and ephemeral: the result of a request to play, as it was for Robert Langham, or the desire to make an impression, as it was for Mendax who mingled his music with tall stories about Florida. On such occasions, music requiring a largely or exclusively strummed technique may often have seemed the most convivial kind to employ. Since guitars were commonly equipped with only four courses the string-array was compact and easy to sweep for an impromptu galliard, an accompaniment for a song or a chord sequence like 'passamezzo antico' or 'romanesca'. This is the kind of playing that the renaissance guitar was especially set up to provide, inside as well as out. Insofar as the internal bracing of sixteenth-century guitars can be inferred from later examples it was simpler than the bracing of a lute, comprising essentially one brace on either side of the sound-hole with a correspondingly thicker soundboard to resist the pull of the strings. The soundboard area above and below the bridge was therefore akin to a membrane; flexing in all directions it responded more quickly to the initial jolt that set the string(s) in motion. The rhythm of the strumming patterns would, as a result, and as experiment shows, be more distinct and idiomatic on the renaissance guitar than on the lute, an effect heightened by the generally smaller size and higher pitch of the former.[1]

To enquire into the currency of strumming techniques during the sixteenth century is partly to ask how later forms of this approach, well documented for the five-course or baroque guitar, emerged; but it is also to investigate whether brushing play may be the renaissance continuation of medieval practices whereby the players of various instruments set all or most of their strings into simultaneous vibration.[2] By these means players had long been able to create a self-accompanying texture of drones, for example, and the most common tunings for the renaissance guitar bear

---

[1] In the later part of this paragraph I am much indebted to a private communication from Alexander Batov.
[2] See Dean, 'Strumming in the Void' and Eisenhardt, 'Baroque Guitar Accompaniment'.

suggestive traces of medieval precedents for fingerboard instruments.[3] There may even be a late survival of such drone accompaniment in 'The hedgynge hay', music for a 'haye' or company dance (Example 5). Taken as it stands, the notation of that piece in the Osborn Commonplace Book shows the lowest course sounding continuously open, without being used to create the change of chord at certain points that the instrument could easily supply. On a guitar equipped with an octave string on the fourth course, a drone sounds throughout this piece both a fourth below the home pitch and a fifth above.

Such techniques were gradually relinquished by the more ambitious string players during the fifteenth century as a trans-European language of counterpoint emerged and began to infiltrate all forms of play that were truly admired.[4] In this language, the intervals of octave and fifth retained the structural importance they had long possessed in the Middle Ages, and remained pure, but thirds and sixths, both major and minor, began to be used with a fluency unprecedented save in England where musicians sang them in a tempered form which began to be widely imitated.[5] The consequences are obvious if one compares a polyphonic chanson – especially the cadence figures – by the resolutely Pythagorean Guillaume de Machaut (d. 1377) with the early songs of a renaissance master such as Guillaume Dufay (d. 1474). The more advanced instrumentalists of the fifteenth century increasingly sought to reproduce, on one instrument such as lute or harp, the counterpoint of chansons, mass movements, motets and other pieces by rendering at least the two-part texture of cantus and tenor that formed a grammatical and self-sufficient duet in any piece competently composed in the new musical language. This comprehensive shift, probably led by keyboard players who were also proficient on stringed instruments, was well underway by the 1480s. By then, according to Johannes Tinctoris (in every way a competent witness), the best lutenists had already put the plectrum aside for some pieces and were playing music in two, three or even four parts by plucking the strings with their fingers.[6]

Printed sources of guitar music from France and Spain before the final decades of the sixteenth century mostly use the instrument as a 'diminutive of the lute', to quote the description of the *Guiterne ou Guiterre* offered by Maurice de la Porte in 1571.[7] Accordingly, they envisage a miniaturised version of precisely the technique that Tinctoris describes for the larger instrument. Some continental players even granted the guitar an ability to

---

[3] Appendix E.   [4] Strohm, *The Rise of European Music*, remains the unrivalled study.
[5] See *Oxford Music Online*, sv 'Medieval', iii (c).
[6] Baines, 'Fifteenth-Century Instruments', 24: 'Alii (quod multo difficilius est) soli: cantus non modo duarum partium: verum etiam trium et quatuor: artificiosissime promunt'. Online text at http://earlymusictheory.org/Tinctoris.
[7] See Appendix G.

play in four parts like the lute. According to *La maniere de bien et iustement entoucher les Lucz et Guiternes* of 1556:

Les instruments ou nous vsons (en ce païs) de ces cordes de trippes sont la Viele, le Rebec, la Viole, le Luc et la Guiterne: desquels les trois premiers ne sont que pour chanter et jouer vne partie. mais la Guiterne en peut jouer seule quatre ... Ainsi demeure la Viele pour le aueugles: le Rebec et Viole pour les menestriers: le Luc et Guiterne, pour les Musiciens, et mesmement le Luc, pour sa plus grande perfection ...[8]

The instruments on which we in this land use gut strings are the viele, the rebec, the viol, the lute and the gittern; the first three of these can only play a single part, but on the gittern a player can perform alone in four parts ... Thus the viele [hurdy-gurdy] is the instrument for the blind, the rebec and viol for minstrels, the lute and gittern for musicians, and especially the lute, for its greater perfection ...

This seemingly overstated claim about the scope of the renaissance guitar is in some measure justified, for many pieces in the French guitar books of the 1550s show sequences of four-note chords, with intervening passage-work, that are capable of being represented, and perhaps of being heard, as four-part counterpoint. In the following instance, from one of the French guitar books of the 1550s, notation on two staves serves to bring out the four 'voices' (Example 7):

Example 7. Extract from a fantasie by Gregoire Braysing (Adrian Le Roy and Robert Ballard, *Quart livre de tabulature de guiterre* (1553), f. 4, measures 18–25). Facsimile in Tyler, *Adrian Le Roy and Robert Ballard: Five Guitar Books*.

The inversions in this example would have been quite out of place in music for the lute, at least when used in this way, and by no means acceptable in composed counterpoint for vocal or instrumental ensembles. Nonetheless, it does not follow that they were considered undesirable. In

---

[8] *La maniere de bien et iustement entoucher les Lucz et Guiternes*, 95–6.

France, the four-course guitar was allowed to raid the polyphonic textures of contemporary compositions in various genres, collect what it could in a small basket and abandon what it could not in a spirit of licensed holiday from the more scrupulous behaviour required of the lute. First and second inversions of chords made that gaiety audible.

A second major development with implications for guitar playing in the sixteenth century was the broadening of performance, especially in Italy, to encompass imitations of musical techniques, both vocal and instrumental, that had not commanded written or printed record hitherto but now began to do so, somewhat transformed. One may call these techniques 'popular', and it is common practice to do so, but only at the cost of relating them, with unwarranted exclusiveness, to a simplified milieu of peasants, street entertainers and singers using non-Tuscan forms of romance such as Neapolitan dialect. From the first traces of the frottola repertory in the later fifteenth century, to the 'canzone villanesche alla napolitana' that appear in printed musical sources by the late 1530s, the lighter and Italianate musical styles reveal a strong feeling for chords as sonorous blocks rather than as the result of contrapuntal parts falling momentarily into the necessary places for the chords to emerge.[9] The idiom reaches its purest state in sequences such as 'passamezzo moderno', which guitarists and lutenists had merely to pluck or strum to find themselves provided with serviceable dance music, or the harmonic support for an extempore setting of a poem. This emphatically chordal music lay within the reach of many more musicians, both amateur and professional, than intricate counterpoint, and was in that sense democratic; but it could also find favour with the social elite, for it was uniquely well suited to a courtier's display of *sprezzatura*, perhaps by the instrumentally accompanied performance of verse.

In France, to which the gittern playing of England owes so much, the traces of an association between the guitar and Italianate lighter idioms appear as early as 1544. In that year the exiled prince of Salerno, Ferrante Sanseverino, sang 'canzone napolitane' to the women of the French royal court at Fontainebleau every night, and there was 'a great quantity of *chitarre*, every lady having her own'.[10] These were perhaps guitars, for there is an obvious affinity between the renaissance instrument, so amenable to the technique of brushed chords, and music that softens contrapuntal priorities in favour of chordal conceptions that the player can carry through by simply shifting the fingers without thinking in terms of constituent parts falling into place and requiring articulation. The guitar of the later 1500s, with a major third between two of its courses and so definitively relinquishing the older drone potential of mixed fifths and fourths,

[9] See, for example, Cardamone, *The* canzone villanesca alla napolitana *and Related Forms, 1537–1570*, and the essays in the same author's *The* canzone villanesca alla napolitana: *Social, Cultural and Historical Contexts*.

[10] Cardamone, 'The Prince of Salerno'.

was a portable and inexhaustible box of chords. Thus when the interlude of *Ralph Roister Doister*, dating from the early 1550s, parodies the sound of the gittern as 'Thrumpledum thrumpledum thrum/Thrumpledum thrumpledum thrumpledum thrumpledum thrum', we should look past the sexual innuendo to some Italianate and probably strummed pieces for the gittern known in England, such as 'The Matizine', the name being derived from a form of dance whose precise nature remains obscure, 'Il Mattaccino' (Example 8):[11]

Example 8.   Extract from 'The Matizine' here underlaid with imitative elements from *Ralph Roister Doister*. Osborn Commonplace Book (Beinecke Rare Book and Manuscript Library of Yale University, Osborn Music MS 13), f. 44 (old foliation), f. 40 (new foliation). The original can be viewed in the Digital Library of the Beinecke.

Thrum - ple-dum   thrum - ple-dum   thrum

With a few further chords, Example 8 can become a brisk 'passamezzo moderno' and 'romanesca' as they appear in 'An instruction to the Gitterne' as 'Les buffons' (Example 9).

The four-course chords here may have been played with a strumming action; alternatively, musicians could have plucked them using what English players called a 'grip' (a downward stoke with the thumb simultaneous with an upstroke of two or three fingers). If the chords were indeed brushed, then the player was compelled to relinquish that action once, or even twice, in each measure to sound the isolated note(s) before strumming again. That is not difficult to accomplish, and it raises the question of whether renaissance guitarists combined strumming and plucking to foster a mixed style, destined to be swamped by the all-strumming music of the 1590s onwards and only to resurface when the strummed/plucked style of Francesco Corbetta and others emerged in the 1640s. Example 9 is

---

[11] Tydeman, ed., *Four Tudor Comedies*, 131. For the date, see Edgerton, 'The Date of *Roister Doister*', and for the author, *ODNB*, sv 'Uddal, [Yevedale], Nicholas'. 'Thrumpledum' combines the echoic verb 'thrum' (*OED*, sv 'thrum', v.³: 'To play on a stringed instrument, as a guitar, harp, etc., by plucking the strings; to play on any stringed instrument in an idle, mechanical, or unskilful way; to strum.'). The verb 'to strum', also echoic in origin like 'thrum', is not recorded in the *OED* before 1775. For the double entendre, see Williams, *A Dictionary of Sexual Language and Imagery*, sv 'thrum', in the sense to couple with. The 1550s may seem rather early for the lewd sense that is only attested from the early 1600s, but it can scarcely be doubted that Udall has such a meaning in mind. Williams finds no tradition of sexual imagery associated with the gittern and has no entry for it (as he has none for 'harp'), in contrast to 'cittern', 'fiddle', 'lute', 'viol' and 'virginals', which all have entries. For 'Il Mattaccino' see MacDowell, 'Il Mattaccino'; Robinson, 'Lute Music for Comic Actors, Fools, Buffoons and Matachins'; Ward, 'The Morris Tune', 329, and *Music for Elizabethan Lutes*, vol. I, 127–8. Compare the 'Matachina' for four-course guitar in Pierre Phalèse, *Selectissima . . . in guiterna ludenda carmina* (1570), f. 79v.

Example 9.   'Les buffons'. From 'An instruction to the Gitterne'. See Figure 16.

Example 10.   A 'Plus diminués' rendering of 'Les buffons', for four-course guitar. From 'An instruction to the Gitterne'. The piece also appears in the 1570 guitar book of Phalèse and Bellère (Brown, *Instrumental Music*, 1570₃, ff. 59v–60). The source for both is the lost guitar tutor of Adrian Le Roy. From the Pennsylvania Leaves. Pennsylvania, University Library, Rare Book and Manuscript Library, Folio MT654.C58.L47 B7 1568. See Figure 16.

immediately followed in the same print by an elaborated version requiring a fluent plucking technique (Example 10). Even here the first chord of the piece, and some others, might have been strummed, but not the second, for it does not use the third course, suggesting the possibility of a mixed style.

II

The remains of music for the Tudor guitar all draw their repertoire from the 1550s or 60s and employ French lute tablature:[12]

1. The five guitar books issued by Adrian Le Roy and Robert Ballard in the 1550s, all of which made their way to England, as a set, at some time in the second half of the sixteenth century. London, British Library, Music Collections K.2.h.12.(1.) This is a very substantial collection of fantaisies, branles, galliards, almandes, chansons (both as instrumental intabulations and as accompanied songs with a separate vocal part in staff notation), basse-dances, tourdions and pavanes presented on four-line tablature grids of great typographical elegance.

2. London, British Library, MS Stowe 389, a volume of statutes in Latin and Anglo-Norman, whose parchment flyleaves carry tablature. Leaf 1, at the front of the book, shows an incomplete 'passamezzo antico' setting on four-line tablature for an instrument tuned guitar-wise. The music trails off in the midst of a florid passage. Four leaves at the end, seemingly in the same hand, carry tablature for a six-course lute. Ward, *Sprightly and Cheerful Musick*, 110–11, gives an accurate reproduction of the gittern tablature, and a more sustained discussion of all the tablatures in *Music for Elizabethan Lutes*, vol. I, 8–13 (with inventory) and transcriptions in vol. II, *passim*. An inscription, in a different ink to the lute tablature, and in a hand that may not be Bowle's, appears above the music for lute and reads: 'The xviij^th daie of maye the same writtin by one Raphe Bowle to learne to playe on his Lutte in anno 1558'. Various later hands have added their names, including Thomas Dent (1602) and James Johnson (seventeenth century). The compiler of the music was perhaps Ralph Bowle of St Lawrence in Thanet, for whom Administration was granted in 1575–6 (see Appendix H).

3. Twenty-one items on four-line tablature for an instrument tuned guitar-wise in the Osborn Commonplace Book, dating from *c.* 1560, in The James Marshall and Marie-Louise Osborn Collection, Beinecke Rare Book and Manuscript Library, Yale University, as Osborn Music MS 13.[13] The pieces for guitar appear on ff. 44–8 (old foliation),

---

[12] I have reluctantly decided to omit a single (?) item, possibly a draft, on six-line tablature but never using more than four lines, for a four-string/course instrument tuned lute-wise (i.e. rising third, fourth, fourth) in a manuscript addition to the bassus partbook of Baldassare Donato's *Il secondo libro di madrigali a Quattro voci* (Venice, 1568), now in the Marsh Library, Dublin, since its provenance is unknown. See Greer and Robinson, 'A Fragment of Tablature in the Marsh Library'.

[13] The standard works on the musical material in this manuscript are both by John Ward: *Sprightly and Cheerful Musick, passim*, with a catalogue of the gittern pieces at 112–29, and *Music for Elizabethan Lutes, passim*, but esp. vol. I, 22–42, with an inventory of both the music and the verse, and vol. II, with transcriptions of all the music in the manuscript, the gittern pieces at 136–46. On Ward's needless division of the pieces into guitar music and gittern music, see Appendix F. The manuscript has attracted some attention for its texts of verse by Henry Howard, Earl of Surrey. See,

ff. 40–4 (new foliation). The book also contains a substantial and important collection of music for lute, recipes and a collection of verse by Surrey, 'T. W.' and others. All the music in the book is the work of a single, elegant and accomplished hand. There are galliards, a 'haye', a 'matachins', settings of grounds (including the Spanish 'Conde Claros', probably through a French intermediary),[14] a 'pavana', a salt-arello with accompanying galliard, variations on the 'passamezzo antico' and pieces with titles taken from the first lines of courtly ballads by Sir Thomas Wyatt and Henry Howard, Earl of Surrey, that could presumably serve as accompaniments for vocal performance or as solo items. An imperfect printing of all the tablatures is given in Ward, *Sprightly and Cheerful Musick*, 49 and 113–29, with transcriptions in his *Music for Elizabethan Lutes*, vol. II, 129–46, but with a superfluous distinction between 'gittern' music and 'guitar' music. *RISM*, BVII, 234–5, mistakenly gives the four-line tablatures of the book to the cittern.

4. Four complete or reconstructable pieces that survive in the recovered leaves of 'An instruction to the Gitterne', published in 1568/9. Figures 14–17.

5. London, British Library, Additional MS 30513, 'The Mulliner Book', compiled by Thomas Mulliner whose name appears in several places. No definitive identification of Mulliner is possible, but there is some reason to believe he had been a pupil of John Heywood (*ODNB*, 'Mulliner, Thomas'; Flynn, 'Thomas Mulliner'). The main contents of this paper manuscript end at 115r, after which ff. 116 and 117 are blank; there then follows a series of tablatures for gittern and cittern, evidently an addition to the main corpus, running from ff. 118r–127r (there are four more leaves ruled with six-line tablature after this, but no music was entered). Two items on six-line tablature, but only using four lines, and with lines five and six cancelled, are for a four-string/course instrument tuned guitar-wise. The first is an ornamented and untitled setting of 'Chi passa' marked 'gitterne' in the margin (Example 26), and the second an ornamented version of the 'passamezzo antico' ground, untitled but almost certainly for gittern also since the next item in the book changes instrument ('Sytherne') and tuning. *RISM*, BVII, 180. For a description of the manuscript see Caldwell, ed., *The Mulliner Book*, xxvii–xxviii and 221–7. Transcriptions of the gittern pieces, together with a representation of the tablature, are at 190–4.

for example, Edwards, 'Manuscripts of the Verse of Henry Howard'. For further on this kind of book, see Craig-McFeely, *English Lute Manuscripts*, 97ff.
[14] Cf. *Le Premier Livre de Chansons, Gaillardes, Pavannes, Bransles, Almandes, Fantaisies, reduictz en tablature de Guiterne par Maistre Guillaume Morlaye ioueur de Lut*, ff. 24v–25v, and *Le Second Livre . . .*, ff. 29r–30r (Tyler, ed., *Simon Gorlier and Guillaume Morlaye*).

All five of the guitar books published by Adrian Le Roy and Robert Ballard came to England as a set some time in the second half of the sixteenth century, perhaps obtained by a player looking for sophisticated repertoire in print, or by an English collector of continental music prints in the manner of Henry Billingsley. A flyleaf at the beginning of the first book, made of a different paper to the main publication, bears the writing of five or six individuals who have recorded their names:[15]

Hand 1 (late sixteenth century): 'Richard Hobson'
Hand 2 (late sixteenth century): 'Humphrey Guyse' (deleted)
Hand 3 (late sixteenth century): *Inueni portu[m] spes et fortuna valete*
  (a Neo-Latin translation of a Greek epitaph)
Hand 4 (? 1560s): 'William Reeve; Maryon my wife' (written partly over
  'Richard' in Hand 1)
Hand 4a/5 (late-sixteenth-century italic): 'William Reeve'
Hand 6 (mid-seventeenth century): 'John Caue'

The current binding of these five books was re-sewn around 1900 using the original boards, the front cover being somewhat crudely stamped with the initials WR. This is evidently for W[illiam] R[eeve], who adds a note on the title page of the first volume that he bought the 'booke' from a certain Mr Banger, a rare name in England that may stand for Bangert, Bongers or Bongaerts, all of which are still in use in the Netherlands.[16] While it remains unknown whether William Reeve was the first English owner of the collection, it seems that the books crossed the Channel as a bound set, for Reeve refers to having bought a 'booke' in the singular and the manuscript additions are confined to the opening of the first volume. The hands suggest that Reeve acquired the material at some time in the second half of the sixteenth century; his name appears several times on the front flyleaf and once in a secretary hand with a high initial stroke of the 'v', consistent with an earlier Elizabethan date; he also gives the name of his wife as 'Maryon', an orthography that gave way to 'Marion' during the later 1500s with the disappearance in the later 1550s of the spelling 'yo' for the glide in words such as *informacyon/informacion*.[17] The music will scarcely have

---

[15] London, British Library, K.2.h.12.(1–5). The flyleaf, not reproduced in the Tyler facsimile, can be viewed via the *Early Music Online* database of Royal Holloway, University of London. I am most grateful to Dr Nicholas Bell, of the British Library, for the information that the Library purchased the volumes on 9 April 1890 from Bernard Quaritch for £16. They formed item 299 in their catalogue no. 102 of March in that year (Quaritch had no record of the seller). The Music section of this catalogue is described as 'Including the Library of the late William Chappell, Esq., and the Collection of Elizabethan Madrigals and Song-Books, from the Library of a Nobleman'. Three other items are listed as coming from the library of the Earl of Crawford.

[16] The inscription has been hatched out; I cannot improve on the transcription given by Ward, *Sprightly and Cheerful Musick*, 16, n.: 'Wm Reeve is the trewe oner [thoner?] of this booke/witnes Mr Banger that sold yt'. This is followed by the name 'Wynterbourne' in a later hand.

[17] In the printed sources searchable through *EEBO*, the spelling 'Maryon' for a woman's name makes its last appearance in 1565; to cite some parallel cases, 'lamentacyon' disappears in 1549 and

seemed out of date in England at this time, given that Pierre Phalèse in France was still recycling Adrian Le Roy's guitar music in 1570. What was admired in France would not have seemed *vieux jeu* in England.[18]

There is a tempting wealth of music in these volumes making them well worth the purchase. The dance pieces comprise galliards, branles, almaines, pavanes and basse-dances, and for the more ambitious players there are preludes and fantasies, many of high quality. Forty-two French-texted chansons appear in Books II and V where the cantus appears separately in staff notation, underlaid with the first verse (the remaining verses stacked below), while the accompaniment for guitar is given in tablature. Two pieces from these books will show the range of approaches they contain, from exacting counterpoint in a small space to something considerably more ambitious. A branle from the *Premiere livre* shows the kind of rigorous two-part writing in which the Parisian repertory often uses the contrapuntal facility of the guitar to good advantage (Example 11).

After a rhythmically stabilising beginning, four measures of running ornament in measures 5–8 prepare a lucid and grammatical duet, beginning in measure 10, which introduces a sudden shift (to use modern terminology, and in relation to the key of the transcription) from sharps to naturals and from naturals to flats. The effect is vigorously swept aside with declamatory block chords in measures 13–14 that put the counterpoint on hold and briefly restore the former harmonic palette; but the flatward move swiftly returns with the notably melodious tenor used again from measure 16 onwards for an ornamented form of the same duet. For a bravura conclusion, the superius gains a rush of energy to close the piece, rising up the instrument with the kind of running stepwise ornamentation that contemporary musicians cultivated with an insatiable appetite, here placed over a tenor of wisely reduced melodic interest, but continuing directional influence. This is indeed *multum in parvo*.

The second example is excerpted from one of the most ambitious pieces in the entire repertory of the four-course guitar: M. Gregoire Braysing's spacious intabulation of a psalm-motet by Josquin, *In exitu Israel*, using just the first part.[19] It says much for the scope of the guitar, as perceived in mid-century France, that such an undertaking was ever attempted; with no apparent sense that the instrument has shortcomings that must ultimately

---

'occupacyon' in 1561; 'informacyon' disappears in 1555 with an isolated outlier in 1631, but quoting a document from the reign of Henry VIII.

[18] Brown, *Instrumental Music*, 1570₄. There is no guarantee that William Reeve was a guitarist; the pages show no obvious signs of use, and there are no manuscript indices, annotations or musical additions of the kind ventured by a continental user of the Gorlier-Morlaye guitar books who thereby gives a valuable insight into the decidedly interventionist way that a contemporary player might use such tablatures. (These can all be studied in the facsimile edited by Tyler.) This does not prove that the volumes in the British Library set were never used for playing, however, for the sixteenth century was not a period when it was customary to buy unnecessary books.

[19] For the original, see Jas, ed., *Motets*, measures 88–97. The intabulation is noted in the accompanying volume of critical commentary (vol. II, 21).

Example 11.   Adrian Le Roy, 'Cinquiesme Branle de Bourgongne' from *Premier livre de tabulature de guiterre*, Adrian Le Roy and Robert Ballard (Paris, 1551), f. 22v. Facsimile edited by Tyler, *Adrian Le Roy and Robert Ballard: Five Guitar Books*.

defeat the enterprise, or make it appear quixotic, Braysing 'reduces' a large and rhetorical composition by one of the great masters of renaissance counterpoint. The performer must shape an extensive piece without the Latin words to which much of its musical rhetoric is wedded. The opportunism of the intabulator, and his disregard for many details of the vocal model, swiftly reach the point where the version for gittern becomes an independent musical entity (Example 12).

The second and fifth books of the Le Roy/Ballard volumes would have given a Tudor player access to the most sophisticated forms of guitar-accompanied song then in print. Book II is entirely devoted to strophic settings of French chansons with the first verse of the poem underlaid to the melody and succeeding verses given as text alone; there are sometimes as many as sixteen, leaving no doubt that these items can be performed as accompanied songs.[20] Book V, another chanson anthology, contains music by various composers, including Adrian Le Roy, but the chief purpose of the volume is to capitalise on the vogue for songs by Jacques Arcadelt. Glancing at this music, one can only conclude that English amateur (or

---

[20] See Lafargue, 'Adrian Le Roy', which counters the arguments of Le Cocq, 'The Status of Le Roy's Publications'.

Example 12.   Excerpt from Josquin's *In exitu Israel de Aegypto* as intabulated in *Quart livre de tabulature de guiterre*, Adrian Le Roy and Robert Ballard (Paris, 1553), ff. 7–10v, beginning at the first measure of f. 9v. Facsimile in Tyler, *Adrian Le Roy and Robert Ballard: Five Guitar Books.*

indeed professional) musicians capable of using such material in the 1550s and 60s would have formed a very select company indeed if they were genuinely at ease with the rhythm signs in the tablature and the mensural notation, with occasional coloration, that is used for the vocal line. The French texts of the chansons would also have posed a problem to many. As Jane A. Bernstein has observed:

Tudor and Jacobean musical manuscripts include some 280 chansons by such composers as Claudin de Sermisy, Sandrin, Crecquillon, Gombert, Clemens non Papa, Sweelinck and Lassus. Often the composers are not named, and in many cases the French titles are either missing or appear in bastardized versions.[21]

Since the accompanying parts for the guitar generally include a substantial amount of melodic material drawn from the superius – in effect, the guitar doubles the voice – many of these items can be performed as instrumental solos, which is perhaps how they were used in England, if used at all. There are indeed cases where the guitar accompaniment of a given chanson appears elsewhere in the set, different in numerous details but essentially unchanged, as a purely instrumental item.[22]

Players in England who did venture to sound the voice parts and the accompaniments together would often have found the result decidedly heterophonic in places. The melody sometimes sounds simultaneously in both plain and ornamented forms as the guitar exploits its own characteristic idioms, especially rapid scalar runs, both against the

[21] 'An Index of Polyphonic Chansons', 21.
[22] Thus the accompaniment to 'J'ay le rebours' in Book II (f. 3) is reworked as an instrumental pavane 'J'ay du mal tant tant' in Book III (f. 7r–v), while the guitar part for 'L'ennuy qui me tourmente' in Book II (f. 12) had already appeared in the 'Galliarde si je m'en vois' in both a plain and a diminished form in Book I (ff. 9v–10).

Example 13. The beginning of Pierre Certon's 'L'Ennuy qui me tourmente' as intabulated in the *Second livre de guiterre* of Adrian Le Roy and Robert Ballard (Paris, second edition of 1555), ff.11v–12. Facsimile edited by Tyler, *Adrian Le Roy and Robert Ballard: Five Guitar Books.*

voice and in the pauses at the ends of texted musical phrases. The guitar part therefore abandons any attempt to duplicate the sonorous and often somewhat overfed harmonies of the vocal originals, which are quite beyond its resources; indeed, the intabulator does not even seek the fullest versions of chords that the instrument can provide; many of those in Example 13 could be more sonorous than they are. Instead, the emphasis shifts from harmony, which is sketched, to an essentially two-part texture of simultaneous melody and diminutions of the same. The concept of diminution in renaissance music is so familiar that one might easily miss its freshness here in a new art of accompanied song using the four-course guitar. In effect, the vocal line in these songs is mildly 'fredonnés': a technical term but one which derives from the heart of the essentially non-technical vocabulary of contemporary French poetry and prose. There it expresses the lightness and elaboration of birdsong, or the freshness of youth.[23]

III

With the main English sources of music for the gittern we enter a different landscape. Music that did not usually command record on the continent, save in a markedly tidied form, now begins to appear in a remarkably naked state. The procedures employed range from the simplest concatenations of riffs, seemingly for strumming, to elegant adaptations of vocal originals in up to three polyphonic parts. The outstanding source, which contains both, is the Commonplace Book of *c.* 1560, now Osborn Music MS 13 in the Beinecke Rare Book and Manuscript Library of Yale University. (Pieces from this manuscript have already appeared above as Examples 1, 3–5 and 8.) All the music therein is the work of a single scribe who copied continental and native pieces for the lute but was also interested in items for a four-string/course instrument tuned to a rising fourth, major third and fourth, almost certainly a guitar. The manuscript shows the guitar *à cheval* between the ideals of written counterpoint on one hand, as adapted for high-status fingerboard instruments such as the lute, and older techniques on the other where the player wove a texture of sound that did not obey (or did not consistently obey) literacy-based notions of chording or counterpoint.

Perhaps the most blatant example of the latter is the 'Morisco gallyard' (Example 14). Seemingly designed to resist any but a vigorous and raking performance, this piece opens with the most emphatic strummed (or gripped) effect to be found anywhere in music for the renaissance guitar and proceeds with sonorous block chords creating disorientating chromatic shifts on the *chanterelle* that sounds the upper surface of the harmony. A series of hemiola patterns, in bare semibreves, wonderfully destabilises and energises the music in measures 7–8 where the texture fractures open and an ornamented version of the same material begins, here signalled by a double bar. Now there is running stepwise figuration that falls very well under the fingers. Again, the music works towards dizzying hemiola patterns to capture a wild and perhaps supposedly Moorish abandon, for this 'Morisco' galliard appears to be no simple Morris dance.

Other pieces in the Osborn manuscript appear to skirt the limits of what one might suppose to be viable candidacy for written record, such as the galliard produced by arpeggiating the chords of the 'passamezzo antico',

---

[23] Huguet, *Dictionnaire*, sv 'Fredonner'.

Example 14. 'Morisco gallyard', Osborn Commonplace Book (Beinecke Rare Book and Manuscript Library of Yale University, Osborn Music MS 13), ff. 44v–45r (old foliation), ff. 40v–41r (new foliation). The original can be viewed in the Digital Library of the Beinecke.

with stepwise passagework introduced for ornamental effect in the second statement (Example 15).

In cases like this, the Osborn tablatures give the illusory appearance of finish and fixity to music created by combining riffs, in a fluent and no doubt largely oral tradition, that passed from one 'piece' to another as readily as they fell under the fingers. A revealing instance occurs in the galliard 'Whan raginge love', whose title is formed from the first three words of a well-known poem by Surrey (Example 16).

Here the music prizes the full sonority of all seven strings (at least one of them presumably with an upper octave) sounding on the strong beats and even on the shorter time-values in the dotted rhythms. The result is an ideal texture for the crisp response of a small, lightly braced instrument operating at a relatively high pitch. Since the number of musical phrases

Example 15. 'Pasy measure' (= two variations on the 'passamezzo antico') from the
Osborn Commonplace Book (Beinecke Rare Book and Manuscript Library of Yale
University, Osborn Music MS 13), f. 47 (old foliation), f. 43 (new foliation). The original
can be viewed in the Digital Library of the Beinecke.

corresponds to the total count of lines in each stanza of the poem, this is
presumably either an accompaniment for a melody not given or an
instrumental adaptation in which the melody is encased, so to speak,
within the block chords and perhaps traced by the various passing notes.
Yet whatever relation the music bears to some performance of Surrey's
lyric that might be envisaged, the first twenty-four minim beats are
virtually identical to 'A galliard' notated a page away. The frontiers
between copying, arranging and composing, as between 'haye' and
courtly ballad, seem to be dissolving in this scribe's hands.

That enterprising individual, in every way our major conduit of music
for the Tudor guitar, remains unknown and unidentified, but there may be
a clue to his or her identity in the manuscript. On f. 37r (new foliation) the
hand responsible for the lute and gittern tablatures has copied a poem
beginning 'The hare and the hownd shall fyrst agre', essentially a series of
impossible conditions that must be fulfilled before the poet will waver in
his devotion to his beloved. The first quatrain runs:

> The hare and the hownd shall fyrst agre
> So shall the see hys water mys
> All fearsnese from the egle shall flye
> Er I forgeat what promis ys

Example 16.   'Whan raginge love', Osborn Commonplace Book (Beinecke Rare Book and Manuscript Library of Yale University, Osborn Music MS 13), f. 40v (old foliation), f. 44v (new foliation). The original can be viewed in the Digital Library of the Beinecke.

A name appears framed in a box drawn freehand at the head of the text: 'Arther blanchinden'.[24] Presumably this is the author. Such attention to the identity of a poet's name is quite exceptional for this manuscript; most of the verse in the Osborn Commonplace Book is either anonymous or carries a pair of initials placed at the *foot* of the text, not at the head as in this case, still less shown framed in this way and with the name given in full.

The surname of Arthur Blanchinden can be found in various forms during the sixteenth century, including Blancherden and Blechenden, and the identity of these forms is proved by the consistency of the heraldry associated with them. The 1530–1 Visitation of Kent gives the arms of James BLANCHERDEN of Aldington as 'Azure a fess nebulée argent between three lions' heads erased or, collared gules',[25] while a paper roll of the arms of Kentish Lords and Knights, dating from *c.* 1594, gives precisely these same arms for the family of BLECHENDEN.[26] The Blechendens were a gentry

[24] Ward, *Music for Elizabethan Lutes*, vol. i, 40, reads the name as 'Blanchindey'. I agree with Ringler, *Bibliography and Index of English Verse in Manuscript, 1501–1558*, TM 1531, that the correct reading is 'Blanchinden'.

[25] Bannerman, ed., *The Visitations of Kent*, vol. i, 2.

[26] MS 112. The manuscript is not listed in the catalogue of Sidney Sussex College manuscripts by M. R. James. I am grateful to Nicholas Rogers for showing me his draft catalogue entry. Further confirmation is provided by the will of the individual mentioned in the 1530–1 Visitation of Kent, James BLANCHERDEN, dated 1556, where his name is given as BLECHINDEN. Canterbury Cathedral Archives, PRC32/27/1.

Figure 22.   The house at Ruffyneshill, Aldington, Kent. Photograph by Steven Collee.

family that owned the house of Ruffyneshill in Aldington where a substantial part of a sixteenth-century brick building still stands, now converted into a farmhouse and incorporating the remains of a two-storied hall (Figure 22).[27] At least two men named Arthur Blechenden, father and son, can be traced in Kent during the 1560s and 70s; was the compiler of the lute and gittern tablatures in the Osborn Commonplace Book a member of that Kentish family with a seat at Aldington?[28] Perhaps we need look no further for the name of the scribe with an interest in the gittern. Who would have held the verse of 'Arther Blanchinden' in higher esteem than the poet himself or a close member of his family?

If the scribe who copied music for the gittern into the Osborn Commonplace Book were indeed a member of the Blechenden family of Kent, then he or she (if not Arthur himself) belonged to a gentry clan that produced benefactors to local parish churches, minor public servants and friends to Members of Parliament, sustained by the usual patterns of land-holding and rents. We may learn a little more about his or her milieu from f. 21v where s/he has copied Surrey's love complaint 'If care do cause men crie' with a textual variant noted between the lines of the second stanza:

---

[27] Hasted, *Historical and Topographical Survey*, vol. VIII, 314ff; Newman, *The Buildings of England: West Kent and the Weald*, 127.
[28] See further Bindoff, *The House of Commons 1509–1558*, vol. ??, sv 'Knight, John II'.

> Synce that amongest them all
> *I know ryght well*
> I dare well say ys none
> So farre from joy so full of woo,
> Nor hathe more cawse to morne

This variant does not correspond to the printed text in Tottel's 'Miscellany' of 1557 (Poem 30), and does not appear to come from the lost broadside edition of the poem,[29] so it was presumably derived from another manuscript source and entered when the compiler collated several copies of Surrey's lyric. Our scribe would therefore seem to have belonged to a coterie of readers exchanging manuscripts of Surrey's poetry, the principal means by which that poet's verse was disseminated before the publication of Tottel's collection in 1557. This suggests a relatively confined network that may one day come into view, for detailed study of Surrey's verse in its manuscript (as opposed to print) tradition suggests that circulation 'seems to have been highly circumscribed'.[30]

There appear to be no concordances between the Osborn pieces and the French guitar books of the 1550s, and very little one might care to suppose was once in the purely French repertoire of 'An instruction to the Gitterne'. Pieces made of constant block chords, or from simple arpeggiations, scarcely appear in the French prints where there is a much more determined emphasis upon counterpoint and a consistently close relation to sophisticated vocal models by Franco-Flemish composers of a kind unknown in the English sources. The gittern may have been valued for being strange or foreign, as Thomas Whythorne reports, but the surviving English repertoire for that instrument often has the flavour of native malt and barley rather than imported wine.

---

[29] The variant probably does not come from the lost broadside printing of the poem of 1557/8 because the compiler does not note the variant in the first line of that text, as listed in the Stationers' Register (Arber, ed., *Transcript*, vol. I, 22v) as 'yf Care *may* Cause men crye' (emphasis added). The want of an authoritative critical edition of Surrey's verse makes it difficult to take the matter further at present.

[30] Edwards, 'Manuscripts of the Verse of Henry Howard', 287. For a different view of the coterie question, see May and Wolfe, 'Manuscripts in Tudor England', 132–3. The earliest traces of Surrey's poetry in print (i.c. before 1547) are summarised in Warner, *The Making and Marketing of Tottel's Miscellany*, 114–15.

CHAPTER 6

The gittern and Tudor song

> The historian who steps away from institutions and instead tries to
> account for [the musical pursuits] of individuals or groups of indivi-
> duals in an urban community – politicians or physicians, lawyers or
> craftsmen, merchants or lower gentry – will usually find that the
> deposits are thin and poor, or have run out altogether.
>
> John Milsom, *Songs and Society in Early Tudor London*[1]

I

All the social groups mentioned by John Milsom in this passage from 1997
have made their appearance during the course of this book, either as
owners or as importers of the gittern. For the politicians there was Sir
William More and for physicians the Cambridge professor Thomas Lorkin
who kept two gitterns in his rooms at Trinity Hall. A lawyer appeared in
the person of Sir William Petre, and a craftsman with the shoemaker
Robart Crispe who took to the open road, gittern in hand. John White,
draper of London, stood for the merchants and William Calley, who
bequeathed a gittern in his will, for the lower gentry. These men give a
reasonable conspectus of the laymen that later Elizabethans called the 'best
sort', a term that somewhat relaxed the old importance of blood in favour
of respectable character, hard work and attainment.[2]

What use did such men have for the gittern if they wished to accompany
song? Here we may broaden the frame of reference for a moment. A
comprehensive survey of the guitar in England from the 1550s to at least
the 1850s would show that even those who criticised the instrument for its
doubtful associations, or its limited musical capacity, often conceded that
it serves very well as an accompaniment to the voice. Yet the traces of
gittern-accompanied song in English musical sources of the sixteenth
century are just what Milsom's words would lead us to expect; the deposits
'are thin and poor', or rather they have 'run out altogether', for no gittern
tablatures are known to survive from Tudor England with a separate and
texted part for a singer. Descriptions in a handful of literary texts, however,

---

[1] At p. 236.   [2] The term 'the best sort' is discussed further below, p. 156.

suggest that the gittern had a place in a vigorous culture of Tudor song where musical and poetic materials were constantly being made, remade and hybridised in a manner that often acknowledged no real boundary between court and street, or chamber and tavern. By collating these literary references with hints in the gittern tablatures we may bring various kinds of song into view, including settings of courtly ballads by Wyatt and Surrey, poems sung over familiar grounds such as 'Tinternell', verses fitted in a workmanlike manner to music that could accommodate them, and English metrical psalms.

Since the material must often be pieced together from hints and fragments, it will be well to distinguish between what we can *reconstruct* and what we must *recreate*. A piece of sixteenth-century music, of any kind, can be *reconstructed* if the surviving materials represent the incomplete and therefore damaged state of a specific entity that, in the normal course of things, would once have existed complete. A set of partbooks with the tenor volume missing, for example, is an invitation to reconstruct the absent part to make performance possible; a case might be made that the three gittern tablatures in the Osborn Commonplace Book whose titles are incipits from identifiable poems are incomplete in a similar sense, the voice part omitted because it was well known. One may therefore venture a reconstruction of what was once there. A *recreation*, on the other hand, is an informed and necessarily somewhat speculative invention corresponding to a kind of repertory that once existed, but not to any specific surviving item, and which has been undertaken because that area of repertoire is mostly or entirely lost and our sense of the musical landscape is impoverished as a result. When evidence emerges in a literary source that verse by Petrarch was sung to the gittern, for example, then one way to bring the possibilities into focus, and to make them accessible for debate, is to invent something in the light of what is known about Tudor procedures and techniques. That is a recreation in the sense that I assign to the term in this chapter. The paradox of such inventions is that they are not real Tudor music and yet in a sense they are more real than anything in the musical sources because they correspond, however conjecturally and imperfectly, to the largely unwritten practices that occupied many gittern players most of the time.

The commonwealth of melody between vocal and instrumental music, and the constant generation of new words for old music, or new music for old words, was very conspicuous to those Elizabethans who appointed themselves adjudicators of value in poetry. In 1586 William Webbe observed in *A Discourse of English Poetrie*, with some annoyance, that fresh verses were devised every day for well-known melodies and grounds used by instrumentalists, such as 'Downwright squire' and 'Trenchmore', together with new poems set to 'Galliardes, to Pauines, to Iygges, to Brawles' and indeed 'to all manner of tunes which euerie Fidler knowes better then my selfe . . .'.[3] Webbe may be employing the term 'Fidler' to mean the player of any stringed instrument commonly used in the street, including the guitar; in 1588, Abraham Fraunce praises 'a good fiddler . . . in respect of his gitterne' without there being any indication, or indeed any possibility (given the context) that the instrument has changed between one reference and the next.[4] Viewed in that light, the song repertoire of the Tudor gittern player, as of many other instrumentalists, seems as wide as ingenuity in a context of limitless opportunity could make it. So whatever we may reconstruct or recreate of gittern-accompanied lyric and then cage, so to speak, within the measures of musical notation, can never be (to sustain the metaphor) more than a few songbirds caught from a vast and clamorous flock that circles beyond our reach where it can be glimpsed but never caught.

II

Some of the most volatile but enticing material arises from the mid-Tudor fascination with Italy. During the reign of Henry VIII many Englishmen went to the Northern and Central cities of the peninsula for a period of study, notably in the schools of law, or to pursue business of a secular or ecclesiastical nature. They returned home, on routes well trodden by diplomats and couriers, with reports of what they had heard in the cities and courts beyond the Alps.[5] The translations of Petrarch's sonnets by Sir Thomas Wyatt and Henry Howard, Earl of Surrey, established the view of these two poets as 'nouices newly crept out of the schooles of *Dante, Arioste*

---

[3] *A Discourse of English Poetrie*, Sig. Fiiij^v. For Elizabethan literary theory concerning the lyric, the texts gathered in the two volumes of Smith, ed., *Elizabethan Critical Essays*, are still invaluable, to which should now be added two collections edited by Alexander, *'The Defence of Poesy' and Selected Renaissance Literary Criticism*, and *The Model of Poesy*. Only a qualified welcome is due to the new edition of Puttenham edited by Whigham and Rebhorn, since the text is modernised. Among studies, the writings of John Stevens (*Music and Poetry in the Early Tudor Court*) provide part of the indispensable foundation for work on English song in the sixteenth century before the rise of the lute song, carried forward by Ward, *Music for Elizabethan Lutes*, vol. I, *passim*, but esp. 79–80 (the Wynne marginalia), 81–3 (music for poems in Tottel's 'Miscellany') and 84–7 (music for poems by Wyatt and Surrey). See also the same author's 'Music for "A Handefull of pleasant delites"'. For more recent scholarship, see the work by Goodwin: 'Some Recent Discoveries in Elizabethan Song'; 'A Few More Discoveries in Elizabethan Song'; *The English Lute Song Before Dowland*, vols. I and II; and 'Philip van Wilder's English Songs'; and by Milsom: 'Caustun's Contrafacta'; 'Songs and Society in Early Tudor London'; and 'Songs, Carols and Contrafacta'. On metrical psalms, see Leaver, '*Goostly Psalmes and Spirituall Songes*'; Marsh, *Music and Society*, 405ff; Quitslund, *The Reformation in Rhyme*; Willis, *Church Music and Protestantism in Post-Reformation England*; Zim, *English Metrical Psalms*. The recent studies on Tottel's 'Miscellany' by Warner (*The Making and Marketing of Tottel's Miscellany*) and the authors of the essays edited by Hamrick (*Tottel's* Songes and Sonettes *in Context*) do not take much interest in music.

[4] Abraham Fraunce, *The Lawiers Logike, exemplifying the praecepts of Logike by the practise of the common Lawe* (1588), Sig. Kiiij.

[5] See Boswell and Braden, *Petrarch's English Laurels*. Much of the raw data is available in the still-valuable study of Parks, 'The Genesis of Tudor Interest in Italian'. See also Coogan, 'Petrarch's *Trionfi* and the English Renaissance'. For the poetry of Sir Thomas Wyatt and Petrarch see now Brigden, *Thomas Wyatt*, and for Surrey, Sessions, *Henry Howard*.

and *Petrarch*', in the words of George Puttenham,[6] and with a markedly
musical emphasis in the case of Surrey. More than half of the manuscripts
that contain material from Surrey's poems 'consist of musical settings,
usually without attribution and often accompanied only by the incipit'.[7]
This suggests how closely English readers of the 1550s and 60s associated
both Surrey and his Italian models with music, inspired by writers such
as William Thomas who reported in 1549 that most Italian cities
possessed 'excellent maisters of musicke to syng and plaie on all maner of
instruments . . .'.[8]

The Tudor gittern converges with the poet at the heart of the Italian
lyric tradition, Francesco Petrarca, in William Painter's *The second Tome
of the Palace of Pleasure*, published in 1567. Painter was a clerk of Her
Majesty's ordnance at the Tower of London, and in the long tradition of
government bureaucrats using their leisure for literary pursuits he translated a number of stories from French and Italian into English. The
published results gave English readers, including William Shakespeare,
versions of tales from continental sources such as the *Heptameron* of
Marguerite of Navarre and the *novelle* of Matteo Bandello. At this stage
in the evolution of Tudor fiction, the advisedness of Painter's undertaking
would have seemed questionable to many on moral grounds, especially if
the translation were made from the language of those most 'busie and open
Papistes' the Italians, always ready to incite good English Protestants to
irreligion and wantonness.[9] Painter's defence, a common one in his day,
was that his book was an inducement to virtue because it revealed the
ugliness of vice, and when one of his heroines begins an adulterous affair
with an earl he duly expresses a real or pretended indignation. The lovers
become the common gossip of Pavia, and songs are made of them; their
infamy is

noised throughout the Citie, and the songs of their Loue more common in eche
Citizens mouthe, than the *Stanze* or Sonnets of Petrarch, played and fained vpon
the Gittorne, Lute or Harpe of these of Noble house, more fine & wittie than those
unsauery ballets that be tuned and chaunted in the mouthes of the foolish
common sort.[10]

At first glance, one might be tempted to suppose that both Petrarch and the
gittern come directly into this passage from Painter's Italian source, and yet
they do not. When he evokes the lyrics of Petrarch that were 'played and

---

[6] Puttenham, *The Arte of English Poesie*, 48; cf. 50: '*Henry* Earle of Surrey and Sir *Thomas Wyat*,
betweene whom I finde very litle difference, I repute them (as before) for the two chief lanternes of
light to all others that haue since employed their pennes vpon English Poesie, their conceits were
loftie, their stiles stately, their conveyance cleanely, their termes proper, their meetre sweete and well
proportioned, in all imitating very naturally and studiously their Maister *Francis Petrarcha*.'

[7] Edwards, 'Manuscripts of the Verse of Henry Howard,' 289; Ward, *Music for Elizabethan Lutes*,
vol. I, 84–6.

[8] William Thomas, *The historie of Italie* (1549), Sig. Aiij. Osborn, ed., *The Autobiography*, 247.

[9] Salzman, 'Placing Tudor Fiction'.   [10] *The second Tome of the Palace of Pleasure*, f. 205v.

fained upon the Gittorne, Lute or Harpe' he is not translating, for Bandello has no corresponding allusions in his tale.[11] Is this therefore an Englishman's attempt (characteristically late in the day) to imagine the art of Italian improvisers such as the renowned Serafino de'Ciminelli dall'Aquila (d. 1500), who trained himself by the intensive study of Petrarch's *sonetti, canzoni e triomphi* that he sang to the lute?[12] This might also be a misreading, however, for Painter's use of the semi-technical term 'feigned' suggests that he has something more definite in mind than an Italianate reverie. As early as the 1440s the wordlist for the use of schoolboys entitled *Promptuarium parvulorum* had framed the definition 'synge lowe' for 'Feynyn yn syngynge', where 'lowe' translates Middle French *bas* and means 'softly sounding'.[13] That is evidently what John Palsgrave intends in his *Lesclarcissement de la Langue Francoyse* of 1530 where, in an invented sentence that may reflect his experience as a tutor to Henry Fitzroy, son of Henry VIII, in 1525–6, he writes:

We maye nat synge out we are to nere my lorde but lette vs fayne this songe; *Nous nosons pas chanter a playne voyx nous sommes trop pres de monsieur chantons pourtant ceste chanson a basse voyx.*[14]

A 'feigned' song for Palsgrave was therefore the opposite of one 'sung out' in the sense of being delivered with the full voice. William Bonde uses the word in a similar sense in *The Pylgrimage of perfection* (1526), enjoining the faithful to sing 'nor feynynge but w^t a full brest and hole voice . . . '.[15] Closer to the period of William Painter, Thomas Wilson reviews the compliments a man might pay in *The Arte of Rhetorique* (1553), and includes 'he feyneth to the Lute marveilouse swetely'.[16]

---

[11] Ferrero, ed., *Novelle di Matteo Bandello*, 122.

[12] According to Vincentio Calmeta's *Life of Serafino*. See Menghini, ed., *Le rime di Serafino de'Ciminelli dall'Aquila*, 1–2: 'ad imparare sonetti, canzoni e triomphi dil Petrarca tutto se dispose, li quali non solo hebbe familiarissimi, ma tanto bene con la musica li accordava che a sentirli da lui cantare nel liuto ogni altra harmonia superavano'. On this *Life* see Kolsky, 'The Courtier as Critic' and on Serafino, Prizer, 'Music at the Court of the Sforza'.

[13] Way, *Promptuarium parvulorum sive clericorum*, 153.   [14] Palsgrave, *Lesclarcissement*, f. 235.

[15] Book III, Sig. HHHiii^v. Bonde is closely following, and largely translating, a passage in Sermo XLVII of the *Sermones in Cantica Canticorum* of Bernard of Clairvaux (*PL* 183, 1011): 'Unde vos moneo, dilectissimi, pure semper ac strenue divinis interesse laudibus. Strenue quidem, ut sicut reverenter, ita et alacriter Domino assistatis: non pigri, non somnolenti, non oscitantes, non parcentes vocibus, non praecidentes verba dimidia, non integra transilientes, non fractis et remissis vocibus muliebre quiddam balba de nare sonantes; sed virili, ut dignum est, et sonitu, et affectu voces sancti Spiritus depromentes.'

[16] Thomas Wilson, *Arte of Rhetorique* (1553), f. 72. Cf. Thomas Cooper, *Thesaurus Linguae Romanae et Britannicae* (1578), sv *incino*: 'to feyne a small voyce; to sowne plesantlye and with melodie'. There may be a connection between 'feigning' in these texts and the terminology of 'feigned voice' (*voce finta*) in later vocal pedagogy, at least in the limited sense that Western writing on good singing bears a longstanding witness to the notion of a vocal production which produces a pleasing result but which in some sense is not real, and therefore counterfeit or feigned. The 'feigned' voice has often been associated with falsetto, widely interpreted to be a manner of singing that keeps the larynx high, with a certain use of the top of chest voice (mingling it with elements of head voice). Bloom, *Voice in Motion*; Stark, *Bel Canto*, 73–4, *et passim*; Miller, *Securing Baritone, Bass-Baritone, and Bass Voices*, 38–9.

A letter of 27 September 1563, now among the papers of Samuel Pepys at Magdalene College, Cambridge, adds the suggestive detail that such 'feigned' singing was regarded, by at least one knowledgeable English judge in the 1560s, to be a characteristic feature of 'Neapolitan' performance. The letter, composed in Madrid by Sir Thomas Chaloner and addressed to Robert Dudley, contains a 'Post Scripta' where Chaloner describes a performance given by the young Neapolitan singer Fabrizio Dentice. This had taken place in Chaloner's lodgings, in Barcelona, the previous March. Chaloner tactfully reminds Dudley that he himself has some talent with the lute, implying that his assessment of what he heard on that occasion, some six months before, should be given due weight. The quality of Dentice's lute playing, with its 'clene handling and depe Musicke and partes withall and excellent fyngeryng in tyme and place', had been truly impressive; what is more, he also sang well 'in a fayning voyce after the Napolitan fashon'.[17]

A further connection between a soft singing voice and a 'Neapolitan' manner of performance is made in George Gascoigne's *A Hundreth sundrie Flowres bounde vp in one small Poesie* (1573). In one of the narrative passages that link the poems in this collection, a gentleman summons musicians with 'violands' and viols, then asks them 'softly to sound the Tyntarnell' while he sings verses, presumably also in a soft voice. Gascoigne says it is all done '*Alla Napolitana*'. Far from being in any way Neapolitan, the text of the gentleman's song is a lyric of ten stanzas in the wholly English and mid-Tudor manner of Surrey and his imitators, a reflection upon the wisdom of loving in poulter's measure:

> In prime of lustie yeares, when Cupid caught me in
> And nature taught the way to loue, how I might best begin:
> To please my wandring eye, in beauties tickle trade,
> To gaze on eche that passed by, a carelesse sporte I made.[18]

The 'Neapolitan' quality of the gentleman's performance therefore seems to reside in the music, embracing not only the implied softness of the singing (in falsetto?) but also the technique of singing – perhaps extemporising – a melody over a ground. This is precisely the kind of accompaniment the gittern could offer singers who might wish to 'feign' settings of Petrarch combining a light, or even falsetto, delivery of the melody over a sequence of chords. Example 17 accordingly recreates a rhythmic and harmonic frame for singing Surrey's translation of Petrarch's sonnet 'Amor, che nel penser mio vive et regna', to elements of the ground 'Tinternell', the chords spelled in a manner idiomatic for the four-course guitar. One full statement of the ground elicits two lines of text, and therefore the ground, in a complete performance of the sonnet, would be performed seven times.

---

[17] Cambridge, Magdalene College, Pepys Library, MS 2502, pp. 213–14.
[18] George Gascoigne, *A Hundreth sundrie Flowres bounde vp in one small Poesie*, 223-5. On the Tinternell ground, see Ward, *Music for Elizabethan Lutes*, I, 11.

Example 17.   Recreated rhythmic and harmonic frame, using a form of the ground
'Tinternell', for singing Surrey's sonnet 'Loue that doth raine and liue within my thought', a
verse translation of Petrarch's sonnet 'Amor, che nel penser mio vive et regna'. Text from
Jones, ed., *Surrey Poems*, 3.

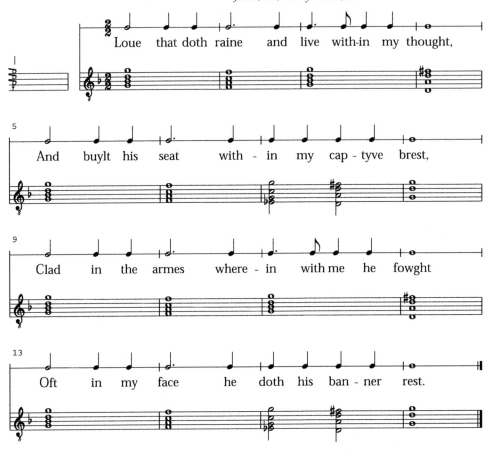

III

William Elderton's sapiential broadside 'Philosophers learnings, are ful of
good warnings' (1569) announces that it may be sung to the tunes of 'my
Lorde Marques Galyarde: or the firste traces of Que passa'. To this we may
add 'A Sonet of two faithfull Louers, exhorting one another to be constant'
in *A Handefull of pleasant delites* (1584) sung 'To the tune of Kypascie',
evidently a corruption of 'Chi passa'.[19] Considered either as a chord
sequence with its melody, or merely as a harmonic ground, 'Chi passa'

---

[19] Facsimile of 'Philosophers learnings' and *A Handefull of pleasant delites* are both available on *EEBO*.
      Edited text of the former in Lilly, ed., *A Collection of Seventy-Nine Black Letter Ballads*, 138–40, and
      of the latter in Kershaw, ed., *A Handefull of pleasant delites*, 87–8. See also Ward, 'Music for "A
      Handefull of pleasant delites"', 166, and for both items Simpson, ed., *The British Broadside Ballad*,
      101–3.

was well known to gittern players, as to many instrumentalists in the late sixteenth century. There is an elaborated setting of the piece for gittern in The Mulliner Book (Example 26), and a further association with the gittern dates from 1586 when Richard Stanihurst remarked that an opponent, charged with expressing opinions unbecoming in a clergyman, had behaved as fittingly as an ass trying to 'twang quipassa on a harpe or gitterne ... ' (see Appendix B, entry 1586₂). It is a relatively simple matter to reconstruct either of these songs with a gittern accompaniment, using the setting in The Mulliner Book as a guide to where the chords might be placed on the instrument. For the purposes of Example 18, the texture is reduced to the bare minimum to allow for interpretations that might range from a simple strum to something more elaborate.

The portability of guitars, and their ability to provide a discreet harmonic support for untrained voices, explains their distinguished history as instruments used to accompany the voice on stage during dramatic performances. Although this can principally be traced from Jonson's *The Gypsies Metamorphosed* of 1621 through to Restoration plays by Porter, Etherege, Shadwell and others, the first trace of a guitar being used in this way appears in Ulpian Fulwell's *An Enterlude Intituled Like Wil to like quod the Deuel to the Colier* (1568, with a second edition in 1587).[20] The action turns upon the doings of the apprentice Nichol Newfangle as he consorts with a cast of lowlife characters such as Tom Tosspot, Hankin Hangman, Ralph Roister and Cuthbert Cutpurse before being finally carried off to hell on the back of his godfather, Lucifer. The action is set in Croydon, south of London on the road leading down from the villages of Battersea and Streatham, known for the trade of charcoal burning in the Elizabethan period, for its blackened inhabitants and for its streets that 'were deep hollow ways and very dirty, the houses generally with wooden steps into them, and darkened by large trees'.[21] A note on the title page states that 'fiue may easely play this enterlude', suggesting that Fulwell envisaged a domestic performance or one to be given by a company with boys, since part of the action turns on the wearing of false beards with the players having no real beards underneath. In an early scene, a stage direction requires that Nichol 'must haue a Gittorn or some other instrument (if it may bee)', but if none is available he and his two companions on stage 'must daunce about the place all three, and sing this song that followeth, which must be doon also although they haue an instrument':

[20] For the author see *ODNB*, 'Fulwell, Ulpian'. I have used the 1568 edition of the play on *EEBO*. There is a modern-spelling edition in Somerset, ed., *Four Tudor Interludes*. For an inventory of the elements of this play, including music and staging, see Wiggins and Richardson, *British Drama 1533–1642*, 34–7.
[21] Anderson, *A Short Chronicle concerning the Parish of Croydon in the County of Surrey*, 170.

Example 18.   'A Sonet of two faithfull Louers, exhorting one another to be constant',
from *A Handefull of pleasant delites* (1584), Sig. Diij[r–v], 'To the tune of Kypascie',
reconstructed as a song to the melody of 'Chi passa', with basic accompaniment devised
with regard to the intabulation of 'Chi passa' for gittern in The Mulliner Book (BL,
Add. MS 30513, ff. 119v–120v). For the tune, compare Ward, *Music for Elizabethan Lutes*,
vol. II, 88, and Simpson, *The British Broadside Ballad*, 101–3.

Tom Colier of Croydon hath solde his coles,
and made his market to day:
And now he daunceth with the Deuil,
for like wil to like alway.

> Wherfore let vs reioice and sing,
>> let vs be mery and glad:
> Sith that the Colier and the Deuil,
>> this matche and daunce hath made.
>
> Now of this daunce we make an end,
>> with mirth and eke with ioy:
> The Colier and the Deuil wil be,
>> much like to like alway.
>   *Finis.*[22]

The stage direction shows that Fulwell's attitude is quite pragmatic; let the actor have a gittern if there is one to hand, otherwise another instrument will do; if there is none he may just sing and dance. When an actor was indeed able to accompany 'Tom Colier of Croydon hath solde his coles' the music was perhaps a simple three-part setting in the manner of one added in manuscript to this very play in one copy, but apparently designed for a later scene.[23] Alternatively, the players may have felt that something more streetwise was required for Nichol Newfangle. The choice of ballad metre (also known as 'Sternhold's metre' because it was so widely used in the metrical psalms that Thomas Sternhold both wrote and inspired) gave the option of adapting melodies currently in circulation with other texts, and provides valuable evidence that songs in this metre (of which more below) were sometimes sung to the gittern.

Writing a decade later than Fulwell, and in a very different vein, Sir Philip Sidney places a gittern in the hands of a singing shepherd in *The Old Arcadia*, the first (and the only complete) version of his pastoral romance completed in 1579/80. Sidney's Arcady is recognisably the place of rustic song and piping, the true home of 'the woodland Muse on slender reed', that Virgil depicts in the *Eclogues*, but it is also a political settlement: a dukedom whose stability and moral welfare depend upon the wisdom and integrity of its governor. The peace of Arcadia is violently disturbed when its people drink too deep during a feast to celebrate the duke's birthday; as the wine heats temper and complexion, they become incensed by his decision to heed the warnings of an oracle and relinquish his throne. The Arcadians make their way towards the quiet place where the duke is lodging in retirement with his wife and daughters; a fight ensues, but the shepherd Dametas avoids the conflict by hiding in a cave. He only emerges, when all is done, to proclaim the virtues of self-serving cowardice in a song accompanied by a gittern:

But as they were in the midst of those vnfained ceremonies, a Gitterne, ill-played on, accompanyed with a hoarce voice (who seemed to sing maugre the Muses, and to be merie in spite Fortune) made them looke the way of the ill-noysed song. The song was this:

---

[22] *An Enterlude Intituled Like Wil to like quod the Deuel to the Colier*, Sig. Aiiij^v -B.
[23] Sabol, 'A Three-Man Song in Fulwell's *Like Will to Like* at the Folger', with transcription.

A Hatefull cure with hate to heale:
A blooddy helpe with blood to saue:
A foolish thing with fooles to deale:
Let him be bob'd that bobs will haue.
But who by meanes of wisdome hie
Hath sau'd his charge? it is euen I.

Let others deck their pride with skarres,
And of their wound[ë]s make lame showes:
First let them die, then passe the starres,
When rotten Fame will tell their blowes.
But eye from blade, and eare from crie:
Who hath sau'd all? it is euen I.[24]

Sidney's allusions to accompanied song in the *Arcadia* have wide-ranging sources that extend through Spanish prose romances of the sixteenth century to deep strata of Old French romance. When a shepherd in another episode prepares to sing by 'tuning his voice to a rebeck', for example, we should look to models such as Jorge de Montemayor's *Diana* of *c.* 1559 and its continuation by Gil Polo, *Diana enamorada* of 1564;[25] virtually every singing shepherd in those spacious romances can play the small bowed instrument that the Spanish writers call 'rabel', for which 'rebec', in various spellings, was the contemporary English and French equivalent.[26] There is no such very clear line of descent in the gittern episode, however, so this may be a passage where Sidney is ranging (as he would say) through the zodiac of his own wit. The song that Dametas sings, with its ragged colloquialism and old-fashioned alliteration, seems designed to disparage both the player and his instrument, yet Arcadia was ever a place to tread carefully. Dametas has been raised far beyond his station, and even further beyond his merits, by a duke of Arcadia who has shown a want of wisdom in this as in much else. The favouritism of the duke, and the position of trust Dametas enjoys in the dukedom, have given this shepherd a liking for courtly fashions and arts which, in this case, consort with neither the inner nor the outer man. Just as he affects a 'courtlike' nonchalance in certain aspects of his dress, being casually 'ill

[24] I take the text from the edition of 1593, ff. 106v–7. Another lyric sung by Dametas in Sidney's text, not to the gittern but to piping and dancing, was set as a round by Thomas Ravenscroft. See Morehen and Mateer, eds., *Thomas Ravenscroft*, 55.

[25] Both are translated in *Diana of George of Montemayor: Translated out of Spanish into English by Bartholomew Yong of the Middle Temple Gentleman* (1598). See for example 2, 3, 7, 29 etc.

[26] There are similar scenes of pastoral rebec playing in the *Espejo de príncipes y caballeros* (Part II), by Pedro de la Sierra. This was rendered into English by 'R. P.' and published in 1583 as *The Second part of the Myrror of Knighthood*, with material offering a close analogue to Sidney's passage: 'This we will do with a very good will aunswered the shephearde: and for that you doo seeme vnto vs, for to be of high estate, we will playe on our instruments, to giue you some comfort, and we will publish our paines and griefes, with our own mouths: and taking the Rebeck in his hand, which was meruailously well wrought, he beganne to playe vppon the same very sweetely, and likewise did associate the musicke with these pastorall verses . . . ' (f. 187).

gartered', so he presumes to cultivate an instrument that seems but 'ill-played on' in his hands.

IV

Two tablatures in the Osborn Commonplace Book bear titles taken from the first lines of poems by Surrey; a third bears the incipit of a poem by Sir Thomas Wyatt, 'Lowe what yt ys to love':

f. 44v (old foliation), f. 40v (new foliation), 'Whan raginge love'. The first words of a poem by Surrey. Text in Jones, ed., *Surrey Poems*, 1–2.

f. 45v (old foliation), f. 41v (new foliation), 'In winters just returne'. The first words of a poem by Surrey. Text in Jones, ed., *Surrey Poems*, 12–14.

ff. 47r–v (old foliation), 43r–v (new foliation), 'Lowe what yt ys to love'. The first words of a three-section poem by Sir Thomas Wyatt making fifteen stanzas in all, arranged in three groups of five. Text in Rebholz, ed., *Sir Thomas Wyatt*, 165.

The Surrey lyrics became well known in the 1550s and 60s; they appear in Tottel's 'Miscellany' of 1557 and licences for printing both as broadside ballads were registered between the summers of 1557 and 1558, although no copies are known to survive.[27] Both poems show the ease of motion, with an even tread of accents, so characteristic of Surrey's manner:

> In wínters júst retúrne |when Bóreas gán his ráigne,
> And éuery trée vnclóthed fást, as Náture táught them pláine;[28]

This form of couplet, called 'poulter's measure' after an ephemeral conceit ventured by Gascoigne (who did not mean thereby to demean it), has attracted unfavourable comment in a long tradition reaching back to the dawn of serious literary criticism.[29] Hence it is obvious that something is amiss, for this measure is often used by Surrey. The poets of Tottel's 'Miscellany', following in his footsteps, employ it often, and this is therefore the metre in which a substantial amount of verse sung to the gittern is likely to have been cast; George Gascoigne describes it as 'the commonest sort of verse which we use now adayes'.[30]

---

[27] Arber, ed., *Transcript*, vol. 1, 22r–v; ballads licensed to John Wally and mistress Toye include 'Whan Ragynge love', 'A ballet in wynters Juste Retorne' and 'yf Care may Cause men crye'.

[28] Jones, ed., *Surrey Poems*, 12. There has been much discussion of metrical issues in sixteenth-century English verse. Warner, *The Making and Marketing of Tottel's Miscellany*, 95–157, examines virtually the entire corpus of Tottel's book and gathers the relevant bibliography. Attridge, *Well-Weighed Syllables*, is still the most lucid, perceptive and balanced account of contemporary attitudes to accentual verse. Smith, ed., *Elizabethan Critical Essays*, gathers most of the contemporary discussions, to which Alexander's edition of *The Model of Poesy* should now be added.

[29] Gascoigne's point in the passage often cited (*Certayne Notes of Instruction*, Sig. Uij) is that the metre has no name and he does not know what to call it 'unless I should say that it doth consist of Poulter's measure . . . ' (i.e. the measure of poultry sellers or 'poulters' who sometimes gave twelve and sometimes fourteen for a dozen). This is meant as a witticism and a convenience, not a condemnation.

[30] *Certayne Notes*, Sig. Uij.

It has been suggested that most people in the sixteenth century 'made their primary contact with poetry or verse when it was accompanied by music'.[31] That is certainly an overstatement, but contemporaries undoubtedly did understand the power of melody not only to articulate the metrical structure of a lyric but also to liquefy certain prosodic features that may seem recalcitrant when they are spoken. In the words of Anthony Munday in his *Banquet of Daintie Conceits* (1588), some verses may seem 'very bad stuffe in reading but ... [it] wyll delight thee, when thou singest any of them to thine Instrument'.[32] This is not to suggest that poems in poulter's measure (a metre that Munday does not employ) were considered 'very bad stuffe in reading' in their day, or that they should be considered in that light now; the point is rather that many poems in that metre are outstanding candidates for music to lighten and grace the cumulative effect. Indeed, George Gascoigne says as much in 1575 when he expresses a wish that poulter's measure should be reserved for 'Psalmes and Himpnes', genres habitually associated with music.[33]

In most renaissance traditions of song, melody advances with an even rhythmic stride, the musical phrases following the underlying pulse. When it is well managed, no due forward movement of that pulse can be either insignificant or distasteful, just as no structural pause, such as the caesura in the first line of poulter's measure, can be meaningless or unpleasant. To compare the gittern piece entitled 'In winters just returne' with the original text in poulter's measure is soon to discover that the music makes the caesura in the first line of each couplet seem light and fluid without in any way seeking to understate it; indeed, the accompaniment vamps a chord during the caesura, marking the time until the harmony moves again and preventing any relaxation or loosening of the underlying pulse. This is our one reasonably sure glimpse of gittern-accompanied song using one of the most common metres of the 1550s and beyond (Example 19).

The tablature bearing the incipit of a poem by Sir Thomas Wyatt offers five variations on a simple three-chord ground of A minor, E major and G major, either arpeggiated or presented with intervening passagework. This is certainly music of modest quality (though it could be lifted by a stylish performance) and the only link with Wyatt's poem is presumably that the chord sequence preserves elements of an accompaniment for singing the text that have here been worked into a set of variations. The music seems singularly tuneless, but that is probably because the tune is missing. One may hazard a recreation of at least a rhythmic frame for the

---

[31] Lindley, 'Words for Music, Perhaps', 10. In 1994 Erik S. Ryding noted, to his credit, that 'even a poem like Gascoigne's "In prime of lustie years", composed in the deadly Poulter's Measure, acquires an unexpected suavity and lyricism when sung to the "Tinternell" melody that Gascoigne specified' (review of Ward, *Music for Elizabethan Lutes*, in *Renaissance Quarterly*, 47 (1994), 441–2). It is significant that one should find oneself praising a critic for making such a basic discovery.
[32] 'To the Gentle and freendlie Reader'.   [33] *Certayne Notes*, Sigs. Ui and Uiij.

Example 19. 'In wynters just returne'. Lower stave: the setting in the Osborn
Commonplace Book (Beinecke Rare Book and Manuscript Library of Yale University,
Osborn Music MS 13), f. 45v (old foliation), f. 41v (new foliation). Text from Jones, ed.,
Surrey Poems, 12. Upper stave: a reconstruction based upon two broadly comparable
melodies for this text offered by lute intabulations in the amateurs' miscellanies Royal
Appendix 58 and Folger V.a.159 (Ward, *Music for Elizabethan Lutes*, vol. II, 22 and 94–5).
In their presentation of the underlying harmonic pattern the two lute sources agree, broadly
speaking, both with one another and with the gittern setting. By collating them we may
arrive at a tentative reconstruction of the melody.

lost song, allowing some of the gittern material to emerge in what may be
its original form as an idiomatic and accompanying part for the renaissance
guitar (Example 20).

v

Might it be possible to recreate the gittern player's share of the well-attested
interplay between courtly verse and music for the lute, virginals, organ and

Example 20.   Recreated rhythmic frame for 'Lo, what it is to love!' using (and repeating) the first statement of the A-E-A-E-A-G-A-E ground bearing that title in the Osborn Commonplace Book (Beinecke Rare Book and Manuscript Library of Yale University, Osborn Music MS 13), ff. 47r–v (old foliation), 43r–v (new foliation). The original can be viewed in in the Digital Library of the Beinecke. Text from Rebholz, ed., *Sir Thomas Wyatt*, 165.

harpsichord during the 1550s and 60s, and even the tradition of the English metrical psalm? Consider Example 21, reminiscent of another tablature from the Osborn Commonplace Book, given above as Example 4. Both are presumably intended to serve as purely instrumental

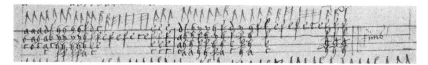

Figure 23. Untitled setting in the Osborn Commonplace Book, f. 44v (old foliation),
f. 40v (new foliation). New Haven, Yale University, Beinecke Rare Book and Manuscript
Library, Osborn Music MS 13. Reproduced by permission.

Example 21. Transcription of the tablature shown in Figure 23.

pieces, but in neither case does the music follow any of the familiar dance
forms, and in this instance the texture shows a swifter rate of harmonic
change, with a richer palette of chords, than in any of the familiar grounds.
The succession of four-course sonorities, without intervening passagework,
supporting a simple but shapely melody on the surface of the harmony,
does not resemble the music in the French guitar books, and appears to
adapt a vocal original (Figure 23).

A prior vocal state, perhaps the intabulator's immediate model, can
be reconstructed with surprising ease, and the result looks very much
like music for a syllabic setting of a text with a regular gait of minims
(Example 22).

In the 1550s a texture such as this could have carried any verse struc-
tured according to the fundamental unit of Tudor lyric, and indeed, it
might be argued, of the entire English verse tradition: a quatrain of four-
beat lines where some beats may be virtual.[34] This means that the music
could carry one couplet of poulter's measure or one stanza of a metrical
psalm in 'Sternhold's metre' such as the following:

---

[34] On this matter see now Attridge, *Moving Words*.

Example 22.   A three-part vocal original reconstructed from the texture of Example 21.

The mán is blést þᵗ that háth not góen   1 2 3 4
    by wýcked réde astráye,   1 2 3r (4 virtual)
Ne sáte in cháyer of péstilènce,   1 2 3 4
    nor wálkt in sínners wáye.³⁵   1 2 3r (4 virtual)

For the use of instruments in the kind of pious, domestic music represented by this stanza we need look no further than the Eglantine Table discussed above in Chapter 1. There is nothing fortuitous about the makers' decision to depict there, crowded amidst the instruments, a four-part anthem by Thomas Tallis, 'O Lord, in thee is all my trust'.³⁶ The makers of the Table might almost be said to have followed what they read on the title page of *The Whole Psalmes in foure partes* (1563), published by John Day, announcing 'psalmes … whiche may be song to al musicall

³⁵ Sternhold, *Certayne Psalmes*, Sig. Aiiij.

³⁶ The tune alone had been published in 1562 (*The Whole Booke of Psalmes*, 389–90), and a four-voice setting was printed in *The Whole Psalmes in foure partes* (1563), also printed by John Day; it appeared again in Day's *Certaine notes set forth in foure and three partes to be song at the morning Communion, and euenyng praier* (1560), and yet again in the summation of that project entitled *Mornyng and Euenyng prayer and Communion, set forthe in foure partes, to be song in churches, both for men and children* … (1565). These collections were all issued in partbooks, but the makers of the Table show the four voices copied in score on what is clearly intended to be a short scroll or *rotulus*. The anthem is edited, but without consulting the musical text on the Eglantine Table, in Ellinwood, rev. Doe, *Thomas Tallis: English Sacred Music*, vol. II, 29–34. Milsom, ed., *A Tallis Anthology*, remedies the omission.

instrumentes, set forth for the encrease of vertue: and abolishyng of other vayne and triflyng ballades'. Day's 1565 collection (I quote from the bassus partbook) also announces that the contents are for performance in church or 'to play on instruments', possibly implying the kind of purely instrumental rendition suggested by the image on the Table where the underlay is confined to the triplex part and goes no further than the first few words. This may also be a manner of performance that Tallis envisaged for his settings in Matthew Parker's psalter of 1567/8; in a somewhat pedantic paragraph, rich in schoolroom learning, Parker (? or Tallis) declares that the four-part settings are for larger choirs and for 'suche as will synge or playe them priuatelye', and reminds his readers that King David was 'an expert musicion in ordering of his instruments'.[37] A prefatory verse to the whole book, presumably by Matthew Parker, encourages performances with lute and harp (precisely the instruments which jostle Tallis's score on the Eglantine Table, together with a viol); this is followed by a poem on the virtues of the psalms, certainly Parker's work, which emphasises how much more the psalms move the spirit when they are uttered with 'tune and tyme'. The faithful should therefore put aside foolish 'songes' and 'sonnets' (conceivably an allusion to the title of Tottel's 'Miscellany', and the poems therein), reserving their instruments for psalms instead:

> Depart ye songes: lasciuious,
> from lute, from harpe depart:
> Geue place to Psalmes: most uertuous,
> and solace there your harte.
>
> Ye songes so nice, ye sonnets all,
> Of lothly louers layes,
> Ye worke mens myndes: but bitter gall,
> By phancies peuish playes.[38]

Metrical translations of the psalms circulated widely from the later 1540s onwards, notably through the medium of print, with musical settings ranging from a single line of melody to four-voice and mostly homophonic counterpoint.[39] Example 23 uses the music of Example 21 to

---

[37] *The whole Psalter translated into English metre*, Sig. VViiij. [38] *Ibid.*, Sig. Bijr.

[39] *ESTC* S119590, with much expanded edition in 1549: *The Psalter of Dauid newely translated into Englysh metre in such sort that it maye the more decently, and wyth more delyte of the mynde, be reade and songe of al men. Wherunto is added a note of four partes, wyth other thynges, as shall appeare in the Epistle to the Readar* (*ESTC* S104580). There are traces of the common metre in Miles Coverdale's *Goostly psalmes and spirituall songes drawen out of the holy Scripture, for the comforte and consolacyon of soch as loue to reioyse in God and his worde* (1535), e.g. 'Let go the whore of Babilon', but neither the syllable count nor the metrical form is as strict as in Sternhold (*ESTC* S121127). For the proliferation of the common or ballad metre in this context see, for example, John Hall, *Certayn chapters taken out of the Prouerbes of Salomon* (1559) (*ESTC* S109536); William Hunnis, *Certayne Psalmes chosen out of the psalter of Dauid, and drawen furth into Englysh meter by William Hunnis seruant to the ryght honorable syr Wyllyam Harberde knight* (1550) (*ESTC* S111771); Tye, *The Actes of the Apostles* (1553)(*ESTC* S91049); *Psalmes of Dauid in Englishe Metre, by Thomas Sterneholde and others* (1560) (*ESTC* S90608); Matthew Parker, *The whole Psalter translated into English Metre,*

Example 23.   The first couplet of Surrey's lyric 'When sommer toke in hand' (text from Jones, ed., *Surrey Poems*, 10) and for the psalm 'Quam bonus Israel' (Psalm 63), as it appears in Thomas Sternhold, *Certayne Psalmes chosen out of the Psalter of Dauid* (1549), Sig. Ciij'. Recreation as gittern-accompanied songs, using the melody of an untitled tablature in the Osborn Commonplace Book (Beinecke Rare Book and Manuscript Library of Yale University, Osborn Music MS 13).

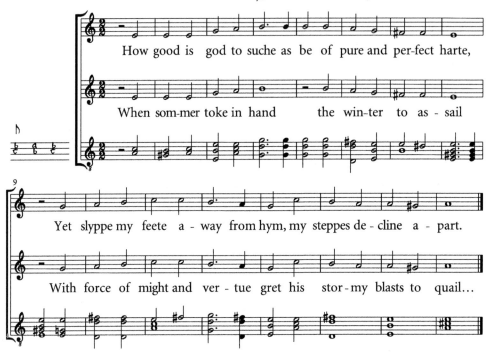

recreate a court ballad in poulter's measure, and an accompanied psalm, both using the same melody and the same reconstructed accompaniment for the gittern. The choice of texts available is very wide, and any selection is bound to seem somewhat arbitrary; for the ballad, the example used is Surrey's lyric 'When sommer toke in hand', printed by Tottel, and for the psalm 'Quam bonus Israel' (Psalm 63), as it appears in *Certayne Psalmes chosen out of the Psalter of Dauid*.

We have made one particular tablature in the Osborn manuscript do considerable work, and yet it can do more. By establishing a link between the gittern and a polyphonic idiom by no means rare in contemporary sources, it points to materials one might use to recreate further examples.

which contayneth an hundreth and fifty Psalmes (1567) (*ESTC* S102297). For literary, musicological and historical scholarship, see Charlton, '"False Fonde Bookes, Ballades and Rimes"'; Leaver, '*Goostly Psalmes and Spirituall Songes*'; Milsom, 'Caustun's Contrafacta'; Quitslund, *The Reformation in Rhyme*; Zim, *English Metrical Psalms*; Willis, *Church Music and Protestantism in Post-Reformation England*, 121–8.

Example 24.   Psalm 28, 'Blessed art thou that fearest God', first verse only, from the Wanley manuscripts (Wrightson, ed., vol. I, 146; used with permission), with editorial intabulation of the entire texture for gittern and then of the lowest three parts for the gittern to play an accompanying role to a single voice performing the superius. The text corresponds to the last item in the ?1547 edition of Sternhold's *Certayne psalms*.

Example 25.   Psalm 3, 'O Lord how are my foes increast', from *Psalmes of Dauid in Englishe metre, by Thomas Sterneholde and others* (1560), 7–8. The following emendations have been made: '*best*ed', minim emended to semibreve; 'wor*ship*', semibreve emended to minim; 'and *thou* holdst,' semibreve emended to minim.

The Wanley manuscripts, probably used in a London church from the late 1540s, contain numerous settings which show how readily the requirements of Edwardian worship, in churches equipped with the necessary choral forces, could result in polyphony that lies well within the reach of the gittern, both for playing alone and as an accompaniment to the voice. It is only necessary to respell some chords by raising the bass by an octave where necessary but without sacrificing any root position chord or losing any defining pitch in the structure of each sonority (Example 24).

There is no obvious reason why such practices should have been confined to polyphonic settings; some players were perhaps more at ease with simple arrangements of the monophonic melodies in *Psalmes of Dauid in Englishe Metre, by Thomas Sterneholde and others … Very Mete to be Vsed of all sorts of people priuatly for their godly solace and confort, laiyng aparte all vngodly songes and ballades, which tende only to the norishing of vice, and corrupting of youth*, published by John Day in 1560. There are graceful and pleasingly elastic melodies in this collection that amply repay the work of recreating idiomatic accompaniments (Example 25).

CHAPTER 7

Thomas Whythorne: the autobiography of a Tudor guitarist

> If you wold haue your sonne, softe, womannish, vncleane ... set him
> to daucing school, and to learn musicke, and than shall you not faile
> of your purpose.
>
> Philip Stubbes, *The Anatomie of Abuses* (1583)

I

Thomas Whythorne, a keen player of the gittern during his youth, and
sometime pupil in a dancing school, commissioned a portrait of himself
in 1569 (Figure 24). By the standards of the day, it shows him at an age
when 'youth's proud livery' was considered worn, for he was then about
forty, but the picture proves that Whythorne wishes to be seen, even to be
studied. He does not share the picture with anything except his coat of
arms; there is no instrument to proclaim his profession as a household
teacher of music, and no prayer book or motto to inspire pious meditation.
With the exception of the 'official' black that he wears, partly to set off his
expensive pendant, Whythorne has dispensed with many conventions of
portraiture favoured by the merchants, physicians, lawyers and clergy of
his time.[1] Yet the picture may not address the viewer as directly as one
might suppose, for the coat of arms which appears there cannot be traced in
Tudor Visitations of Somerset whence Whythorne's family came. He had
read in Gerard Legh's *The Accedens of Armory* that arms could be conceded
to those of 'clean life', loyal to their word and knowledgeable in one or all
of the liberal arts; perhaps he simply assumed this heraldry, thinking well of
himself in general and of his musical talents in particular.[2]

It would be characteristic of Whythorne to have done so, for he
contrived means to emblazon and fictionalise himself in portraiture,
print and text throughout his life. His literary effort in this vein was *A
book of songs and sonets*, a substantial collection of his song verse connected

---

[1] There is an enlightening discussion of such conventions, and their meaning, in Cooper, *Citizen
Portrait*, 11, *et passim*.
[2] For the Visitations of 1531, 1575 and 1591, see Weaver, ed., *The Visitations of the County of
Somerset*. Osborn, ed., *The Autobiography*, 243, n., identifies the passage on f. 115 of the 1576
edition of Legh's text.

Figure 24.　Portrait of Thomas Whythorne, in his forty-first year (1569) by (?) George Gower. Oil on board, 42.3 × 36.4 cm. Yale University, Beinecke Rare Book and Manuscript Library, 1980.389. Reproduced by permission.

by an extensive autobiographical narrative which constantly outgrows the stated purpose of relating the poems to the circumstances that inspired them. The work has elements of a courtesy book, a romance, a collection of aphorisms in the manner of his teacher John Heywood, a tract on the ages of man and a warning about the wiles of women (an admonitory common-place of contemporary lyric verse). Whythorne began it around 1575 but never saw it through the press, for which it was surely intended.[3] In the

[3] The manuscript is now in Oxford, Bodleian Libraries, MS Eng. Misc. c. 330. Osborn, ed., *The Autobiography* (edition of 1961), edits the text in Whythorne's spelling. At lx–lxiv, Osborn gives

course of the narrative, he makes three principal references to his dealings with the gittern, all relating to the period that began with his move to London in the later 1540s. These allusions have a unique value since they offer the reflections of a player – perhaps only the letter of Robert Langham comes close to what Whythorne provides – but we do not have to read very far to recognise that none of the 'pryvat and secret affayrs past' he is prepared to disclose, including his cultivation of the gittern, can be simply isolated from the whole in the service of our (or any other) particular interest.

For *A book of songs and sonets* is a moral and devout work, designed to meet some disconcertingly simple demands of the course of a Protestant life as time passes: the obligation 'to grow holier day by day, while being mindful of God, never backsliding, and preparing for death'.[4] Thus although the text appears to contain nearly all the verse that Whythorne wrote, even there his purpose has a stern aspect, suggested by the title page that he carefully wrote out to imitate a printed book:

> A book [of s]ong[s and son]ets.
> with lo[n]ge discoors[es s]ett with
> them, of the chylds lyfe, to-
> g[y]ther with A yoong mans
> Lyfe, and entring into the old
> mans Lyfe. devysed and
> written with A new Orthografye
> by Thomas Whythorne gent.

As this title indicates, Whythorne hopes to engage with the particularities of one life – his own – by seeking what is universally true in the span of

---

details of the manuscript. Whythorne's life is summarised at xvii–liii and in *ODNB*, sv 'Whithorne, Thomas'. In 1962 Osborn published a second edition, under the same title, but in modern spelling. All quotations from Whythorne's book in this chapter are given in his own orthography. Although he was no Thomas Wyatt, the reasons for quoting him in his own spelling are the same as they are for retaining the old spelling found in the works of that much greater poet: 'to keep a measure of the distance between then and now, between him and us, his language of heart and mind, and ours' (Brigden, *Thomas Wyatt*, ix). See Palmer, *Thomas Whythorne's Speech*, and for context, Suárez, 'The English Spelling Reform'. The book is widely regarded as an innovative attempt to portray a recognisable subject with an inner life, a *self*. See Shore, 'The Autobiography of Thomas Whythorne' and 'Whythorne's Autobiography'; Hodgkin, 'Thomas Whythorne and the Problems of Mastery'; Mousley, 'Renaissance Selves and Life Writing'; Bedford, *et al.*, eds., *Early Modern English Lives*; Flynn, 'Thomas Mulliner'; Skura, *Tudor Autobiography*, 98–125. Whythorne's account of a failed courtship is deftly analysed in Cressy, *Birth, Marriage and Death*, 237–9. The most recent sustained study of Whythorne as a musician is Nelson, 'Thomas Whythorne and the Social and Professional World of Tudor Musicians', which is highly recommended; see also the same author's 'Love in the Music Room'. Whythorne's songs for three, four and five voices in his 1571 collection have been edited by McQuillan.

[4] Ryrie, *Being Protestant in Reformation Britain*, 441–2. Cf. Osborn, ed., *The Autobiography*, 141–2 (Whythorne's mind troubled by an outbreak of the pestilence; he turns to reading 'godly and grav books'), 145 (he is perturbed by fear of death), 147–9 (he ponders divine punishments), 158–9 (on the fear of death), 255–67 (an extensive meditation upon the Lord's Prayer in prose and verse).

human life considered as a drama of three phases: 'the chylds lyfe ...
A yoong mans Lyfe ... the old mans Lyfe'.[5] He writes to show that the
poems he composed for music, such as 'Give not thy mind to heaviness',
should be read as salutary reflections upon some specific experience in
one of the three phases. So it will be for the gittern: whatever Whythorne's
transactions with that instrument (light in every sense) will prove to be,
we may be sure that they will possess a certain weight.[6]

II

At the age of ten, Whythorne was sent from his father's house in Ilminster,
Somerset, to the household of a relative near Oxford. Young men who
remained in the country house of their fathers until their late teenage years
were widely believed to sink into the 'rusticitie' and 'clownish speech' of
butchers, fishmongers and other tradesmen, familiar figures on the fringes
of a rural household. Whythorne had the good fortune to be settled with
one of his uncles, and when he showed an interest in music rather than the
Church, medicine or the law, his uncle approved. In 1538 he entered
Magdalen College School in Oxford and remained there as a chorister for
six years, followed by one year as a full member of the College. By 1545
he was a pupil in the household of the musician, poet and dramatist, John
Heywood. According to Whythorne's own account, and using the orthography he devised, he was to be

---

[5] For Ages of Man schemes, see Shepard, *Meanings of Manhood*, 54ff. For the sense of 'sonet' at this
date see Shrank, '"Matters of Love as of Discourse"'. In one of the most remarkable passages of the
autobiography, Whythorne appears to make a much smaller claim for his work. He reports a
conversation with his publisher, John Day, in which he received the dispiriting news that sales of
Songes for three, fouer and five Voyces were not what Day had hoped (Osborn, ed., *The Autobiography*,
220). Whythorne responded that the fault lay partly with Day's poor reputation as a printer of music;
what is more, the book had not been sufficiently brought to the attention of potential buyers. Having
thus unwisely set his publisher against him, Whythorne then told Day he had written a book which
sounds very much like a first version of *A book of songs and sonets*. It contained 'all þe songs and sonets
which I had mad to be sung with my miuzik', and Whythorne thought it would be a good idea to
print the book, not only as an advertisement, in effect, for the 1571 collection but also to provide
longer versions of the song texts than it had been feasible for Day to print in that volume.

[6] Osborn, ed., *The Autobiography*, 3. In general terms, not all relevant to this chapter, I believe
Whythorne's book is animated by a belief that the future of musical art as a respectable profession,
and as a literate pursuit, lies with men whose position has not yet been configured, in the new days of
the reformed religion, with either the security or the status that those persons deserve. These men are
the teachers of music in households – like Whythorne himself – who are as yet caught between the
role of gentleman guest and domestic servant, never more so in Whythorne's case than when those
positions are confounded and he finds himself the object of predatory sexual attention. The best role
as yet available for them is 'skoolmaster', a class for whom Whythorne has no great respect since
many of its representatives are unskilled and merely 'pettifoggers of miuzik'. The autobiography
shows that musicians of the necessary talent, inwardness and breeding already exist, for Whythorne
emerges from the text as one such man, but it also reveals that they are more dependent upon the
whims of their patrons than are the singing men whose professional security, in the days before the
Reformation, Whythorne is perhaps inclined to overestimate, and are constantly at the mercy of
circumstance.

both hiz servant and skoller, for hee waz not only very well skylled in Muzik, and playeng on þe virȝinals but also such an English *poet*, az þe lýk, for hiz witt and invension . . . waz not az þen in England, nor before hiz týme sinse Chawser's týin.[7]

By the time he left John Heywood's service after 'three yeer and mọr', probably in 1547/8, Whythorne had passed into the second Age of Man that he calls 'Adolescency'.[8] The sheltering period of household dependency he had known since birth now came to an end and he was required to secure an income and a reputation, or what he calls his 'kreditt and estimasion'. For company and for peers, he looked to 'yoong folks' and 'gentilmen' who are probably to be identified with the better kinds of London apprentice and the sons of gentry at the Inns of Court. To cultivate the sportive pursuits favoured by such young men, he joined schools of fencing and dancing:

I being þen dezyrows to hav and enrich my self with sum mọr such exersýzes and qualyties az yoong folks for þe most do delýt in, went to þe daunsing skool, and fens skooll . . .[9]

Whythorne had learned the lute and the virginals during his period of apprenticeship with Heywood, so his musical accomplishments probably placed him well ahead of most of his peers in at least one department of what has been called the courtly trivium. Yet he planned to use those instruments to earn his livelihood, and that brought him dangerously close to minstrelsy and the associated state of vagabondage.[10] During the early-to-mid-1570s, when Whythorne began to compile his autobiography, the Elizabethan government was much concerned with legislation against minstrels and what he himself calls their 'vakabond' life.[11] The reformed religion did not accommodate itself easily to many of the old pastimes; 'minstrels, rather than mass priests' proved to be the Protestant preacher's principal enemy, and such musicians were commonly regarded by the authorities as little better than masterless itinerants at a time when the expansion of Elizabethan London was responsible for a substantial rise in vagrancy, mostly among young, unemployed and homeless males.[12] As early as 1566, Sir William Cecil had made notes listing 'fensers, berewardes, *mynstrells*, pedlars, tynkers' (emphasis mine) as examples of vagabondage.

---

[7] *Ibid.*, 13. On this orthography, see Palmer, *Thomas Whythorne's Speech*. Although this is nominally a sound-per-letter system, Palmer shows that Whythorne conceals some phonetic features of his own West Country speech.

[8] The question of whether adolescence, as now understood, was a recognised phase of life in the early modern period has been much discussed. See Griffiths, *Youth and Authority*, 21; Smith, 'The London Apprentices as Seventeenth-Century Adolescents'; Shepard, *Meaning of Manhood*, 207ff.

[9] Osborn, ed., *The Autobiography*, 19.

[10] *Ibid.*, 245–6, where the delicacy and sensitivity of this issue for Whythorne are evident.

[11] *Ibid.*, 233–4, on minstrels and their 'vakabond' life; 242–3 (a story at the expense of a minstrel); 244–5 (another); 246–7 (on minstrels again, among others).

[12] Collinson, *Birthpangs of Protestant England*, x; Beier, 'Social Problems in Elizabethan London' and *Masterless Men*.

Whythorne had no choice but to recognise that he belonged with those who used music to 'furþer þeir lývings þerby', like any minstrel.[13] Upon his arrival in London, therefore, he decided that it was time to learn two instruments associated with a free and companionable amateurism that we have already met in the person of Francis Saunders from the Middle Temple. Whythorne

learned to play on þe Gyttern, and Sittern. which ij° instruments wer þen stranʒ in England, and þerfor þe mor dezyred and esteemed.[14]

The social aspect of Whythorne's decision to cultivate these two instruments, but especially the gittern, was clearly of prime importance to him, for it ranked him as a gentleman:

þe which instriument [i.e. 'þe Gyttern'] az A sytting mat, lieng mat, and walking mat, I þen yvzed to play on very often, yea and almost evry howr of þe day, for þat it waz an instriument much esteemed and yvzed of gentilmen, and of þe best sort in þoz dayz.[15]

If we are encouraged by this passage to describe the gittern as a new 'fashion', or even as 'fashionable', in the days of Whythorne's youth, we do well to ask what it means to employ such terms in a sixteenth-century context. Tudor writers often use the word 'fashion' in the literal sense of 'a making', keeping the meaning close to its Latin ancestor formed from *facere*, 'to make'. A 'new fashion' in this sense was the novel appearance or design of a manufactured object. The objects most often spoken of in this way are garments designed in a strikingly new manner, like the cut shoes and slashed hose sported by the Newcastle apprentices in November 1554 (the root of the modern sense of 'fashion' as something especially pertaining to the garment industry began under the first Tudors).[16] The gittern was a new fashion in this sense, for although bowed instruments with figure-of-eight bodies had been known in medieval England for centuries, the 'new fashion' of the renaissance guitar with its combination of incurved sides, frets, a circular sound-hole, a fretwork or perforated parchment rose and a plucking technique must have been very apparent to the eye, and largely accounts for its reputation as an unusual or foreign instrument in the later 1540s. An allusion to a 'costly cradel, made after the new fashion', mentioned in 1568 as something that a wealthy or aristocratic family might possess, adds an important dimension by showing how the notion

---

[13] Osborn, ed., *The Autobiography*, 245.   [14] *Ibid.*, 19   [15] *Ibid.*, 30.

[16] The modern use of the word 'fashion' to mean especially some new form of clothing endorsed by those in a position to influence custom among others, and liable to enjoy only an ephemeral fame, was already very well established in the sixteenth century, but mostly in a negative context. See, for example, *Here begynneth the booke which the knyght of the toure made and speketh of many fayre ensamples and thensygnementys and techyng of his doughters* (1484), Ch. 20: 'But god haue mercy on vs at this day; after that som haue herd that ony newe facion or nouelte of goune or arraye [is available, they] shall neuer reste till they haue therof a Copye, And shullen saye to their lord or husbond dayly: "Suche thyng, and suche shold become me wel and it is right faire; I praye yow that I may haue it".' [my punctuation].

of something 'made in a new fashion' was already poised in the late 1560s to drift towards the something 'made in a new way which the illustrious and wealthy can afford and which others, though less prosperous, might wish to imitate'. The gittern may have begun its English career in London among gentlemen, but the signs of aristocratic and court patronage for the instrument can be traced to at least the early 1550s, and continental makers were producing opulent examples, with some components and decoration using exotic woods, that would have made the most luxurious gitterns into enviable examples of a 'new fashion' in musical instruments.

This shows that the gittern was not only played by gentlemen but was also a mark of gentility that Whythorne thought himself well advised to adopt. It was precisely because such negotiation of one's social position was possible in the sixteenth century that the title of 'gentleman' was so often claimed and contested in pamphlets and polemics at the time when Whythorne wrote. How valid was the relatively new notion of the gentleman as lawyer or university man who, in the words of John Webster, 'only smell'd of a ink and counters'? Was a true gentleman one who made rare visits to London, perhaps when his legal affairs compelled him to do so, and who then returned swiftly home to his estate, his tenants and his store of weapons rather than 'sylke Garmentes'? The time had now arrived when a man could choose to adopt a gentlemanly style of life, unknown to his ancestors, by taking certain steps. Whythorne's account of his youthful days in London shows him working for the title of gentleman, not simply bearing it.

That is why Whythorne associates the gittern not only with gentlemen but also with 'þe best sort' in the passage quoted above. That phrase is not a synonym for 'gentlemen', though it might appear so at first sight; instead, it belongs to a relatively new vocabulary of social discrimination, better able to accommodate those, like Whythorne himself, with social and professional aspirations. The older system had long acknowledged gradations of social rank running downwards from nobleman through gentleman to yeoman, citizen and burgess, husbandman, artisan and labourer; this is the one Whythorne evokes by speaking of 'gentlemen'. The newer language, however, distinguished different 'sorts' of men, somewhat relaxing the importance of lineage and gentry descent in favour of the reputation that hard work and an honest life could confer. The 'best sort' encompassed those who were deemed fit to serve on juries, or to be buried within parish churches because they were prominent and respected in their communities: a superiority of experience, authority and wealth that had been earned.[17] Some men had worked hard to reach the stage where they

---

[17] Wrightson, '"Sorts of People" in Tudor and Stuart England', 28–51, and Thomas, *The Ends of Life*, 114ff.

might take up a gentleman's form of life, including playing the gittern, and Whythorne did not forget it.

Judged in purely musical terms, something exceptional happened when Whythorne began to cultivate that instrument himself. Someone who thought no man worthy to be called a 'miuzisian' unless he could compose correctly in four parts or above, who was a highly conservative composer himself and who was a competent player (one may suppose) upon the lute and virginals, nonetheless put those sophisticated and versatile resources aside in his enthusiasm for an instrument whose repertoire was sometimes in no parts at all, and which made liberal use of first and second inversions of chords in 'ungrammatical' positions. It was all very well for the author of *La maniere de bien et iustement entoucher les Lucz et Guiternes* to praise the gittern for being able to play in four parts, making it a fit instrument for *musiciens* rather than *menestriers*, for as a Frenchman he knew a rich and literate tradition of music for the four-course guitar. In England, French material was certainly known but in general terms the case was different; so little repertoire remains in writing that we must assume much of the music played on the gittern was ephemeral and easy to learn by ear, making much more liberal (indeed unchecked) use of inversions than any save the most unusual pieces in the French prints. Whythorne's liking for the gittern suggests the tolerance of even the educated Tudor ear in response to harmonic effects that the literate and notated tradition mostly censured and rarely broached. A world of sonority evidently existed that was related to the harmonies emerging from 'correct' and composed counterpoint but which nonetheless formed an exuberant and independent dominion.

The most fitting musical illustration to associate with Whythorne is a setting for gittern of Filippo Azzaiolo's 'Chi passa per questa strada' that appears within a set of additions, for both gittern and cittern, in the paper volume of keyboard music prepared by Thomas Mulliner. The biography of this Tudor musician remains very uncertain, but there is a note on f. 2r in which the book announces itself as Mulliner's (*Sum liber thomae mullineri*) and a very similar hand has added, in different ink, and probably at a different time, *iohanne heywoode teste*. It is likely that this 'witness' to Mulliner's ownership of the book is Thomas Whythorne's master, the musician, poet and dramatist John Heywood; if Mulliner is the individual he is commonly supposed to be – a clerk at Magdalen College, Oxford in 1557/8 and later the 'organorum modulator' at Corpus Christi College – then he and Whythorne shared a background in the ecclesiastical music of Oxford.[18] The setting of 'Chi passa', untitled but marked 'gitterne', is

---

[18] The page is reproduced in Caldwell, ed., *The Mulliner Book*, xli; in *ODNB*, sv 'Mulliner, Thomas', he remains scrupulously impartial ('The John Heywood recorded in the inscription could have been the vicar-choral of St Paul's (*c.* 1490–1574), John Heywood the court dramatist and entertainer (*c.* 1497–1578), or someone else of that name.') See Flynn, 'Thomas Mulliner'.

Example 26.   The first section of ['Chi passa'] from The Mulliner Book (BL, Add. MS
30513, ff. 119v–120v), marked 'gitterne'. Barring as in the original.

given as Example 26. The texture shows an essentially two-part idiom,
punctuated by four-note chords (there is barely a three-note chord to be
found) and abounding in second inversions; the result is a lively and even
bravura alternation between running, ornamented passagework on one
hand and plucked or strummed chords on the other. The tablature
includes two signs for ornaments (+ and a dot) whose meaning is uncertain,
but since both appear on the top string in adjacent block chords at one
point, where there is limited room for manoeuvre, they presumably mean
an upper or lower mordent, though that is not necessarily their meaning in
every case.[19]

III

The relative ease and appeal of these techniques set the gittern of later-
sixteenth-century England on its course to become the instrument of the

---

[19] For ornamentation signs in the lute sources, see Poulton, 'Graces of Play', 112–14, and Shepherd,
'The Interpretation of Signs for Graces'. The piece is edited in Caldwell, ed., *The Mulliner Book*,
190–1. One does not readily depart from the choices made by such an experienced editor, but I have
not seen the need to add the bass of the 'Chi passa' chord sequence; there is nothing in the music
that departs from standard four-course guitar idiom in a way that suggests it needs to be supple-
mented; nor am I convinced of the need to add the 'lost' measure that Caldwell inserts between
square brackets.

wayward apprentice as well as the gentleman, of the card-sharp as well as the scholar, but above all of the young male out and about in town. Whythorne cultivated the gittern as part of what he calls 'A yoong mans Lyfe', but it is the nature of Whythorne's writing and reflection to be forever 'entring into the old mans Lyfe' (again the phrase is from his title page) as his account unfolds. This moral vigilance results in an autobiography that seems a remarkably unmasculine account of young days in Tudor London. Where are the alehouses, the bowling alleys, the gambling dens, the brawls, the pranks and the nocturnal trips with doubtful watermen to the Southwark side? Whythorne appears to relish the memory of his youthful sports with gittern, foil and galliard, but the reasons for disavowing those pleasures, even while recalling them, seem to come swiftly to mind as he recognises the danger of censure from others almost as quickly as he finds himself sitting in judgement upon his younger self. He discerned 'many follies in yoong men'.[20]

This is certainly true of his allusion to learning the gittern which, together with fencing and dancing, is one of the very few activities where we sense that Whythorne is constructing a recognisably male and homosocial identity for his young self in a way that offers and may even court an association with youthful misrule. An entry in the memoranda of the Court of the Governors of the Bridewell for 1575 shows how unfavourably young male players of the gittern (and other instruments with more resilient reputations) might appear in the eyes of their elders at about the time when Whythorne began his autobiography. The text records that some servants and apprentices appeared before the Court in October of that year; in their various depositions they spoke of plans to go overseas, of nocturnal visits to a widow in Lambeth to whom many 'gentlemen' were accustomed to resort, of rich fabrics misappropriated from the house of one of their masters and of a stolen ring. They had repeatedly dined at the house of a certain John Hardinge, a Thames waterman; on one occasion 'they came at iiij of the Clocke in the mornynge and broughte a sett of vialls with them, & then spente there iiij d. & so appointed a suppar'. On another they came with a lute, a gittern and cittern:

And also he [John Hardinge] saieth on sondaie was sevenighte there was certcyne of them with a lute a gittorne & a Cittorne & that they were there, aboute iij quarters of an hower, And also that they were there one tyme, when they broughte in a side & a hautch of venison.[21]

As late as 1592, a player of the gittern strikes no better figure than this in Robert Greene's *A Dispvtation between a Hee Conny-catcher and a Shee Conny-catcher*:

---

[20] Osborn, ed., *The Autobiography*, 4. Griffths, *Youth and Authority*, provides an excellent discussion and analysis of this theme. See also Shepard, *Meanings of Manhood*.

[21] Bethlem Royal Hospital Archives and Museum, Item bcb-02, ff. 184v–5.

It fortuned that as many sought to win me, so amongst the rest there was an od companion that dwelt with a Gentleman hard by, a fellowe of small reputation, and of no lyuing, neither had he any excellent quallities but thrumming on the gittron: but of pleasant disposition he was, and could gawll out many quaint & riba[l]drous Iigges & songs, and so was fauoured of the foolish sect for his foppery.[22]

We cannot simply conclude that the 'scandal of the gittern', as it might be called, is absent from Whythorne's text on the grounds that he is referring to a time long past, or 'þoz dayz', when there was no issue to be addressed. His autobiography is in some measure a book about folly addressed to the scions of gentry families, or 'yowthfull Imps',[23] and the very quality that commended the gittern, according to his account, namely that it was considered 'stranʒ', is transparently ambivalent. The root sense of the word is 'foreign', derived through Middle French *e(s)trange* from Latin EXTRANEUS meaning 'foreign' or 'that which is from without'.[24] At the highest social level among nobles such as Robert Dudley, Earl of Leicester, the taste for strangeness in the positive senses of the word was a necessary form of cosmopolitanism to be expressed, for example, in dress and architecture; it showed that a man belonged to the international community of chivalry and was familiar with the opulent forms its material culture could take in distant courts.[25] The virtues of the gentleman, however, were not conceived in such grand terms, and a liking for 'strange' novelties was therefore a hazardous taste for anyone who sought to appear a gentleman in Elizabethan England much beyond the sphere of his friends or like-minded associates. Many conservative commentators (which is to say most commentators) deplored the desire to covet novel and imported forms of dress, or any other foreign commodities, as vehemently as they inveighed against strange doctrines in religion. The wide and alarming hinterland of the word that Whythorne uses of the gittern now comes into view. A foreign land, likely to be a source of decadent imported fashions, was a 'strange' country; unfamiliar or affected words introduced into English from abroad were 'strange' terms; and 'strange' goods included imports such as ostrich feathers, dyed silks, satins and perfumed gloves. At a time when there was much discussion of the common weal, the tendency of many to dress like foreigners, repudiating established forms of dress, and to adopt strange usages, could cause exasperated comment.[26]

---

[22] Sig. D4.
[23] Osborn, ed., *The Autobiography*, 2. 'Imp', literally 'a graft', here carries its obsolete figurative sense of 'Scion (esp. of a noble house); offspring, child (usually male)' (*OED*, sv 'imp', 3a).
[24] See *OED*, sv 'strange', adj., especially senses 1/1a 'Of persons, language, customs, etc.: Of or belonging to another country; foreign, alien', and 7. 'Unknown, unfamiliar; not known, met with, or experienced before', and *LEME*, entries for 'strange', notably John Palsgrave, *Lesclarcissement de la Langue Francoyse* (1530) and *The Dictionary of syr Thomas Elyot knyght* (1538).
[25] On Dudley in this regard, see Morris, '"I was never more in love with an Olde House"'.
[26] Sherman, 'Anatomising the Commonwealth'. See also Warneke, 'A Taste for Newfangledness'.

This is one of Whythorne's reasons for emphasising that the gittern was his companion as he walked, sat and lay down. A book that is in some measure about folly maturing into wisdom, stuffed with verse that offers good counsel and 'lessons large', was bound to make more of the gittern than the cittern, for there was no comparable scandal of the latter. The cittern somehow established itself as English, domestic and (at first) genteel; there were some critics of the cittern because there were always Tudor commentators inclined to regard the art of music, especially among the nobility, as an undesirable consequence of the progress of opulence, and one from which they should be deterred by the example of Nero; thus Johann Rivius in *A Notable discourse of the happinesse of this our age, and of the ingratitude of men to God for his benefites* (1578) inveighs against 'Noble mens gorgious buildings, and goodlie houses, nothing else almost (by their leaues) is done, but daily dice playing, iollie tossing of beere potts, daunsing to the sound of the Citterne, or Lute'.[27] Yet even here the context for the cittern is implicitly conceded to be aristocratic. Not yet associated with barbers' shops during most of Whythorne's lifetime, the cittern was more consistently acceptable in social and musical terms during the second half of the sixteenth century, and more durably associated with a gentleman's 'exercises', than the gittern. The proposal of Humphrey Gilbert (d. 1583) for 'an achademy in London for educacion of her maiestes wardes, and others the youth of nobility and gentlemen', addressed to Elizabeth I, requires 'one Teacher of Musick, and to play one the Lute, the Bandora, and Cytterne', but there is no mention of the gittern.[28] Thomas Preston's *A lamentable tragedy mixed ful of pleasant mirth* (1570) can insouciantly place the cittern in royal company; there seems to be no irony, and nothing tragicomical, in the innocence of the pastoral setting as the lovers go 'to walke a brode/On Lute and Cittern there to play a heauenly hermony'.[29]

Whythorne describes both the gittern and cittern as strange, so why did the 'strangeness' of the gittern prove by far the more damaging? We have seen that there was no native tradition of manufacturing gitterns, or virtually none that can be traced beyond the set possibly produced by John Rose. In contrast, there is some evidence that citterns were made in England and assimilated into a musical culture dominated by the bright sound of plucked wire strings on virginals, harpsichord, citterns, bandoras and orpharions. The effects of Robert Mallet of Oxford (d. 1612), manciple of St Edmund Hall in Oxford, included some incomplete instruments including '2 citternes unfinisht', and working tools.[30] A native tradition of cittern manufacture would explain why Vincenzo Galilei could write in 1581 that the *Cetera*, presumably meaning the cittern, was used in Britain before any other nation, and that the players of that isle

---

[27] Sig. Piiij[v].   [28] Furnivall, ed., *Queene Elizabethes Achademy*, 261.   [29] Sig. Ci[v].
[30] Fleming, 'Some Points', 302.

had brought it to a state of *eccellenza*, while the enthusiasm of Michael Praetorius for what he calls the 'Klein Englisch Zitterlein' is well known.[31]

IV

One last reference to the gittern in Whythorne's autobiography is perhaps the most revealing. He was once employed in an unspecified household with 'dyverz young women', settled in a chamber that appears to be part of a house that is opulent and extensive enough for the room to be entirely his own. One of the female servants took a fancy to him; stealing into his chamber, she left an amorous message in English verse, folded 'between þe strings of a Gittern'. This room was Whythorne's private space in the sense that unauthorised entry could be deemed a kind of intrusion; the young woman's entry had to be clandestine, and Whythorne accordingly says that she delivered her message 'in sekret wýs'. He appears to be employed in the kind of residence where the 'quiet rooms', the 'tight-fitting doors' and the general sense of space, denied to so many, were available to him.[32]

In recent years historians have explored the ways in which men and women in early modern England knew themselves as autonomous and private beings with movements of inner life which they could scrutinise before the many inherited discourses for transforming those motions into illustrations of what was wise or foolish, virtuous or corrupt, in the general life of Mankind asserted their authority. Suspecting that this sense was enhanced in the sixteenth century, but generally anxious to escape the renaissance 'discovery of the individual', historians and literary critics have examined changing notions of privacy, often in questionable connection with architectural innovations in the design and arrangement of chambers securing some anticipation of 'the state or condition of being alone, undisturbed, or free from public attention, as a matter of choice or right'.[33]

Private prayer, reading and meditation in chamber or closet have attracted special attention, but there is one element conspicuously missing from these accounts: the sustained and often solitary work of practicing a

---

[31] *Dialogo di Vincentio Galilei nobile della musica antica e della moderna*, 147; *Syntagma Musicum: De Organographia*, Ch. 31 and Fig. 16. For studies of the cittern in England, see Danner, 'Dd.4.23'; Abbot and Segerman, 'The Cittern in England Before 1700'; Forrester, 'Citterns and their Fingerboards'; Gill, *Wire-Strung Plucked Instruments*; Grijp, 'Fret Patterns of the Cittern'; Segerman, 'A Short History of the Cittern' (with reply by Forrester in *GSJ*, 2008); Stauder, 'Zur Entwicklung der Cister'; Ward, *Sprightly and Cheerful Musick, passim*. Digital images of what may be the only surviving cittern of English manufacture are currently available at www.cittern.theaterofmusic.com/old/1600.html. Aspects of the cittern in England were regularly debated in the pages of *FoMRHI Quarterly*, the Bulletin of the Fellowship of Makers and Researchers of Historic Instruments, notably by Forrester and Segerman. These are now available online at www.fomrhi.org.
[32] Ryrie, *Being Protestant*, 158.
[33] *OED*, 'privacy, n. 1. See Orlin, *Locating Privacy in Tudor London*, and Shaw, 'The Construction of the Private in Medieval London'.

musical instrument, or simply playing it for pleasure when alone. The association between privacy construed as a desired solitude and instrumental playing in the early modern period has yet to find its chronicler, and can only be very lightly sketched here, starting from what one may reasonably assume: that the work of becoming proficient upon a musical instrument, in the sixteenth century, as today, was accomplished in full knowledge that others might wish to avoid contact with it, and was therefore necessarily conducted alone, amongst those who were wealthy enough to have domestic interiors sufficiently complex for such isolation to be possible.

Some texts of the later sixteenth century suggest a surprisingly thin partition between the art of string playing and the 'tuneable fashion and practyse' of living a devout life:

But as in a harpe, a lute, or a vyol . . . euery string with other must be tuned, and none lefte vntuned, leste thereby some vnpleasant soundes, and discords might be vttered, so we muste putte all and euerye the commaundementes of God, to theyr tuneable fashion and practyse, lest that yf any be left vnused or of vs, there might to the pure and cleane eares and iudgemente of Almyghtye GOD, come thereby some vnpleasaunte sownde, and vnswete reporte of our lyues and doynges.[34]

The art of living a devout, prayerful life and the art of the string player cease to be held together by the force of a familiar metaphor and become literal partners in the developing genre of the Protestant spiritual diary. In both of the outstanding cases the player is a woman, one with an orpharion and the other with a lute. On 25 January, 1599, Lady Margaret Hoby reported in her diary that

After priuat praers I went about the house and then I reed of the bible tell dinner time: after diner I dressed vp my Clositte and read and, to refreshe my selfe beinge dull, I plaied and sunge to the Alpherion . . .[35]

The power of music to inspire a discerning scrutiny of the self, or at least a diagnosis of one's own changing moods, is very apparent here; so too in the spiritual diary of Grace, Lady Mildmay (d. 1620), much of whose material is hard to date but is plainly sixteenth century. Her composing, lute playing and prayers weave a seamless garment of profitable works:

Wherein I found that as the water pierceth often the hard stone by dropping therevpon; So the continuall exercyse in the word of God, made a deepe impression in my stony hart, wt an apteness to inclyne vnto the will of God, & to delight in the meditation therof vpon euery occasion. Also euery daye I spent some tyme in playing on my lute, & setting songs of 5 partes therevnto & practised my voyce

---

[34] Bonner, *A profitable and necessarye doctrine with certayne homelyes adioyned therunto set forth by the reuerend father in God, Edmunde Byshop of London* (1555), Sig. Ff1ᵛ.

[35] Meads, ed., *The Diary of Lady Margaret Hoby*, 99. On the traditions of spiritual diaries, see Ryrie, *Being Protestant*, 298–9.

in singing of psalmes, & in making my prayers to God, And confessing any sinnes . . .[36]

Playing an instrument, like the private prayer and meditation that might be conducted in the same place, and seemingly on the same occasion, required 'continuall exercyse' and self-scrutiny, and like private prayer, music refreshed the spirit, bringing what Whythorne calls 'A fors with it lẏk vnto A heavenly inspirasion'.[37]

Perhaps one may view Thomas Whythorne through the experiences of these two women who were his younger contemporaries, and players of the orpharion and lute respectively: self-examination and devout reflections converged increasingly with work that required scrutiny of the operations of the limbs, informed by a careful sifting of the impressions delivered to the mind by a bodily sense straining towards something that is physically produced but remains intangible. It was the gittern that Whythorne practiced most intensely, virtually 'every hour of the day'. No doubt he genuinely enjoyed playing the instrument, but it is hard to tell whether he is cultivating the instrument or the instrument is helping to cultivate him.

v

The third woman in this story, the young servant who stole into his chamber and therefore inspired him to record the episode of the clandestine message, failed in her suit, but she succeeded in reversing a favourite tale by playing the lovelorn Criseyde to a cautious Troilus. She also managed to make herself the only woman in all our sources whom we find touching a gittern. Whythorne and other gentlemen presumably learned it to be an addition to mixed company, not just their own; that was certainly the case with Robert Langham in 1575, who would sometimes 'foot it with daunsyng: noow with my Gyttern, and els with my Cyttern', and who found himself (according to his own report) surrounded by female admirers crying 'anoother good Langham anoother'. The previous year, the court servant Edward Hellowes translated a passage from the Spanish of the bishop Antonio de Guevara about the behaviour of young men in love and inserted a reference to playing the gittern where Guevara's Latin original has none. Thus we learn from an English court servant of 1574 that amorous youths made poor messengers because they wished to spend their time 'writing letters, watching at corners, playing on

[36] Martin, 'The Autobiography of Grace, Lady Mildmay', 59–60.
[37] Osborn, ed., *The Autobiography*, 230. The practice of an instrument in private, as part of a developing inner life of self-scrutiny, should not be too briskly associated with a 'style of experimental Calvinist religiosity which had become fashionable in the late 1580s', since solitary prayer was a foundational practice of medieval Catholicism for those that could attain to it. Cambers, 'Margaret Hoby's Marginalia', 213, and on the closet, Orlin, *Locating Privacy*, 296–326, esp. 301.

gitterns, climing on walles, and vewing of windows'.[38] Presumably these young men were using their gitterns like the Parisian gallants of the late 1540s who thought themselves 'to be passing excellent and singular good players on the Lute and Gitterne, and do nightly walke the streates before their louers gates, tearing the poor strings of their instrumentes . . . '.[39]

Yet despite the curiously enduring place of the gittern in the armoury of amorous young men, Whythorne never suggests in his autobiography that he played in the kind of social context evoked by Langham, and he neither says nor implies that women might play the instrument. To some extent, the gendering of the gittern that inflects all the Tudor sources surveyed in this book may be an illusion created by forms of gender inequality before the law, with profound effects upon the content of the records that survive, and by the slender documentary trace of the part played by women in maritime trade and the institutional structures of the livery companies. A complete absence of female gittern players in sixteenth-century England seems a curious preparation for the appearance of guitars in the private accounts of women in the first half of the seventeenth century, such as Rachel, Countess of Bath,[40] or indeed the abundant material from Restoration London documenting female players with their foppish guitar masters. John Playford, writing in 1666, was surely not the first to believe that the 'natural' inclination of women to vanity and social emulation drew them to this intermittently fashionable instrument: 'Not a City Dame though a *Tap-Wife*, but is ambitious to haue her Daughters Taught by Mounsieur La *Novo Kickshawibus* on the *Gittar* . . . '.[41]

The gittern in England during the second half of the sixteenth century was strongly associated with the many gendered freedoms of young males: their liberty of access to higher learning and the law via the universities and the Inns of Court; their freedom of movement in the common street that often brought censure but rarely an enduring disgrace; their liberty to take an apprenticeship and be sent abroad to Antwerp, or elsewhere, as a factor by their master; their freedom to become known as accomplished poets in the almost entirely masculine and frequently misogynist manner of Tottel's 'Miscellany'.[42] The amorous gittern players described by Edward Hellowes climb walls and peer in at windows, seeking out the frontiers and apertures behind which the women they admire, with no such right of the street, are ensconced. The Parisian serenaders walk the streets and seek out another liminal spot where women are confined: 'their louers gates'. The Tudor guitar was a potent image of the liberty and licence enjoyed by the male.

---

[38] *The Familiar Epistles of Sir Anthony of Gueuara* (1574), 115.   [39] See Appendix B, 1547₁.
[40] See Gray, ed., *Devon Household Accounts*, 2nd vol., 178, 223 and 232.
[41] *Musick's delight on the Cithren*, Preface. The sense of 'Monsieur . . . Kickshawibus' (< French *quelque chose*, with a Latin dative and ablative plural termination to create a macaronic word) is something like 'Mr . . . Geegaw'. *OED*, sv 'kickshaw'.
[42] Heale, 'Misogyny and the Complete Gentleman'.

Conclusion

There may be no better way to develop a deceptively peaceable view of English society in the sixteenth century than to trace the history of a Tudor musical instrument. As we review representations of the quarry in the visual arts, or sift archives and literary texts for germane references, any sense that Tudor England was a small country, threatened by encircling powers of a competing faith, is liable to fade. The battle to keep hunger at bay, which blighted the lives of so many, seems to be won as imported instruments come to the wharves of London in substantial quantities and enthusiasts fill their commonplace books with tablature. On one hand, this may not be so very misleading. Contemporaries repeatedly praised music for its power to give comfort and to revitalise the intelligence; only the trumpet in time of war, John Milton's 'sonorous mettal blowing Martial sounds', showed that music could also be a summons to conflict (as opposed to conflict of opinion). On the other hand, however, to treat any musical instrument of the sixteenth century merely as a civilised pastime is to sunder it from its raw materials, the craftsmanship required to make it, the aspirations of its owners and the political circumstances, sometimes fraught, which affected its circulation.

Stringed instruments, fragile and relatively expensive creations, were luxuries in the sixteenth century that counted for most amongst those for whom they represented the most significant expense. This obviously does not mean the nobility or great families like the Kitsons of Hengrave Hall – though gitterns are found among them also – but rather the 'middling sort' whose instruments represented their aspirations, and therefore their struggles. Inventories made for probate show that many men and women of this broad category lived in houses that were inhabited larders with sacks of rye, barley and peas competing for space with bedding and furniture; the presence of a stringed instrument in such documents, especially if it be a gittern and therefore perhaps the cheapest variety available, ranks with the appearance of a gaming table, an array of pewter or a few books as the sign of someone who aspired to surround himself with possessions suggesting there might be more to life than the grind of business and the danger of a lean harvest.

At all social levels below the nobility, the number of persons wishing to learn a musical instrument as an accomplishment mounted in later medieval England as the constituency aspiring to forms of life associated with gentry status expanded. Vernacular instructions for tuning harp and lute appear in a few commonplace books of the later fifteenth century; some may be derived from independent 'bills' that could be purchased from minstrels,[1] but the manuscript culture of the later Middle Ages in England did not generate a substantial tradition of such instructions. In contrast to treatises on hawking, for example, some of which can be traced passing from script to print, there were no published manuals for musical instruments in England until the later 1560s to suggest an antecedent circulation of such instructions in manuscript, and even when printed tutors eventually appeared, most of the recorded examples (and all the surviving ones) were translations from French. Viewed in a European context, this want of material in the vernacular until surprisingly late is anomalous; it presumably means that amateurs generally studied with a minstrel, a friend or perhaps a singing man from a nearby church, with only the most basic information deposited in writing, or none at all. Perhaps it also implies that they did not reach the same level of musical literacy as their continental counterparts. Be that as it may, the gittern had evidently gained enough currency with purchasers of secular and vernacular printed works by the late 1560s for 'An instruction to the Gitterne' to be published within the first wave of such tutor books in English. This 'reading public' may be cautiously envisaged as descendants of the 'merchants, clergy, members of provincial landed families, lawyers, officials, and court servants' who bought the secular works printed by William Caxton a generation or two before.[2]

The guitar came from abroad with a gradual enrichment of material culture, especially enhanced by maritime commerce despite inflation and the variable fortunes of the Elizabethan economy. The technology necessary to build the instrument, and the economic circumstances required to support it, differed from those of its medieval predecessor, the pear-shaped gittern with body, neck and peg-box carved from a single piece of timber. There are some indications that this older technology survived into the guitar-making period; generally speaking, however, the builder of a guitar in the sixteenth century, as today, bent thin strips of wood for the sides and then assembled them, with back and soundboard, into a box joined securely to a neck. These were precisely the difficult operations that the older method of carving the medieval type from a split trunk or branch had

---

[1] Some of these bills could evidently be quite substantial. One of the documents that George Cely purchased from his teacher, the harpist Thomas Rede, was 'a byll ffor to lerne to teune the leute' for which Cely paid the considerable price of three shillings and sixpence, more than ten times the price of the bill with dancing steps that he also bought from Rede. Comparison with contemporary copying rates suggests that Cely's bill of luting, undoubtedly at this date in manuscript, may have possessed at least twenty-one leaves, making forty-two sides. See Page, 'The Fifteenth-Century Lute'.

[2] Yu-Chiao Wang, 'Caxton's Romances and their Early Tudor Readers'.

been designed to avoid; as a result, the task of manufacturing the new gittern was best left to experienced artisans organised in small ateliers.

By the second half of the sixteenth century, such workshops in Paris and Lyon were manufacturing gitterns in substantial quantities, many of them no doubt for export; inventories reveal their large stocks of raw materials, together with worked but as yet unassembled components suggesting streamlining of procedures for maximum output. There is no sure trace of such gittern building in England, however, where the volume of man-ufacturing in general was inadequate to secure basic hardware (such as nails) in the necessary quantities, and where artisans possessed such an indifferent reputation for quality abroad that foreign merchants rarely came to London for fine or finished goods. The three gitterns that John Rose gave to Queen Elizabeth in 1559 were surely very fine, but no other English craftsman of the period can be associated with the production of gitterns, probably because it was impossible for native makers to match the quality of imports and to undercut their price. Foreign competition was simply too strong.

There are various ways in which the output of such foreign workshops could have reached England: with returning ambassadors or merchants, with apprentices coming home after serving their masters abroad, and with 'diplomats' who might be asked to obtain foreign goods for friends and patrons at home. (The dangers of the international situation involved the Elizabethan government in frequent negotiation, intrigue and espionage requiring journeys back and forth across the Channel.) With the exception of Sir William Petre, however, whose encounter with the gittern in France can plausibly be surmised from his private financial accounts, no case of such informal importing can be securely documented. Our best informa-tion is therefore to be found in the official records of imports, the Port Books. The volume for 1567/8 reveals, with especial importance and clarity, merchants importing musical instruments as part of a wider com-merce in textiles, hardware and haberdashery; one of them, the London draper John White, ranks as the closest approximation to a dealer in musical instruments from the Elizabethan period and is the only known sixteenth-century importer of gitterns. All the merchants in the 1567/8 book who imported musical instruments or strings brought in a much wider range of goods than their membership of one livery company would imply; save perhaps for John White, instruments were just another com-modity into which a merchant might sink some capital now and then, depending upon the state of his finances, his ability to command credit overseas and the quality of his foreign agents.

The gittern therefore had a place within a maritime economic system, but one that was vulnerable to disturbance. A domain of economic activity we might suppose to have been regulated by mercantile rationalism was always threatened by the intervention of monarchs and counsellors whose reaction to a royal birth, a military defeat or an intercepted letter of seditious intent could be profoundly influenced by their belief that the wishes of an omnipotent and supernatural participant were manifest in them. Throughout the twelve-month period covered by the 1568/9 Port Book the English government feared a Catholic conspiracy between the Pope, the King of France, the King of Spain and Mary Stuart; the quantity of instruments imported between Michaelmas 1567 and the same feast in 1568 was so high – eighty lutes, for example – that we may surely suspect a spate of panic buying by merchants anxious lest the worsening international situation between England and the Catholic powers should threaten the maritime link between London and Antwerp. Trade with that city was indeed suspended within months of the last recorded shipments our merchants commandeered, and was soon thereafter lost for good. The implications for the commerce in imported instruments seem to have been severe.

One player of the gittern, Francis Saunders, comes to light in September 1562 because he was a prisoner in the Tower of London held at the same time as several Catholic gentlemen and a number of the Marian prelates. If Saunders were being held because he was himself a Catholic charged with some kind of offence to the Queen or the government, which seems very likely, then we may suspect he enjoyed the privilege of taking a gittern into his cell precisely because he was deemed to be potentially dangerous and was therefore, it would seem, 'close and severallie kept'. Despite the trouble of holding prisoners in separate cells, Catholic inmates of the Tower could not be allowed to share a room and plot, or celebrate clandestine masses, unless the Lieutenant of the Tower received special instructions that it was safe to put them together. In that winter of 1562, Francis Saunders was playing the gittern by his own private fire as a political prisoner. Upon his release, whose date remains unknown, he presumably returned to the society where we can place him with considerable confidence: the Middle Temple.

Saunders may be identified with a young gentleman, of Norfolk stock. The gittern was often the choice of young men; valued especially for being eminently portable, it suited those who wished to 'nightly walke the streates before their louers gates' or to be deemed the kind of person who might have such nocturnal adventures. The gittern was therefore associated with a particular construction of manhood: the masculinity of the youth who was still technically in service, perhaps as an apprentice, who was past puberty, keen to let his beard grow and to wear fashionable clothes, but by no means ready or equipped to accept the responsibilities of maturity and a settled adulthood. The type is superbly (if hyperbolically) delineated in 'An Act for the Apperell of Appryntyses', issued with some virulence by the Masters of the Merchant Adventurers of Newcastle in 1554. We can probably trace other versions of it at the universities; in 1562, a young man at Oxford asked his servant to write home for the money to buy a gittern, a bow and a set of arrows, 'the wyche . . . be necessarye . . .'. Not necessary for his studies, certainly, but perhaps essential to being a young *man*. Everything depended upon the context in which the gittern was played and the nature of the player. When a gentleman like Robert Langham used it at court, the more riotous associations of the instrument were softened and a ready air of conviviality, without ceremony, took its place; when an apprentice took his instrument over the Thames to the Bankside, he could play the Inn of Court gallant, the university man, the errant apprentice or the gentleman, as he chose.

This breadth of association rested upon the unusually accommodating nature of the gittern's range of techniques. Much of what has been said above turns on the simple fact that the sixteenth-century guitar was relatively easy to play in the sense that it yielded passable results quickly to those who were of modest ability but were also impatient to get a return on their investment of time. The Osborn Commonplace Book contains galliards that demand little more of the player than today's intermediate music for the ukulele. In some respects, the history of this approachability reaches far back. The four-course guitar emerged from experiments conducted across Western Europe in the later 1400s, albeit with a Southern and Mediterranean emphasis, that also produced the viol and the Spanish vihuela. Instrument makers sifted the legacy of medieval fingerboard instruments and tried them with or without frets; they sounded them with a plectrum, plucked them with the fingers or swept them with a bow; bridges could be flat or slightly rounded; some instruments had no bridges at all but a guitar-like string holder. Several of these dispositions allowed the player to sound all or most of the strings at once, brushing them with the bow or sweeping them with the fingers or with a plectrum. It is very likely that these sounds and playing techniques were principally used in relation to largely unwritten repertories, especially forms of accompanied narrative such as the 'historiae' that Johannes Tinctoris heard accompanied by the bowed *viola*, or the 'old romances' ('romances viejos') that Juan Bermudo in 1555 still associated with the 'old' tuning of the *guitarra* and with its 'struck' or strummed music. The renaissance guitar can be defined, in musical terms, as the only instrument of medieval ancestry that retained a link with swept-string techniques when it finally emerged in a consolidated form from these later-fifteenth-century experiments. The viol and the vihuela were products of the same ferment in the workshops of instrument makers as the guitar, and they became the vehicles for polyphonic repertoires of great sophistication; but while the guitar also acquired an elegant polyphonic repertory in the sixteenth century, it never entirely relinquished its ties to much older oral and improvised forms of playing involving swept (strummed) chords and no doubt drones.

The English have long been accustomed to speak of the 'Spanish' guitar, a term now relinquished by most of the other European languages, but the more sophisticated guitar playing of later-sixteenth-century England was in large measure an avatar of practice in Northern France. The potent ethos of the guitar there is captured by the remarkable set of epithets for the instrument that Maurice de la Porte commended to poets in 1571: 'Hauteine, gentile, resonnante, damerette, ioyeuse, mignarde ou mignonne, portatiue, hebenine, plaisante, babillarde, chansonniere, amoureuse, cheuillee.' (See Appendix G.) Some native echo of what the guitar meant to the French was part of its appeal in England, but this was by no means the same as having a taste for Frenchmen, who were commonly associated with Catholic superstition, insurgence against the English crown and the French pox. The Tudor guitar was therefore strongly touched by the complex discourse of the foreign in Elizabethan England: the conflict between a xenophobic and isolationist insistence on the homely, honest values of an imaginary English past (its Catholicism conveniently forgotten) and the taste for foreign goods sharpened by a real or affected dislike of homespun manufacture.

The most sophisticated repertoire in circulation was certainly French. The printed tablatures for the renaissance guitar known in England include a full set of the five guitar books published in Paris, during the 1550s, by Adrian Le Roy and Robert Ballard, all of which made their way across the Channel at some time during the second half of the sixteenth century. They offered any player who encountered them a wealth of galliards, pavanes, branles and decorated grounds with intabulations of chansons and motets, material for the guitar that was still fashionable on the continent as late as 1570. The printed material also encompasses one gathering from the otherwise lost publication 'An instruction to the Gitterne', mentioned above. Thus it is that the only 'terms of art' we know Tudor guitarists encountered, and which they perhaps employed, are French. An intabulation with some degree of diminution in the top part was 'plus diminuée' than its model, or if the divisions were more elaborate still it was 'plus fredonnée', the latter drawing on a very expressive usage well known, in a much broader context, to the French poets of the Pléiade.

Although the art of literate guitar playing was essentially something that English gentlemen had caught from 'abroade in forayne lande', there are vigorous signs of native traditions by *c.* 1560 in the Osborn Commonplace Book. The compiler of this collection, whose cosmopolitanism should not be underestimated, recorded music for the gittern in a state that may be neither final, nor always especially felicitous, but was to hand without the labour of having to create the core material again. However simple, even rudimentary, some of the pieces may seem, there is no sign that the compiler thought the gittern items less worthy of record than the items for lute. The liberal use of first and second inversions, sometimes with hints of residual drone effects, and successions of four-course chords so thick and continuous they invite a strumming technique, creates a result that is often quite contrary to the grammar of contemporary part writing but was evidently relished as the characteristic musical dialect of the instrument. 'An instruction to the Gitterne', though surviving only in fragments, provides a vivid sense of gittern music at both extremes of ambition, from a simple and perhaps strummed ground of block chords to an elaborate and contrapuntal fantasie in the best manner of Adrian Le Roy.

No source of gittern music from sixteenth-century England contains a separately notated vocal part or any text beyond an incipit, but literary sources leave no doubt that the instrument was used to accompany the voice. In several cases, gittern-accompanied song has lowlife associations, the instrument once again skirting the edge of riot, criminality and bitter censure. The Osborn Commonplace Book, however, contains two tablatures with incipits drawn from poems by Henry Howard, Earl of Surrey, and one that alludes to a poem by Sir Thomas Wyatt. The phrase structure of the music in every case fits the metrical structure of the texts, showing that these textual cues are not merely associative or arbitrary. One especially revealing but untitled tablature in the Osborn Commonplace Book even offers a glimpse of how three-part vocal music, probably a setting of a court ballad or metrical psalm, might be adapted for the gittern to create a sophisticated intabulation, apt for carrying any Tudor lyric in the much misunderstood poulter's measure or in ballad metre, opening the gates to a wide range of verse, including the courtly balladry of Surrey and his many imitators in the pages of Tottel's 'Miscellany', but also to many metrical psalms. Perhaps the most tantalising reference to the performance of lofty verse, however, is William Painter's *The second Tome of the Palace of Pleasure* (1567), with its curiously precise (even quasi-technical) allusion to 'feigning' stanzas by Petrarch on the gittern and some other instruments. Were the stanzas sung to well-known or new melodies over standard grounds or harmonic sequences? This is a well-attested practice that makes some of the simplest gittern music (the chord sequences of 'An instruction to the Gitterne', for example) into some of the most suggestive. What looks like a simple exercise for a beginner might also be the genetic code for a whole body of lost Tudor song.

The fashion for the four-course guitar seems to have faded in the last decades of the sixteenth century and just beyond. A poem published in 1599 refers to the 'ancient Gittern', while a play of 1603 calls for a character to enter playing 'an old getterne'. By 1608, gitterns had disappeared from the official rate books listing imports into the Port of London and the duties payable on them. While it lasted, however, the fashion gratified the taste of the age for hybrids. The gittern on the Eglantine Table looks across to the grotesquerie of creatures that are part serpent, part human and part bull in an Elizabethan version of the mannerist taste transmitted northwards by prints and title pages. The appeal of the gittern was in some measure the appeal of the hybrid in the sixteenth-century sense of a creature of mixed generation, sometimes found at court, sometimes in the street, sometimes in the hands of gentlemen, and sometimes of miscreants. It was an instrument, 'as a man would say, halfe wild'.

The terms 'gittern' and 'cittern'

The parent of the English word 'gittern' is Old French/Anglo-Norman *guiterne*, also recorded in various spellings and often assumed to be a derivative of Latin *cithăra*, 'lyre'. Strictly speaking, this cannot be correct. In most words of the 'guitar' family in the Western European languages, such as Spanish *guitarra*, or indeed Received Pronunciation English 'guitar', the prominent syllable is in second position, just as it is in Greek *kithára*, but not as in Latin, where the prominent syllable is in initial position, thus *cíthara*. The word probably passed from Byzantine Greek into Arabic, where it appears as *qithăra* in Abu Abdallah al-Khwarizmi's *Keys to the Sciences (Mafatih al-'ulum)* in the late tenth century.[1] From there, together with direct transmission from the Greek, it passed into the various romance languages through trade and travel in the twelfth and thirteenth centuries. The tendency for short 'a' before 'r' in an accented syllable to be raised to 'e' in the forms of proto Romance from which French and Catalan are derived (compare CARO > Fr *cher*) explains the Middle French form *guiterre*, if it did not arise by consonantal assimilation from *guiterne*.

This leaves the –ERNE suffix in *guiterne* (essentially a peculiarity of French terminology, and therefore of its English derivative) unexplained. An attractive hypothesis, first mentioned in passing by the Romanist Lazăr Şăineanu in the 1920s, is that the suffix is a deliberate exoticism like the invented names for Saracen cities which appear in Old French 'chansons de geste' of the twelfth century, such as 'Califern'. One might also cite the modifications of some genuine names in these same texts so that Valtierra becomes 'Valterne', partly on the model of Southern Mediterranean cities such as Salerno ('Salerne' in the 'chansons de geste') and Palermo (which appears as 'Palerne').[2] On this interpretation, the term *guiterne* was a

---

[1] I am grateful to Professor Charles Burnett for advice on this matter.

[2] See Sainéan (publishing under the French form of his name), *Les sources indigènes de l'etymologie française*, vol. II, 312–13. The *Trésor de la langue française*, vol. IX, sv GUITERNE, disputes the view that the unexplained –ERNE suffix in 'guiterne' is due to the influence of Saracen names in the 'chansons de geste', the word 'semblant peu attesté dans ce type de texte', but this is because the word appears to have become current in France during the later thirteenth century (as pointed out long ago by Wright, 'The Medieval Gittern and Citole', 10), by which time most of the 'chansons de geste' had been written. Further discussion in Wright's study, *passim; FEW*, sv CITHARA; Coromines, ed.,

coinage, evoking the Arabo-Byzantine Mediterranean with which the instruments in question were perhaps associated, given that their name – and perhaps they themselves – had passed into Western Europe from territories where Greek and Arabic were spoken. This is evidently an explanation in which the terms 'guitarra sarracenica' and 'guiterne moresche' may have a place.[3]

The fortunes of the English word 'gittern' continued to track those of its French parent well into the early modern period. By the second half of the seventeenth century *guiterne* had became a vulgarism in France, *guiterre* was a prestigious archaism, and *guita(r)re* was established as the norm. In 1672, Gilles Menage dedicated a section of his *Observations ... sur la langue françoise* to the question of 'whether one should say *guitâre*, *guiterre*, or *guiterne*'; he concluded that *guiterre*, underwritten by the usage of Ronsard, represented the characteristic pronunciation of the sixteenth century, with *guitâre* being the favoured and well-established form in his own day. As for *guiterne*, he claims he has never heard it used by well-bred speakers, and indeed that he only remembers hearing it once, when it was employed by an individual 'who was not only of the common people but the very dregs of the common people'.[4] Robert Alcide de Bonnecase chose to be more succinct in his *Remarques sur les principales difficultez de la langue françoise* of 1673: 'Guitarre, non pas guiterre ny guiterne.'[5]

Matters are rarely as straightforward as grammarians would wish. The form *guiterne* can be found in French writings well into the seventeenth century, especially in sources prone to a certain degree of duplication and even ossification of material, such as dictionaries (including rhyming dictionaries) and translations from Scripture. It was also used in freer forms of composition; *guiterne* even appears, for example, in some works of translation from Spanish, including *Les Novvelles de Migvel de Cervantes Saavedra* (1633), without the Castilian *guitarra* in the original having any effect upon the translator's choice of form in French.[6] Nonetheless, the basic picture is clear, for *guiterne* did indeed yield to *guitar(r)e* in standard French usage, and Gilles Menage, like Robert Alcide de Bonnecase, either saw that it had been accomplished by the early 1670s or wished to urge a well-developed process onwards towards its conclusion.

English usage shows signs of following the same path, probably under French influence. There appear to be no traces of the form 'guitar' (in any

Diccionari etimològici complementari de la Llengua Catalana, vol. IV, sv GUITARRA; Coromines and Pascual, *Diccionario crítico etimológico castellano e hispánico*, vol. II, sv GUITARRA.

[3] Wright, 'The Medieval Gittern and Citole', 11.

[4] Menage, *Observations ... sur la langue françoise*, 87–9: 'je ne l'ay jamais oui dire qu'une fois, et a un homme, non seulement du peuple, mais de la lie du peuple'.

[5] Bonnecase, *Remarques sur les principales difficultez de la langue françoise*, 298.

[6] Rosset and d'Audiguier, *Les Novvelles de Migvel de Cervantes Saavedra*, 217, 219, 221, 223, 226, 229–30, 242, 244 and 532.

spelling) before Ben Jonson's masque *The Gypsies Metamorphosed* of 1621.[7]
The form 'gittar', stressed on the second syllable in the romance manner (as
in Modern English), appears in the printed text of *Britannia triumphans*, a
masque presented at Whitehall before the king on Twelfth Night in 1637.[8]
In 1642 the household accounts of John Manners, Eighth Earl of Rutland,
record a substantial payment of £4 2*s.* 6*d.* to 'the gittarman' that taught
Lady Francis, Countess of Rutland, for two months, and for her 'book'.[9]
The material accumulates as Lady Sussex writes to Mary Verney about a
'gittarre' from Paris, 'the most beautiful that I could find for it was of
Ebony enlayed with Mother Pearle',[10] as Sir Kenelm Digby ponders the
report of a baboon playing on a 'guitarre'[11] and as John Milton alludes to
'the lutes, the violins, [and] the ghittarrs in every house', all in the same
year of 1644.[12] By now the form 'gittern' was well on the way to becoming
an archaism associated especially with the writings of Geoffrey Chaucer.

In the term 'cittern', the initial consonant points to a different line of
development definitely via the Latin form *cithara* but crossed, at least in
France, with the Latin SISTRUM (which denoted a very different form of
instrument). The most common name for the cittern in sixteenth-century
France was *cistre*; the 's' in the consonant group 'st' was no doubt sometimes pronounced under the influence of SISTRUM, but one would expect it
to be silent, to judge by the spelling 'citre' reported by von Wartburg
(*FEW*, sv CITHARA) and thus in accord with the loss of 's' before 't' in Old
French (whence, for example, STELLA > *ESTELLA > *estoile* > *étoile*). It is
revealing, and consistent with our reasoning so far, that the word was
borrowed into Castilian as *sitre*.[13] The English form 'cittern' appears to be
essentially the pronunciation represented by the French spellings 'citre', or
the Castilian 'sitre', with the -ERNE suffix, reduced to a nasal consonant,
imported by analogy with 'gittern'. Variant spellings of both words in
English sources, such as 'gytron' and 'cythren', suggest a strong first-
syllable stress with an emphatic, dark 'r' articulated to the point where it
was sometimes impossible to tell whether the vowel had come before the
'r', as in 'cittern' and 'gittern', or after it, as in 'cythren' and 'gytron'. The
spellings used in sixteenth-century sources reflect that ambiguity.

FALSE GITTERNS

An order for a Canterbury procession of 1532/3 begins with 'gyantes then
the gyttern',[14] while a list of the workmen and labourers serving the royal

---

[7] Knowles, ed., *The Gypsies Metamorphosed*, 488 and 533.
[8] Jones and Davenant, *Britannia triumphans a masque*, 17.
[9] HMC, Rutland MSS, IV, 532. The same page shows a payment of 7*s.* to 'the gittarman',
    presumably the same individual, for 'mendinge an instrument for my Ladie Fraunces'. See also 537.
[10] Verney, *The Standard Bearer*, 92.   [11] *Two treatises*, 319–20.   [12] *Areopagitica*, 16.
[13] Romanillos Vega and Winspear, *The Vihuela de Mano*, 490 (document of 1591).
[14] Gibson, ed., *Records of Early English Drama. Kent*, vol. I, 144.

fortifications at Calais and Guînes in 1541 includes two 'gyttorne bearers'.[15] There are other references to the ceremonial use of such gitterns; a letter written by Sir John Wallop while serving Henry abroad in 1542 reports how a mounted gentleman rode 'with his gyttorn, and with himself was carried another not so great as a standard',[16] while the rearguard for the French wars in 1544 included, in each company, a mounted 'gythorne', taken by a recent historian of the Anglo-French conflict to be a mounted 'gittern player'.[17] These references evoke some pleasingly picturesque images, but unfortunately they are almost certainly irrelevant to the history of Tudor musical instruments and their terminology. It has not been recognised hitherto that they all employ a Middle English word which is derived from Middle French *guidon*, meaning a small flag or pennant leading a company of cavalry. Spellings include 'gettorne' and 'guytorne', among others.[18] The sense fits perfectly into each of the passages cited above. The mounted instrumentalists of the Tudor army are but phantom horsemen.

How is it possible to establish that the gitterns mentioned in other documents are musical instruments and not some form of pennant or banner like the 'gyttern' required by a Canterbury procession of 1532/3, or the 'gythorne' carried by a member of Henry VIII's forces in 1544? The answer is that we cannot resolve every case, but that context is often a reliable guide towards a solution. Some probate inventories and wills list a gittern in the company of other instruments, which settles the matter in the case of gentlemen such as Sir William More of Loseley Park, Sir William Petre of Ingatestone, William Calley of Hatherden and Sir Richard Worsley of Appuldurcombe. In some other sources, the meaning is clear from the narrative context. The diabolical apprentice Nichol Newfangle did not dance to a pennant in Ulpian Fulwell's *An Enterlude* of 1568, and the decayed gallant of William Bullein's *A Dialogve bothe plesaunte and pietifull* (1564) would have had some difficulty getting music from a banner when he sought to make an impression in a tavern. There are, to be sure, cases where an explicit contextual control is lacking. The Cambridge butler John Walker, for example, owned a gittern that might

---

[15] Gairdner and Brodie, *Letters and Papers Foreign and Domestic of the Reign of Henry VIII*, vol. xvi, 416.
[16] *Ibid.*, vol. xvii, 612.   [17] Potter, *Henry VIII and Francis I*, 231.
[18] Godefroy, ed., *Dictionnaire*, supplement, sv GUIDON: 'étendard d'une compagnie de grosse cavalerie'; *OED*, sv 'geton'. Compare the anonymous fifteenth-century poem 'The Assembly of Gods' where a host appears that 'was of a gret leyngth/Among whom were penowns and guytornes many a score'. Chance, ed., *The Assembly of Gods*, 969–70. The term 'guytorne' is glossed 'small flags' by the editor, no doubt correctly. Compare the account of captured Spanish ships in Daniel Archdeacon, *A true Discourse of the Armie which the King of Spaine caused to bee assembled in the Hauen of Lisbon, in the Kingdome of Portugall, in the yeare 1588 against England* (1588), 15: 'some of them of great name, with their ensignes, banners, stremers, and gitterns'. The *Nomenclator omnium rerum propria nomina variis linguis explicata indicans* of Hadrianus Junius, published in Antwerp in 1583, sv 'Signa', treats both 'banner' and 'gyttarne' as equivalent English words. Junius spent some years in England between 1544 and 1550 as tutor to children of the Howards.

have been a standard or pennant, but it is perhaps unlikely. A 'guythorne' in that sense was above all a piece of military or ceremonial equipment like the 'Pynnons, baners and Guytons' that a knight might bequeath to a church, or the three 'Small gittons of Sarstinett' listed in the great royal inventory of 1547.[19]

---

[19] NTA PROB/11/4, the will of Sir William Oldhall, 1460, bequeathing 'Pynnons baners and Guytons' to the Carmelite convent in Fleet Street. Starkey, *et al.*, eds., *The Inventory of King Henry VIII*, vol. I, item 15150.

References to gitterns from 1542 to 1605

The following texts were gathered using (1) a search of numerous property inventories in various classes of TNA, notably E 154 and probate inventories in PROB/2; substantial runs of unpublished inventories were also examined in Norfolk County Record Office and Leicester County Record Office where holdings are especially large; (2) a search of printed probate inventories, which are now abundant; (3) the probate inventories printed in Leedham-Green, *Books in Cambridge Inventories* (*BCI*; all readings have been checked against the originals in the University Archives); (4) a search of electronic databases, including *EEBO; OED; MED; Google Books; British History Online; Oxford Scholarly Editions Online; ODNB; LEME; National Archives; English Poetry 600–1900; Early Modern Festival Books Database* (the character recognition software used by some of these sources (notably *EEBO*) is fallible); (5) studies by Ward (especially *Sprightly and Cheerful Musick*), Woodfill (*Musicians in English Society*) and Helms (*Heinrich VIII*, notably the valuable conspectus of private inventories at 419–43), and articles rich in data, particularly those by Fleming and Kisby;[1] and (6) material from the countrywide archival work undertaken for both the published and as yet unpublished volumes of the *Records of Early English Drama* series, since the editors graciously shared their materials with me. I have not made a comprehensive search of probate inventories for those who died in the first half of the seventeenth century, although the terminal date has here been extended beyond the death of Elizabeth to 1605 in order to show the kind of material that might emerge.

NOTE: This Appendix omits texts translated into English from foreign languages or from Latin, unless they are of some relevance to interpreting the situation in England (whence 1547_1, concerning Paris, and 1577_2 on the use of ebony for manufacturing gitterns). Travelogues using the word 'gittern' to describe the instruments of other civilisations are also omitted.

---

[1] I am grateful to Dr Michael Fleming for sharing materials with me.

1542₁

Thomas Elyot, *Bibliotheca Eliotae. Eliotis librarie* (1542), sv 'fidicula': 'FIDI-
CULA, a rebecke or gytterne'. The pairing of rebec and gittern is explained by
the fact that both were small instruments and therefore their names provide
adequate alternative glosses for a Latin term formed with the diminutive –
ULA. The same gloss is taken from here into Richard Huloet's English/Latin
Dictionarie newelye corrected, amended, set in order and enlarged (1572), but
naturally in reverse, thus with 'Gitterne, or rebecke' as the headwords.

1542₂

RECM, vol. VII, 387. Inventory of possessions of Henry VIII at Westminster.
'Item. four Gitterns with 4 Cases to them.' This document was first brought
to notice by Pearsall ('Tudor Court Musicians', App. B).

1547₁

Philibert de Vienne, *Le philosophe de court* (1547 and 1548), translated by
George North as *The Philosopher of the Court, written by Philbert of Vienne
in Champaigne* (1575), 32:

Walke one night through *Paris*, and you shall finde a companie of yong gallants,
some braue and in good order, and others smothly combed for the purpose, courting
and woing their Ladies: and for that they are so vnskilfull howe the knowledge of this
Philosophie maye bring them into their mistres fauour, beleeue of themselues to be
passing excellent and singular good players on the Lute and Gitterne [*Lutz ou de
Guyterne*], and do nightly walke the streates before their louers gates, tearing the poor
strings of their instrumentes, as it were in despite of *Mercurie*.

1547₂

TNA LR 2/115, f. 75v. Inventory of the goods of Thomas, Duke of
Norfolk, following his attainder, 23 October 1546, and goods of the
Earl of Surrey at his residence of St Leonards by Norwich. After Surrey's
execution for high treason in 1547, the government swiftly arranged for his
chattels to be inventoried. The relevant section bears the marginal heading
'Hanginges of Tapestrie Testors Canapies Cussheons and other like necessary Implements', and includes a 'Gyttorne' listed in close proximity to two
ensigns marked with Surrey's arms and immediately before twenty-four
partisans, a type of spear often decorated with a pennant.

1547₃

RECM, vol. VII, 393 and Starkey, *et al.*, eds., *Inventory* (followed here; post-
mortem inventory of possessions of Henry VIII, the section headed

'Instrumentes at Westminster in the chardge of Philipp van Wilder'). 'Item foure Gitterons with iiij Caeses to theim they are caulled Spanishe vialles.'[2]

c. 1547 TO *c.* 1575

Osborn, ed., *The Autobiography of Thomas Whythorne*, 19–20 and 30. Probably written from the mid-1570s onwards, but here referring to a period from 1547/8 into perhaps the mid-1550s. Whythorne recalls that he learned to play 'on þe Gyttern, and Sittern' while a young man in London. He reports that both instruments were much cultivated by 'gentlemen', by those 'of the best sort', and were valued all the more for being unfamiliar or 'strange'.

1549

The praise of Folie. Moriae Encomivm a booke made in latine by that great clerke Erasmus Roterodame. Englisshed by sir Thomas Chaloner knight (1549), Sig. O. Chaloner renders the familiar topos of the ass and the lyre, an emblem of ignorance and stark insensibility, which Erasmus gives in Greek, 'as if an asse were set to plaie on a gyttarne' (compare the entry for 1586$_2$ below). This allows the term 'gyttarne' to intrude into a long tradition in English of presenting this familiar classical trope in terms of an ass and a harp. That is the formulation carrying the authority of Chaucerian precedent, and the one regarded by Richard Sherry in 1550 as a 'common saying';[3] Chaloner actually employs the Chaucerian and 'common' form three times elsewhere in this same translation, whereas 'gyttarne' appears just once. The irruption of a 'gyttarne' into the tradition is novel and unexpected.

1550

Essex County Record Office D/DP/A4, neither foliated nor paginated, the personal accounts of Sir William Petre. On 11 June 1550, a payment 'for a gyttron vjs', together with some other instruments and accessories.

c. 1552–4

Nicholas Udall (d. 1556), *Ralph Roister Doister*, in Tydeman, ed., *Four Tudor Comedies*, 131. This interlude, composed probably some time in the

---

[2] For the 1547 text in full context see Starkey, *et al.*, eds., *The Inventory of King Henry VIII*, vol. I, items 11872–11952 *et passim*. See also String, *Art and Communication in the Reign of Henry VIII*, 123–31, and Wilson, 'The Keyboard Instruments of King Henry VIII'.

[3] Sherry, *A treatise of Schemes and Tropes very profytable for the better vnderstanding of good authors*, Sig. Kiij^v. Cf. Erasmus (trans. Chaloner), *The praise of Folie*, Sig. Div^v.

reign of Edward VI or early in that of his successor, contains an imitation of the sound of the gittern.

1554₁

Brussels, National Archives, Audience, n° 384, fol. 591v. Letter dated 8 March 1554 in which two imperial ambassadors, the Count d'Egmont and Simon Renard, inform their master Charles V that Queen Mary of England and her council are certain that Edward Courtenay, Earl of Devonshire, 'avoit un ziffre avec pierre caro tailée sur une guitarre' which he used to pass a secret message to Sir Peter Carew.

1554₂

Merchant Adventurer's Book of Orders, 'An Act for the Apperell of Appryntyses' (Newcastle, November 1554), in Anderson, ed., *Records of Early English Drama: Newcastle upon Tyne*, 25. The senior members of the company register what they see as a decline in moral standards among their apprentices, 'lewde libertye in stede of the former virtuous life'. Since the Masters believed, with good reason, that they were training the next generation that would hold the fortunes of the company (in every sense) in their hands, they objected to the wanton behaviour of their juniors. The apprentices, placing too much value on their independence, and too little upon the profitable use of their time, indulged in 'dyseng. cardeng. and mummyng ... typlinge: daunseng and brasenge of harlotes ... garded cotes. Iagged hose. lyned with Silke. and cutt shoes ... gitterns by nyght ...'.

1556

Washington, DC, Folger Shakespeare Library, L.b.550, f. 2. Inventory of the chattels of Sir William More of Loseley House, written by him 20 August 1556. In the parlour were various musical instruments, one of them a 'gittorne', valued at eight shillings, nearly five times the worth of the portrait of Henry VIII in the same inventory, and (most surprisingly) more than the bass lute, which is valued at just under seven:

Item. a payre of virginals	xls.
Item. a base lute	vjs. viijd.
Item. a gittorne	viijs.

1557

Songes and Sonettes, written by the right honorable Lorde Henry Haward late Earle of Surrey, and other (first edition, 5 June 1557), otherwise known as

Tottel's 'Miscellany', ff. 70v–71. This collection includes numerous poems of tribute, some of them epitaphs for distinguished individuals such as Lord Maltravers, Captain Thomas Audley and Ann Parr, Countess of Pembroke. The anthology includes amongst its poems by uncertain authors an elegy for a player of the lute (and by implication the gittern) named 'Philips' who is probably to be identified with the celebrated court lutenist and composer Philip van Wilder (d. 1554).

1558₁

Hampshire Record Office 1559B/020/1–2. Testament and probate inventory of William Calley, gentleman of Hatherden in Andover parish (1557–8). The will includes the following bequest: 'Item I gyve and bequaethe to my brother Thomas Calley my brother [*sic*] my grey geldynge with all my Raymentt iij bose with all my Arrows my lute and my gyttorne whyche lute ys at mr Alfordes.'

1558₂

TNA C 66/920, 4 and 5 Philip and Mary, Part III, ff. 12d to 22d. The Book of Rates of the Custom House for 1558 as enrolled in the Patent Rolls. This is the first of the Rate Books to specify the duty for gitterns arriving as imports in consignments of a dozen.

1559₁

Record of the New Year's Day gifts to the monarch, 1559, in Lawson, ed., *The Elizabethan New Year's Gift Exchanges*, 44. The presents given to Queen Elizabeth by those who ranked as 'gentlemen' included 'oone Chest with thre Getternes in it', presented on behalf of John Rose. For another reference to gitterns in a boxed 'set' of three, see 1563.

1559₂

RECM, vol. vi (1558–1603), 393. Court inventory, 1 May 1559. Payment for '4 new lockes wth scochions for 4 Guytterne cases wth their haspers, Joyntes and keyes ...'. Presumably these are the four in the 1547₃ inventory ('Item foure Gitterons with iiij Caeses to theim they are caulled Spanishe vialles.').

1559/60

Cambridge University Library, University Archives, VCCt Invs. 2. Probate inventory of the goods of John Walker, Butler of Peterhouse College,

Cambridge, 24 January 1559/60, including 'a gittourne' valued at 12*d*.
BCI, vol. 1, 252.

1560

Cambridge University Library, University Archives, VCCt Invs. 2. Probate
inventory of the goods of George Allsope (or Hawsopp), Fellow of Queens'
College, Cambridge, 27 September 1560, including a 'gyttourne' valued at
20*d*. Venn, *Alumni Cantabrigienses*, Pt I, vol. 11, 338. *BCI*, vol. 1, 264.

1561₁

Oxford, Bodleian Libraries, MS Tanner 103*, ff. 177–9v. Album of items
excerpted from MS Tanner 103, a miscellany of mostly seventeenth-
century documents, including Latin plays, and a few prints. Folios 177–
9v give two versions of a curious letter in verse, dated 'le 3. Iour De Aprell
1561' and addressed (on what is clearly the original packet) to 'ower
lovynge frendes/the Crewe of Candelwike/Strette') and sent from associates in Deventer. Candlewick Street, now Cannon Street, was a drapers'
quarter. The letter alludes to a certain John Graves, otherwise unknown,
who plays the 'gyttourne':[4]

> John Graves we here saye, ys on of yowr Crewe
> Wch newes vnto vs, dyd come verrye newe,
> And knowynge that he, the good fellowe can playe
> Owr mynde ys to haue hym in, for on by the waye.
> In playenge of the vergenall, he ys well skyllynge
> And on his fyddel manye tymes well willing
> allso on the gyttourne he playes verye well
> Yett Hamers Clyffe on the lewte doth him far excel.

1561₂

Proceedings of the Court of Mayoralty, Norwich, for Wednesday, 11 July
1561, in Hudson and Tingey, eds., *The Records of the City of Norwich*,
vol. 11, 179:

Wheareas one John Felde, seruaunt to Robart Crispe of Seynt Stephans, confessith
that he ded absent hym selfe from his master his service and went runnyng aboute
the contry wth a gitterne, for that defawte he was commytted to prison and there
remayned thre dayes, and therupon was admytted to his master ageyne.

In 1560 Robart Crispe was a cordwainer, and so presumably in 1561.[5]
Craftsmen did not always take up their freedom immediately after

---

[4] Morfill and Furnivall, *Ballads from Manuscripts*, vol. 11, 148 and 152.
[5] Millican, ed., *The Register of the Freemen of Norwich 1548–1713*, 41: 'Cordwainers: Rob'tus Cryspe,
appr. Willmi Brierton, Frid. Feast Inv. H.C. 2 Eliz.' (i.e. 17 November 1559 to 16 November

finishing their apprenticeship, so Crispe was perhaps a journeyman who set up in business in 1560, for which he would need to be a freeman, employing a servant, John Felde, who then decided on another form of life. It remains unknown whether Felde's brief turn to a life of minstrelsy or vagabondage (which many contemporaries did not distinguish) was made in response to mistreatment. Such cases were not rare.

1561–2

Inventory drawn up for the Chancellor's Court, University of Oxford, 17 October 1561–2, in Elliott, *et al.*, eds., *Records of Early English Drama: Oxford*, vol. I, 106. Lists the goods of one Ralph Allen, of Balliol College, Oxford, and includes 'a gytterne the brydge beyng off'.

1562₁

Letter of 18 June 1562 from Thomas Madock, the servant of a John Somerford, to Charles Mainwaring of Croxton, probably Somerford's guardian, in Baldwin, *et al.*, eds., *Records of Early English Drama: Cheshire including Chester*, vol. II, 834. Madock writes that Somerford, then a student at Oxford, needs 'a gitterne and bowe and arrows the wyche I thinke to be necessarye for hym . . .'. Presumably John Somerford required the instrument to become known as one whose pursuits were both gentlemanly and in the new guise; Roger Ascham's treatise on archery from 1545, *Toxophilvs*, provides ample material for reading Somerford's request for a longbow in much the same way.

1562₂

TNA SP 12/24/39, letter dated 19 September 1562 from Edward Warner, Knight Lieutenant of the Tower of London, to Sir William Cecil, Secretary of State, concerning the prisoners in his care. Among Warner's most important charges at this time were the deprived Marian bishops of Lincoln, Ely, York, Worcester, Exeter and Bath, together with several earls and Lady Katherine Grey, sister of Lady Jane. In such company as this the prisoner named Francis Saunders, probably of the Middle Temple, seemed a minor figure, and one purpose of Warner's letter is to urge Lord Burghley that Saunders should be held captive somewhere else. In what appears to be a facetious moment, Warner informs Burghley that the Lieutenant of the Tower 'shall be fayne to take the sound of hys

---

1560). The Feast of the Invention of the Holy Cross was on 3 May, so the entry dates from 1560. I am grateful to David King for his guidance.

[Saunders'] gytterne for payment of his dyets', meaning the costs incurred for buying food, fuel and candles.

1563

TNA DL 44/96. Inventory of the property of Henry Neville, late Earl of Westmorland at Raby Castle and other places, 19 October 1563. The list includes, in addition to a pair of virginals, a case with three 'gittrons'.

1564

William Bullein, *A Dialogve bothe plesaunte and pietifull wherein is a goodly regimente against the feuer Pestilence* (1564), f. 67. The character of Mendax, a mendicant and confidence trickster, plays the gittern in a tavern. Quoted above, p. 57.

1565

Newport, Isle of Wight Record Office, JER/WA/36/7. Inventory of the goods of the late Sir Richard Worsley of Appuldurcombe, Captain of the Isle of Wight, including a 'Gitthorne'.

? *c.* 1565

Hengrave Hall, Suffolk; painted overmantel of uncertain date, but possibly of around 1565, showing two guitars. See Figure 7.

c. 1567

Hardwick Hall, Derbyshire; Eglantine Table, with marquetry showing numerous instruments including a seven-string (presumably for a four-course) guitar. See Figures 5 and 6.

1568₁

The Bishops' Bible, with a partially concealed representation of a guitar in the decorative border of the portrait of Robert Dudley, Earl of Leicester. See Figures 2 and 4.

1568₂

Ulpian Fulwell, *An Enterlude Intituled Like Wil to like quod the Deuel to the Colier* (1568), Sig. Aiiij^v (stage direction).

1568_3

NTA E 190/4/2, the Port Book of the Port of London, Michaelmas 1567 to Michaelmas 1568. Registers imports of native and Hanse merchants only. John White, draper, imports a consignment of '12 chests with 6 sytternes, 6 gittornes, 4 *parv.* lutes and 6 lutes in cases' with a total value of £6 on the *Spledegle* out of Antwerp and '1 case with 6 slight citerns, 8 giterns and 2 *parv.* lutes' with a total value of £5 3s. 4d. on the *Sea Rider* out of Antwerp.

? 1569

London, Royal Academy of Music, Robert Spencer Collection, 161921–1001, four pages of 'An instruction to the Gitterne'; and Pennsylvania, University Library, Rare Book and Manuscript Library, Folio MT654. C58.L47 B7 1568, four pages of 'An instruction to the Gitterne'. These eight pages are almost certainly derived from *The breffe and playne instruction to lerne to play on the gyttron and also the Cetterne* that James Rowbothum registered with the Stationers' Company in 1568/9. The title in Andrew Maunsell's *Catalogue of English Printed Bookes* (1595) is *A briefe and plaine instruction for to learne the Tablature, to Conduct and dispose the hand vnto the Gitterne*, thus without the cittern. The book was an English version of a lost French tutor for the four-course guitar, the *Briefve et facile instruction pour apprendre la tablature a bien accorder, conduire et disposer la main sur la Guiterne*, devised and published by Adrian Le Roy. There were editions in 1551 (arguably the least well attested), 1567 and 1568.

1571

London, Lambeth Palace, MS Tenison 807/1, p. 61. A paper ledger kept by John Whitgift while Master of Trinity College, Cambridge, containing the private accounts of George Clifford, Third Earl of Cumberland, while a pupil of the Master. The entry, 'A gitern lute xs', appears in a section dated 1571. There is an edition of the accounts by S. R. Maitland, *The British Magazine*, 32 (1847), 361–79, 508–28, 650–6, and 33 (1848), 17–31, 185–97, 444–63. For another 'gitern lute' see 1584_2.

1574

Hellowes, Edward (trans.), *The Familiar Epistles of Sir Anthony of Gueuara* (1574), 115.

1575_1

Bethlem Royal Hospital Archives and Museum, Item bcb-02, ff. 184v–5. Memoranda of the Court of the Governors of the Bridewell hospital and prison recording how some young men, servants and apprentices, appeared before the court in October of that year. They had repeatedly dined at the house of a certain John Hardinge, a Thames waterman; on one occasion 'they came at iiij of the Clocke in the mornynge and broughte a sett of vialls with them, & then spente there iiij d. & so appointed a suppar'. On another they came with a lute, a gittern and a cittern.

1575₂

Robert Langham, *A Letter: whearin. part of the entertainment vntoo the Queenz Maiesty, at Killingwoorth Castl, in warwik Sheer in this soomerz Progress 1575. is signified: from a freend officer attendant in Coourt vntoo hiz freend a Citizen, and Merchaunt of London* (1575), 84. Modern edition in Kuin, ed., *Robert Langham*, 39 (I take the text from the 1575 print). There has been much discussion about the authenticity of this text. Goldring, '"A mercer ye wot az we be"', plausibly argues that 'the Letter began life as a bona fide missive from Langham to his fellow mercer Humphrey Martin, which, though envisioned for circulation in manuscript, was almost certainly not – in the first instance at least – intended for publication'. The letter describes the entertainments staged at Kenilworth Castle in July 1575 by Robert Dudley, Earl of Leicester. Quoted above, p. 48.

1577₁

Probate inventory of goods belonging to Leonerde Temperleye, Gentleman, of the parish of Witton Gilbert (now in County Durham), in Raine, ed., *Wills and Inventories*, vol. 1, 422. Lists an 'olde syttrone and j broken gyttrone', together valued at one shilling. The instruments were kept in 'the Chapel Chamber' among 'His Apparell'.

1577₂

Eden, Richard, *The History of Trauayle in the West and East Indies, and other countreys . . . done into Englyshe by Richarde Eden. Newly set in order, augmented, and finished by Richarde Willes* (1577), 210–11:

There are also a kynde of hygh Date trees, and full of thornes: the woodde of these is most excellent, beyng very blacke, and shynyng, and so heauye that no parte thereof can swymme aboue the water, but synketh immediatly to the bottome . . . Furthermore of this wood the Christians vse to make dyuers musicall instrumentes, as Claricymballes, Lutes, Gitterns, and suche other, the which besyde theyr fayre shynyng colour lyke vnto gete, are also of a good sounde, and very durable, by reason of the hardnesse of the wood.

1578₁

'A letter written to M. Richard Staper by Iohn Whithal from Santos in Brasil, the 26. of Iune 1578', in Richard Hakluyt, *The Principal Nauigations, Voyages, Traffiqves and Discoueries of the English Nation* (1599–1600), 703. Among many other commodities ordered from Staper in London, Whithal asks for 'Foure mases of gitterne strings'.

1578₂

Thomas Cooper, *Thesaurus Linguae Romanae et Britannicae* (1578), sv Fidícula: 'Fidícula, fidículae, f. g. pen. cor. Parua cithara. Cic. A litle lute: a rebecke: a gitterne.'

1579/80

Philip Sidney, *The Old Arcadia*. Sidney places a gittern in the hands of a singing shepherd in the first (and the only complete) version of his pastoral romance completed in 1579/80.

? *c.* 1580

Victoria and Albert Museum, London (A.12–1924). Painted overmantel of carved and gilded oak showing Apollo and the Muses, one with a guitar. See Figure 8.

1584₁

Norwich Archive Centre, DN/INV 2/114. Probate inventory of the goods belonging to Dennys Bucke [yeoman] late of Walsingham Magna, 9 September 1584. In the parlour chamber was 'a gittorne, xijd'.

1584₂

Record of the New Year's Day gifts to the monarch, 1584, in Lawson, ed., *The Elizabethan New Year's Gift Exchanges*, 337. The presents given to Queen Elizabeth by those who ranked as 'gentlemen' included 'By Mr. Lychefelde a spannyssche Gyttorne lute in a Case of blewe vellat edged with a passamayne of golde.' For another 'gittern lute', see 1571.

1586₁

Case, John, *The Praise of Mvsicke: Wherein besides the antiquitie, dignitie, delectation, and vse thereof in ciuill matters, is also declared the sober and*

lawfull vse of the same in the congregation and Church of God (1586), Sig. Bij:
'What shall I speak of the Lute, Citterne, Violle, Rebeck, Gittorne, Pandore, Dulcimer, Organes, Virginals, Flute, Fife, Recorders, of the Trumpet, Cornet, Sackbut, and infinite other sortes so excellent and pleasant in their sundrie kinds, that if art be any way faultie for them, it is for being too riotous and superfluous.'

1586₂

Stanihurst, Richard, *A treatise conteining a plaine and perfect description of Ireland* (1586), 16. An opponent is charged with expressing opinions unbecoming in a clergyman, declaring that '. . . trulie they beeset a diuine as well, as for an asse to twang quipassa on a harpe or gitterne, or for an ape to strike trenchmore in a pair of buskins and a doublet'.

1588₁

Probate inventory of the goods belonging to Anthony Hall, gentleman, of South Newington, 1588, in Havinden, ed., *Household and Farm Inventories in Oxfordshire*, 263. In the chamber was 'an old paire of Virgynalls out of repaire one githorne and an old lute vjs viijd'.

1588₂

Abraham Fraunce, *The Lawiers Logike, exemplifying the praecepts of Logike by the practise of the common Lawe* (1588), Sig. Kiiij:

A double Elench lurketh in this place, one of composition an other of diuision: for composition thus. *Humfrey Crowther* is a good fidler, therefore hee is good: and this fallacian is from the whole, because those two thinges so ioyned togither seeme to make vp the whole, wherevpon afterward the part may bee concluded, as though in this example, *Humfrey Crowther* were a whole integrall thing, made and consisting of these two partes, goodnesse and fidlery. Some other call this *à dicto secundum quid, ad dictum simpliciter,* when wee apply that absolutely and generally which was spoken but in part and in respect, as heere *Humfrey* is called good, not generally, for his good conditions, but particulerly in respect of his gitterne.

1588₃

Lancashire Records Office, DDKE/acc. 7840 HMC/f.10d. Presentments within the parish of Rochdale, 15 April 1588:

Adam Stolte, gentleman, vpon the Sabbothe daye, in the eueninge, beinge eyther the last Sundaye in December or the fyrste in Januarie, had a minstrell which plaied vpon a gythorne a[t] his howse, with a greate number of men and women dauncinge . . .

The wife of Lawrence Collendge

had a minstrell playinge uppon a gythorne at hys howse, uppon a festivall daye in Christenmas laste, in the eveninge, and many yonge folkes dauncinge.

1591

Cambridge University Library, University Archives, VCCt Invs. 5. Probate inventory of the goods belonging to Thomas Lorkin, Regius Professor of Physic in the University of Cambridge. Among his effects, which included an extensive library of 631 volumes, were 'a lute with a case and 2 Gittornes', with a comprehensive valuation of 20s. Venn, *Alumni Cantabrigienses*, Pt I, vol. III, 106. *BCI*, vol. I, 493–4.

1592₁

Robert Greene, *A Dispvtation between a Hee Conny-catcher and a Shee Conny-catcher* (1592), Sig. D4.

1592₂

Hunfrey Barwick, *A breefe discourse, concerning the force and effect of all manuall weapons of fire and the disability of the long bowe or archery, in respect of others of greater force now in vse* (1592), Sig. B3:

It dooth cause me to remember one *Cornelius* a Gentleman and a Souldiour in the French Kings seruice, who could haue plaide of a Lute or a Gitterne excellent well: but his condition was such, that if the best Lord or Lady in Fraunce had requested him to haue plaied, hee would not haue doon it, the reason was that he doubted, that he should haue been taken for some foolish Musition, and yet was he to be brought to haue plaied without intreatye, as thus: if any of his acquaintance had taken the Lute or Gittern in hand, the worse that he or they had played, the sooner would *Cornelius* haue taken the same foorth of his freends hands, and thereon would haue plaide right pleasantly.

1595₁

Anthony Copley, *Wits Fittes and Fancies. Fronted and entermedled with Presidentes of Honour and Wisdome* (1595), 183 (from the section on similes): 'One seeing an other thrust out his head as though he stood harkening to somewhat, said, it was like the head of a Gittern.' Also 193 (from the section on leanness): 'One seeing a grosse man and a lean man standing together, sware, that he neuer in all his life saw a Lute and a Gitterne better consorted.'

1595₂

Andrew Maunsell's *Catalogue of English Printed Bookes* (1595) lists *A briefe and plaine instruction for to learne the Tablature, to Conduct and dispose the hand vnto the Gitterne* (see ? 1569).

1599

Tailboys Dymoke, *Caltha poetarum: or The bumble bee* (1599), Sig. Ei^v:

> The Kingly Harp, for and the courtly Citheren,
> the Solace, Vyols, and the Vyolins:
> The litle fidling Kit, and ancient Gittern,
> with those same faire and famous Orpherins,
> With Bagpipes, Cornets, and the Cymphanins.

1601

Thomas Wright, *The Passions of the Minde in Generall* (cited from the 1604 edition), 159: 'The Spaniards play their Zarabanda vpon the Gittern, which moueth them (as I heare reported) to daunce, and doe worse.'

1603₁

Samuel Purchas, *Purchas his pilgrimes In fiue books* (edition of 1625), Book VIII, Chapter XII: 'A Voyage set out from the Citie of Bristoll at the charge of the chiefest Merchants and Inhabitants of the said Citie with a small Ship and a Barke for the discouerie of the North part of Virginia, in the yeere 1603. vnder the command of me MARTIN PRINGE', 1242: 'and there is no trauelling in the World so easie as this, for you may lye, or sit, and play on a Gitterne all the way if you will, for so the Spaniards doe'. See also entry for 1603₃.

1603₂

William Percy, *The Faery Pastorall*, in Fenn, 'William Percy's *Faery Pastorall*', 226. The play was completed in 1603 and may have been given – assuming it was ever performed – for the visit of James I to Syon House in that year. A prologue shows that Percy intended it to have a court performance. The play survives in three holographs of the 1640s, fixing the date of composition in a final note ('Finis 1603 Wolues Hill my Parnassus'). A stage direction requires the character Salomon, described in the *dramatis personae* as 'A schoole Boye', to begin Act III, Scene 3 'with an old getterne playing and walking . . .'. Gair (*The Children of Paul's*, 64) supposes that Salomon is the child actor Solomon Pavey, whose untimely death was lamented by Ben Jonson. But Pavey died in 1602, the year before *The Faery Pastorall* was written. The error, offered as a speculation rather than an established fact, is repeated in *ODNB*, sv 'Pavey, Solomon'.

1603₃

Samuel Purchas, *Purchas his pilgrimes In fiue books* (edition of 1625), 1655. A few months after the death of Queen Elizabeth on 24 March 1603, the Tudor guitar made landfall in New England. An extraordinary scene occurred soon thereafter, somewhere along the banks of the Piscataqua River in present-day Maine. Members of the Abenaki people, 'wearing feathers in their knotted hair', came down to eat beans and fish with a party of British adventurers led by Martin Pringe (see entry for 1603₁), 'a man very sufficient for his place'. A young man from one of the ships produced his gittern, and the Abenaki warriors, 'somewhat taller than we, strong and swift', began to dance around him:

We had a youth in our company that could play vpon a Gitterne, in whose homely Musicke they tooke great delight, and would giue him many things, as Tobacco, Tobacco-pipes, Snakes skinnes of six foot long, which they vse for Girdles, Fawnes skinnes, and such like, and danced twentie in a Ring, and the Gitterne in the middest of them, vsing many Sauage gestures, singing *Io, Ia, Io, Ia, Ia, Io*: him that first brake the ring, the rest would knocke and cry out vpon.

1603/4

Two images of guitars in engravings of the triumphal arches built for the entrance of James I to London in March 1603, devised by Stephen Harrison and engraved by William Kip, *The Arch's of Triumph Erected in honor of the High and mighty prince James the first of that name* (first edition, 1604). See Figure 9.

1605

Cambridge University Library, University Archives, VCCt Invs. 7. Probate inventory of the goods of Edward Liveley, who entered Trinity College, Cambridge in 1564/5, and was Regius Professor of Hebrew from 1575 until his death. He was the son-in-law of Thomas Lorkin (see entry for 1591). The goods 'In the studye' included 'a gitterne in a case'. Venn, *Alumni Cantabrigienses*, Pt I, vol. III, 92. *BCI*, vol. I, 546–50.

The probate inventory of Dennys Bucke (1584)

The document is transcribed here so that one instance of gittern ownership may be presented in its full material, economic and domestic context.

Norwich Archive Centre, DN/INV 2/114

THE INVENTARYE of all and singuler the goods and cattells of Dennys Bucke late of walsingham magna in the county of Norfolk deceased prised and valued the nynthe daie of September Anno domini 1584 by Richard Burton Robert Warren Thomas Bullocke Thomas Halman Robert Andrewes John Smyth and James Alee

INPRIMIS in monye	xs
Item his apparrell	xls
Item in the parlor chamber ij bedsteads	
fower fetherbedds	
iij paier of blankets	
ij coverings	
iiij pillowes	
iij boulsters	
a warming pann	
a chaier	
vj stoles	
a framed table	
iij glasses	
a brusshe	vli xijs
Item a chest or deske	ijs vjd
Item an old maser and a silver spone	xs
Item by estimation iiij oz. of broken silver	xvijs viijd
Item a gitterne	xijd
Item xij paier of sheates and one sheate	xxxvjs
Item six pillowbeares	xs
Item two bordclothes and fower table napkins	xs
Item v peire of new lynnen clothes	xs

In the ynner chamber

Item a bedstede as it standeth with blankets and an old covering
    three ould chests
    a table and ij trestles
    two firkins
    a chest racke and certaine chestes   xliiijs
Item a sadle for a woman and a bridle furnished   xxxs

In the hall or parlor

Item a table and ij cownters   xs
Item two curtens and a table carpett   iijs iiijd
Item a paier of bellowes
    a paier of tongs
    a fier pann
    two speates
    a paier of cobbirons and ij hakes   vs

In the kitchin

Item ten platters
    viij pewter dishes
    vij porringers
    three sawsers
    a bason and a pewter cupp   xviijs
Item two candlesticks
    two chafing dishes and a grate   xxd

[second leaf]

Item a morter and a pestel   iiijs
Item two brass potts
    ij posnetts
    iiij brasse panns
    a copper pann
    a frieng pan
    a brandlett
    a chopping knife
    a hoke and a hatchett   xxxs
Item a paier of mustard quearnes   xijd
Item a chest presse
    vij milking boules
    a paile and certaine tubbes   xs
Item a paier of stoles   ijs
Item a stave and a bottell   vjd

Item a dozen trenchers

    two carthing potts and a picherd   xijd

In the corne chamber

Item in wheate iiij bushels   viijs
Item vj bushels rye   viijs
Item iiij combs malte   xxs
Item one combs oats   ijs
Item ij stons of woolle   xviijs
Item two stons dimidium of hempe   iijs iiijd
Item x handbasketts and iij leapes   ijs
Item a cradle   xxd
Item ould yron   xijd
Item iij rakes   iijd

In the barne

Item in barley by estimation twentie combes   iiij li
Item a lode of pease   xs
Item two oulde chests

    an oulde coubborde

    dyvers bords

    a ladder

    a ruddle and a dore stale   xxs
Item in the yarde certaine tymber and two trees   vs
Item a myngyng troughe and a table   xxd

In cattell

Item six milche neate and one hefkar   vii li
Item xij ewes ij rammes vj lambes   iij li
Item ij Swyne   vs
Item xij geese   iiijs
Item xij hennes

a capon and a cocke   iiijs

Item at Henrye Grayes a bedsted and a paier of blanketts   xijs

Debts

Item due from William Mason   viij li
Item due from John Bucke   xxi xvjs viijd
Item a lease of v acres and dimidium rode of lande of the

    late prior of Walsingham   v li
Item at John Bucks a pompe a balke and a safron kill   vjs
Item a paier of quearnes   ijs vjd

Item a fann	iiijd
Item a combe of malte lent to John Bucke	vs
Item xij duckes	iijs
Item a sadle for a man	ijs
Summa	lxxix ^{li} vj^s j^d

Exhibitum fuit huiusmodi Inventarium per Aliciam Bucke Relictam dicti defuncti decimo quarto die mensis Septembris Anno domini 1584 pro pleno et recto etc. Que in presenti ad certam omnis notitiam pervenerunt sub protestacone de addendo quod si etc

GLOSSARY

cobbirons	'One of the irons on which a spit turns', obsolete save in dialect (*OED*, sv 'cob-iron', n.).
combe	'A dry measure of capacity, equal to four bushels, or half a quarter' (*OED*, sv 'coomb'/'comb', n. 3).
hakes	hooks, especially pot hooks (*OED*, sv 'hake', n. 2)
hefkar	a form of 'heifer' (*OED*, sv 'heifer', n.).
leap	a basket, now dialectal (*OED*, sv 'leap', n. 2).
speates	a form of 'spit'.

Octave strings on the fourth and third course

The more guitar ancestors were impelled, in some spheres of play, towards the duplication of composed vocal and polyphonic textures during the later fifteenth century – a process continuing in the sixteenth – the more it became essential, in the judgement of many, for the fourth course of the guitar to include at least one low-octave string, or bourdon, to provide extra capacity for grammatical counterpoint. This is made clear in the earliest printed music for the guitar, prepared by Alonso Mudarra in 1546. Mudarra provided a note that the player should have a low-octave string or *bordón* on the fourth course. This implies that Mudarra expected there would also be a higher-octave string in the pair, since he speaks of *bordón* in the singular, and further implies that some guitars had no bourdon at all – hence the need for a preliminary warning – but only a pair of strings at the higher octave. In 1555, Bermudo confirmed that musicians 'are accustomed to put' (*suelen poner*) a higher-octave string on the fourth course of the *guitarra*, 'which they call *requinta*' (*Declaracion*, Book IV, Ch. 39).

This disposition, with an octave pair for the fourth course, bears directly upon the sound-picture of any music for which it is deployed, especially if the higher string is placed in an 'outside' position, rather than 'inside', and is therefore the first to be struck by the thumb. When the high-octave string is placed on the inside it may receive only a light skim of the thumb, or may even remain untouched, if the instrument is not carefully set up, since the higher string is necessarily much thinner than its neighbour. An octave string placed outside, however, produces an intermittent scintilla of sound, or glitter of high harmonics, as the texture variously commandeers or releases the fourth course. This effect, heard as a colouristic device, and as a means to lend high harmonics to the duller sound of the thickest gut string on the instrument, was apparently welcome even to such an exacting contrapuntalist of the mid-sixteenth century as Mudarra.

Special difficulties, notably with regard to the issue of a high-octave string on the *third* course, are presented by the tuning instructions for the gittern in *Selectissima elegantissimaque gallica italica et latina in guiterna ludenda carmina*, published by Pierre Phalèse in 1570. These have been discussed in detail, with facsimile, by Heartz ('An Elizabethan Tutor for the Guitar'), but it fell to Dobson, Segerman and Tyler, expounding an argument further explored and developed by Vanhulst, to show that the tuning instructions given by Phalèse are either derived from those for tuning a cittern in Sebastian Vreedman's cittern book the *Nova Longeque Elegantissima Cithara Ludenda* (1568, published by Phalèse) or from a common cittern original (Dobson, Segerman and Tyler, 'The Tunings of the Four-Course French Cittern'; Vanhulst, 'Édition comparative'). The following text of the Phalèse instructions is edited from the facsimile in Heartz, 'An Elizabethan Tutor', 8.

Modus tendendi neruos in Guiterna

[1] Postremò vt Musices amatoribus omnibus quibus potuimus modis succurramus, modos ali/quot subiunximus qua quisque facile neruos seu fides ipsius Guiternae ad suam quam debe*n*t/habere intentionem te*n*dere poterit.
[2] In primis itaque minores chordae primi Bassi ita tendi/debe*n*t qua*n*tum sine earum lesione fieri potest commodissime, m[a]ior vero neruus ad octauam in/fra à predictis paruis distet.
[3] Proxime deinde sequentes chordas ita concordaueris si digitum si/nistre manus applicas ad F spacium quarti nerui primi Bassi ac ita attraxeris minores neruos vt/par sit sonus illi qui à precedentibus minoribus editur in neruo tertio nullo applicato digito./
[4] Maior vero per octauam à minoribus disiungantur quemadmodum de precedentibus dictum/ est.
[5] Deinde vero secundum neruum sic tendes vt rursum digito in E spacio super tertium ner/uum collocato sonus fiat tertii nerui sono, maxime vero illi qui a minoribus editur.
[6] Primum de/nique neruum [sic intendes ut digito in] F spacium secundi nerui posito parem reddat sonum secu*n*do neruo.
[7] His rite ob/seruatis Guiternam quam perfectissime intensam reperies secundum figuram hic proxime su/biectam.

TEXTUAL NOTES

[1] subiunximus] subuinximus
[2] paruis] parius
[4] There is evident disturbance of the text here, for there is a singular subject and a plural verb: *Maior [chorda] . . . disiungantur.* In Vreedman it is correct (*disiungatur*).
[6] The emendations in square brackets follow Vreedman's text and resolve the evident problem of the dangling ablative *posito* in Phalèse.

TRANSLATION

The manner of tuning the strings on the Gittern

1 Finally, so that we may be of assistance to all lovers of music in all the ways that we can, we subjoin the ways with which anyone will easily be able to tune the strings or chords of this same gittern to its correct tuning.

2 First, the smaller strings of the First Bass should be stretched as far as may most conveniently be done without damage to them; let the greater [gut] string stand an octave below the aforesaid small [strings].

3 Afterwards, you will have put the strings which follow into accord if you apply the finger of the left hand to the F space [= the space before the fret denoted by the tablature letter F] of the fourth course [that is to say] of the First Bass, and so draw up the lesser strings [of the third course] so that the pitch is equal to the one rendered by the aforesaid smaller strings [of the fourth course] with no finger applied.

4 The greater [string] lies an octave apart from the lesser [strings] as was said with reference to the preceding.

5 Afterwards you stretch the second [gut] string so that when the finger is placed in the E space [= the space before the fret denoted by tablature letter E] on the third string the [second string] gives the pitch of the third, especially that which is rendered by the lesser [strings].

6 Stretch the first string so that it gives the same sound as the second string when the finger is placed in the F space of the second string [= the space before the fret denoted by tablature letter F].

7 By following this method you will find the Gittern most perfectly tuned after the manner of the figure immediately following.

There are clear signs of textual disturbance in the Phalèse text, notably a singular subject and a plural verb in [4], which is not present in Vreedman, and the loss of material in [6], leading to a measure of grammatical incoherence, which can be restored and repaired using Vreedman's text, in certain respects the more dependable witness. In the Phalèse text, confusion is also caused by the residual allusions to triple stringing on the lowest two courses of the cittern, and by the way the instructions appear to treat the high-octave string on the fourth and third course as the constitutive element in the tuning steps. Thus the tuning procedure begins with pulling up the higher-octave strings [*sic*, the grammar is plural] of the fourth course to the point where there is a risk of damage (which presumably means breakage, or perhaps 'undue stress'), then the bourdon is adjusted to stand an octave below. Next, the higher-octave strings [*sic*] of the fourth course are stopped at fret F and the higher-octave strings [*sic*] of the third course are tuned to it; then the bourdon of that same third course is adjusted to stand an octave below. Now the second course is to be tuned by stopping the third course at fret E with the second course being tuned to give the same pitch as the *higher-octave* strings [*sic*] of the third course.

Despite this haze of problems, the text is quite clear in [3] and [4] that there should be a high-octave string on the third course of the guitar as well as the fourth. Reference is actually made to *several* high-octave strings (*minores neruos*), but until a more plausible explanation can be found, this can be regarded as a relic of the cittern-based original. It is uncertain how much weight should be given to this particular testimony about the octave string on the third course, since it appears in a text transmitted in a less than ideal manner and state. Nonetheless, the statement in the *main* text of Phalèse's tutor that 'the third … string comprises a small and a thicker string' ('tertium … neruum constans parua et vna maiori chorda') is quite clear, and removes the puzzling reference to multiple higher strings.

The fiddle tunings of Jerome of Moravia, swept strings and the guitar

Self-accompanying techniques based upon drones are already apparent in the earliest evidence for the tuning and technique of a Western fingerboard instrument: the treatise on playing the five-stringed *viella* or fiddle that a Dominican friar named Jerome drew into his substantial compendium of Latin music theory, the *Tractatus de Musica*, on the verge of the fourteenth century. Jerome gives three tunings for the *viella*, all apparently designed for instruments with flat or slightly curved bridges where the player sounds all or most of the strings at the same time, thus embedding any melody to be played in a changeable chordal block.[1] This approach is most clearly implied by Jerome's tunings 1 and 2, which form an accordatura, with the d-string in the first called the *bordunus*, running to the side of the fingerboard so that it cannot be stopped. In the following, the pitches are relative, and should not be taken to imply that the instruments sounded as low as the notation suggests:

d| G g d′ d′   d G g d′ g′

These tunings suggests a pattern of single and double courses:

d| Gg   d′d′   d Gg   d′   g′

Presented in this way, Jerome's information of around 1300 appears to include, some two-and-a-half centuries *avant la lettre*, several characteristic devices of guitar tunings first recorded in the sixteenth century: a mixture of unison courses with octave courses creating elements of a re-entrant tuning, together with the terminology of *bordunus* for a low-pitched string.[2] During

---

[1] I cite the text in Page, 'Jerome of Moravia'; the best practical discussion of these tunings is now Zaerr, *Performance and the Middle English Romance*, 90–104, which gathers the relevant bibliography. See further Page, *Voices and Instruments*, 50–76 and 126–38.

[2] For terms *bordunus/bourdon*, see Page, *Voices and Instruments*, 118–19. Jerome of Moravia's testimony to swept-string techniques is not isolated. The author of the fourteenth-century *Summa Musicae* associates fingerboard instruments with tunings in 'octave, fourth and fifth', which can be read as a recipe for various kinds of accordatura suited to sounding the entire string band at once. Page, ed., *Summa Musicae*, 87 and 169: 'alia chordalia [i.e. not harps and psalteries] temperantur autem per consonantias diapason, diatessaron et diapente, et per diversas digitorum interpositiones artifices ipsorum formant sibi tonos et semitonos . . .'.

the Middle Ages, these enrichments of the sound-picture were often employed for narrative repertoire whose music has mostly vanished, leaving only text behind. In France, players of the fiddle described by Jerome of Moravia were widely associated with the long verse accounts of martial exploits, feuds and crusading, the 'chansons de geste',[3] and such narrative material, taking many different forms, was long-lived in relation to various instruments, some bowed and some plucked, including the guitar. In the early 1480s, Johannes Tinctoris still knew of narratives or 'historiae' performed to the bowed *viola*, while Juan Bermudo in 1555 associates 'old romances' ('romances viejos') with the 'old' tuning of the *guitarra* and with its swept-string music, *Musica golpeada*.[4] This 'old tuning' required the player to lower the fourth course by a tone, creating a fifth between the lowest two courses that becomes ideal as a drone block for melodies on the higher strings.

---

[3] Page, 'Le troisième accord'; Zaerr, *Performance and the Middle English Romance*, 90–104.
[4] Baines, 'Fifteenth-Century Instruments', 24: 'Viola vero cum arculo: non solum ad hanc usum: sed etiam ad historiarum recitationem in plerisque partibus orbis assumit.' Bermudo, *Declaración*, f. xxviijv. For further important discussion see ff. xcvjr–xcvij.

The mandore *and the wire-strung gittern*

There is a widespread and well-founded agreement amongst historians of musical instruments that French *guiterne* and its English derivative 'gittern' both denoted a pear-shaped, plucked and fretted instrument during the later Middle Ages, whose body, neck and peg-box were generally carved from a single block.[1] The pictorial record of such instruments in English manuscript painting, sculpture and stained glass becomes somewhat thin and repetitive by about 1450–75,[2] and we have already seen that a number of references to 'gitterns' from the reign of Henry VIII (d. 1547) concern banners or pennants, not musical instruments (Appendix A). It is signifi-cant in this context that the only fifteenth-century description of the medieval gittern by an informed observer, Johannes Tinctoris of Brabant, shows that it no longer commanded the respect of a trained musician, at least in its traditional form. Tinctoris, who knew the musical scene of Europe from Nivelles to Naples, describes the *guiterra* or *ghiterne* of the early 1480s as a much smaller version of the lute with the same shape, manner of stringing and 'touch' (*contactum*) as the larger instru-ment. He also reports that Catalan women played it to accompany their love songs, but that it had generally fallen out of use, 'because of its thin sound' (*propter tenuem ejus sonum*).[3]

---

[1] Wright, 'The Medieval Gittern and Citole', remains the seminal study that established this position. For a discussion of Wright's theory, see Burzik, *Quellenstudien*, 385ff. For the term 'gittern', see Appendix A. Most studies of the gittern published before the appearance of Wright's article are actually concerned with the citole. See Remnant, 'The Gittern in English Mediaeval Art'; Remnant and Marks, 'A Medieval Gittern'; Brown, 'St. Augustine, Lady Music, and the Gittern'; Young, 'Zur Klassifikation'; Rey, 'La guitarra en la baja Edad Media'; Spring, *The Lute in Britain*, 1–30; Kevin, *et al.*, 'A Musical Instrument Fit for a Queen'. See also Peters, *Musical Sounds*, 250, *et passim*.

[2] The substantial gallery of medieval instruments depicted in English ecclesiastical sculpture, assembled by Gwen and Jeremy Montagu, suggests a terminal date for the gittern somewhere around 1420 (*Minstrels and Angels*). Spring's smaller yet broader list, gathering depictions of the lute and gittern in English manuscripts and stained glass as well as sculpture, proposes nothing for the gittern later than *c.* 1460 or the later fifteenth century in cases where precise dating is impossible (*The Lute in Britain*, 21–2). Wright's list of gittern players mentioned in historical documents ends in 1471 ('The Medieval Gittern and Citole', 12).

[3] Baines, 'Fifteenth-Century Instruments', 23 and 25: 'Quinetiam instrumentum illud a Catalanis inventum: quod ab aliis ghiterra: ab aliis ghiterna vocatur: ex lyra prodisse manifestissimum est: hec enim ut leutum (licet eo longe minor sit) et formam testudineam: et chordarum dispositionem atque contactum suscipit . . . Ghiterre autem usus: propter tenuem ejus sonum: rarissimus est. Ad eamque

This explicit comment, and the apparent fading of the iconographical record, might lead one to suppose that the medieval gittern became obsolete, or at least unfashionable, towards 1500 and perhaps on a European scale. That would be a fair assumption, providing we recognise that the medieval gittern was destined to enjoy a long and continuous history after 1500 in a significantly modified form. This was largely because makers began to crossbreed it with the lute at precisely the time when it might otherwise have lost favour and declined into oblivion. The 'quintern' depicted by Sebastian Virdung in *Musica getutscht* (1511), Sig. Bij, for example, has a body built from ribs like a lute, not carved from a solid in the manner of the two extant medieval gitterns;[4] it also has a fixed bridge, like a lute, as opposed to the floating bridge, with strings running down to one or more hitch-pins, that characterise many of the gitterns shown in later medieval art. In effect, Virdung's 'quintern' is a miniaturised lute, and it is suggestive that references to the 'quintern' virtually disappear from the archives of cities and towns of German-speaking lands during the 1400s, perhaps because the instrument was increasingly regarded, for most purposes, as a small lute and had begun to shed its own name of 'quintern' as a result.[5]

In France, these mini-lutes were commonly called *mandore*. They achieved a very wide currency to judge by inventories of workshops in later-sixteenth-century Paris which reveal them being made in considerable numbers.[6] Curious as it may seem, there appears to be no clear evidence that these instruments crossed the Channel. There seems to be no trace of the term *mandore* in any English document or literary text of the Tudor period; even the Books of Rates that itemise the musical instruments imported from abroad do not use the word.[7] There is no sign that the two (lost) methods for *mandore* issued by the firm of Adrian Le Roy and Robert Ballard in Paris were ever translated into English, unlike the

---

multo sepius Catalanas mulieres carmina quaedam amatoria audivi concinere: quam viros quicpiam ea personare.' Online text at http://earlymusictheory.org/Tinctoris.

[4] The two surviving medieval gitterns are the instrument manufactured by Hans Ott, probably in Nuremberg, around 1450 (Wartburg Stiftung, Eisenach) and that of 1350–1450 discovered during archaeological excavation in the Old Town area of Elblag, in Poland, in 1986. See Hellwig, 'Lute-Making', for the former and Poplawska and Czechak, 'The Tuning and Playing of a Medieval Gittern', for the latter. For a poor copy of a rare photograph showing the soundboard of the Hans Ott instrument removed see Burzik, *Quellenstudien*, 405.

[5] Polk, *German Instrumental Music*, 22–4, advances the argument with due caution. The name 'quintern' may have arisen from some specific technical aspect of the instruments so named ('having five strings or courses', 'tuned a fifth higher', or whatever else might be alleged), but it may be best to assume that name was an invented one, simply meant to imply high pitch; compare Geoffrey Chaucer's nonce word 'quynyble' for a high voice in *The Miller's Tale*, line 3333.

[6] Documents in Lesure, 'La Facture instrumentale'. The seminal study is still Tyler, 'The Mandore'.

[7] There appears to be nothing in English before an entry for the term – as a French word, not an English one – in Randle Cotgrave's *A Dictionarie of the French and English Tongues* (1611), and it is clear from the definition Cotgrave offers that the term was for him entirely French: 'MANDORE. f. A Kitt, small Gitterne, or instrument resembling a small Gitterne.'

methods for guitar and lute issued by the same Parisian firm.[8] No such translations were registered with the Stationers' Company and Andrew Maunsell knew of none when he drew up the music section of his *Catalogue of English Printed Bookes* in 1595, where the tutor for *Gitterne* (= four-course guitar) finds a place. The possibility that *mandores* were imported and simply called 'gitterns' cannot be discounted, but there is no evidence (as yet) to suggest that this was so, and it is not obvious why the English should simply have abandoned the French name. The cognate and near homonym 'bandore', which came into use during the Elizabethan period, was used for quite a different instrument.

Nothing identifiable as a *mandore*, as opposed to a small lute, has yet been identified in any English pictorial source between the reigns of Henry VIII and James I. To be sure, Tudor musical iconography is not abundant; a great deal of material has undoubtedly been lost or was deliberately destroyed in later periods; despite this shortage of pictorial sources, however, the guitar manages to make four appearances, or rather seven if we count the French woodcut from Adrian Le Roy's treatise on the guitar and then add the two examples shown on the ceremonial arches built for the coronation pageants for James I in 1603. This is a small but not a negligible tally, representing about half the count for the cittern during the same period.[9]

Another form of gittern, strung with wire, is first described in seventeenth-century English documents.[10] The composite picture that emerges shows a small cittern with four courses of wire plucked with a quill, tuned guitar-wise to a rising fourth, major third and fourth (so quite unlike the re-entrant tunings of the 'Klein Englisch Zitterlein' described and illustrated by Michael Praetorius in 1618/19 and 1620). John Playford's *A Booke of New Lessons for the Cithern and Gittern* (1652) uses the same woodcut, but reversed, and with the pitch-letters of the strings changed from a re-entrant order, for both the cittern and gittern. For Playford, the principal difference between the gittern and cittern lay in the guitar-wise tuning of the former. The illustrations compiled by the herald Randle Holme (d. 1700) for *The Academy of Armory*, an immense visual encyclopaedia of objects almost masquerading as a set of notes for heraldic blazons, show 'a Gitterne or a Citterne' as a lute-shaped instrument with raised fingerboard extending onto the belly and strings running over the bridge to a hitch-pin.[11]

---

[8] Brown, *Instrumental Music*, [1578]$_2$ and [1585]$_7$.

[9] I am grateful to Peter Forrester for advice on this matter.

[10] In various publications, John Ward always entertained the possibility that the wire-strung gittern may have been in use as early as the mid-sixteenth century. On this instrument and its relation to the 'small English cittern' described by Praetorius, see Gill, 'The Seventeenth-Century Gittern'. I am grateful to Peter Forrester for advice here.

[11] Illustrated in Ward, *Sprightly and Cheerful Musick*, Plate II.

The most important literary source for the wire-strung gittern is the work of a noted scholar and antiquary, Sir Peter Leycester. In a comprehensive set of notes on various musical instruments written in 1656 for the instruction of his son, Leycester describes the gittern that he knew:

Like vnto this [the cittern] is the Ins/trument, we now vsually do/~~tearme a Kit, some~~ call ~~it~~ a Gitterne, wch indeed/is only a Treble Psittyrne; beinge./somewhat lesse then/the other, yieldinge a more/Treble Smart Sound, havinge/the same number and the/same Order of Wyre-stringes/and playd vppon with a Quill/after the same order as/the ~~gittern~~ Psittyrne: onely/some variation in the tu/ninge, wch may also be varyed/in the Psittyrne at pleasure.[12]

This gittern is 'onely a Treble Psittyrne', and Leycester implies on another folio of his notebook that it is derivative of a larger and more established cittern when he refers to 'the Psittyrne, and *from/thence* the Gitterne' (emphases mine).

When did the treble cittern tuned guitar-wise come into use under the name 'gittern'? The London Port Book of 1567/8, discussed above in Chapter 3, mentions 'slight' citterns, which are presumably small and therefore treble citterns, but calls them 'citterns' not 'gitterns'; the latter appears elsewhere in the same Book and is therefore presumably a different instrument, here assumed to be the renaissance guitar. This would indicate that the treble cittern did not have a distinctive name of its own in the 1560s, be it 'gittern' or any other. It is also of importance that the wire-strung gittern of the seventeenth century was almost certainly not an organic development from the medieval pear-shaped gittern despite somewhat resembling it in form (but not in construction or the shape of its back). The evidence lies in the fundamental matter of string materials, for in this respect the medieval gittern and its wire-strung namesake known to Sir Peter Leycester and John Playford belonged to different traditions. The medieval gittern used strings of gut. Jean Corbechon's 1372 translation of the famous encyclopaedia *De proprietatibus rerum* by Bartholomaeus Anglicus records that 'guisternes' were strung with 'cordes faictes de boyaulx', and the Dutch translation of the same passage, published in 1485, names the 'ghytaern'.[13] The 'quiterne' is listed among the instruments strung with gut in Jehan de Brie's *Le bon berger* of 1379, and almost exactly a century later, Johannes Tinctoris reports that the lute-shaped *guiterra/ghiterne* – this is plainly still the medieval instrument, and evidently passing out of common use – is strung in the same manner as the lute, implying the use of gut.[14] Cases of medieval and early modern stringed instruments crossing from one string-material tradition to another are rare. Gut-strung psalteries, for example, or metal-strung fiddles, if they

---

[12] Cheshire Records Office, DLT/B33, 85v–86. See *ODNB*, 'Leycester, Sir Peter'.

[13] Page, *Voices and Instruments*, 236 (18c and 18f).

[14] *Ibid.*, 242, and Baines, 'Fifteenth-Century Instruments', 23. Online text at Johannes Tinctoris, http://earlymusictheory.org/Tinctoris.

ever existed as more than isolated experiments, seem to be unrecorded in medieval sources. Johannes Tinctoris reports that some Germans were experimenting in the 1480s with a few low-pitched metal strings on the lute, otherwise strung with gut, but the experiment seems to have yielded no permanent results.[15] Metal-strung harps were always recognised as forming a distinct or 'Irish' tradition set apart from the gut-strung harps of the European mainstream, and were valued for precisely the contained and separate tradition they embodied. In the vital matter of their string materials, the medieval gittern and its wire-strung namesake did not share their DNA.

During the early 1600s there was a shift in guitar terminology in England, with forms of the word 'guitar', destined eventually to triumph, entering the historical record beside the longstanding 'gittern' (Appendix A). This probably coincides with the gradual adoption of the five-course guitar in England. The four-course treble cittern tuned guitar-wise (Playford's 'gittern') was probably devised during the changeover period and designed for those whose ambitions ran no further than playing on four courses using the established guitar-wise tuning but who sought something new and fashionable; the new and invented hybrid added the attraction of metal-string sonorities at a time when the gut-strung guitar was both acquiring a fifth course and shedding the old name 'gittern' in favour of 'guitar', thus leaving the former free to become attached to what was in effect a treble cittern tuned guitar-wise.

---

[15] Baines, *ibid.*, 22.

APPENDIX G

The ethos of the guitar in sixteenth-century France[1]

The gittern playing of sixteenth-century England was especially indebted to practice in France, and it is French sources of the period that reveal, with especial vividness, the kind of ethos for the renaissance guitar that we glimpse, here and there, through the words of Thomas Whythorne.

In a manner that Whythorne certainly does not care to acknowledge, guitars were widely associated in the sixteenth century with itinerant musicians, as revealed in a poem by the laureate Mellin de Saint-Gelais (1491–1558). This is the angry soliloquy of a guitarist whose serenade has failed. He is half frozen to death; the midnight bell rang some hours ago and the temperature has fallen. He can only remain staring at a closed wooden door:

> Et quel grand Diable est cecy?
> Veult-on que je couche icy?
> Seray-je encores longtemps
> En ce maigre passetemps?
> Mynuict est pieça sonné.
> Par Dieu, c'est bien promené.
> Je fay bien de leur vallet,
> D'icy trembler le grelet . . .
> Adieu, belle, je m'en vois.
> Par Dieu vious n'aurez de l'an
> Moy ny ma Guiterre, bran![2]

And what the devil is this? Is it intended that I sleep here? Will I have to keep up this poor game much longer? Midnight sounded long ago. By God, I have been led here and there. I am certainly playing their servant to stand here shivering with the cold . . . Good bye, fair one, I'm going; by God, you will have neither me nor my *guiterre* again this year, *merde*!

This poem bears an unexpectedly discursive title: 'Cecy est sur la chanson des neigres sur la guiterre: *Se lo commo non me dan*' ('This is [based] on the song of the blacks on the guitar: *Se lo commo non me dan*'). Saint-Gelais has

---

[1] For the thematic concerns of this Appendix, see Zecher, 'The Gendering of the Lute', 'Ronsard's Guitar' and *Sounding Objects*. The essay by Jeffery, 'The Idea of Music in Ronsard's Poetry', is excellent. Lesure, 'La Guitare en France au XVIᵉ Siècle'; Vanhulst, 'Édition comparative'; Heartz, 'Parisian Music Publishing under Henry II'; Dobbins, *Music in Renaissance Lyons, passim*.

[2] Stone, ed., *Mellin de Saint-Gelais*, vol. 1, 215–16.

209

apparently modelled his poem upon a pre-existing lyric, and perhaps he intended that his poem should be sung to the melody of this model accompanied by a guitar; one of the scribes who copied the poem certainly thought so, and duly added the explanatory title 'Pour chanter sur la guiterre'.[3] Saint-Gelais gives the incipit of the model poem in the original language which is essentially Spanish or a romance argot meaning perhaps 'If I eat it, it does me no good/it does not bother me'. The accompanying assurance that the poem is modelled on a 'song of the blacks' associates the guitar with musicians who are perhaps to be identified with Spanish Moriscos, nominally converted Muslims who sought to escape the impoverished conditions of their dwellings, in major urban centres such as Seville, and the intermittent hostility of their Catholic neighbours. The term 'guitar of the Moriscos' or *gitarra morisca* was already established in Old Spanish by the middle of the fourteenth century, perhaps well before, and to that legacy the colonial ventures of the sixteenth century added the black player of the *guitarra*, mocked as early as 1580 in Antonio Riberyro Chiado's *Auto da natural invenção*.[4] Such players did not inspire Saint-Gelais to evoke a guitarist worthy of any esteem. The musician who delivers the soliloquy in the poem is so little accustomed to the ways of good French society that his response to a lady's refusal of his serenade is the scatological oath that closes the poem.

Yet that is by no means the only understanding of the guitar that Saint-Gelais has to offer. If he knew the instrument as a resource of itinerant Moriscos, he had also seen it played in quite a different context. With this poet's various references to the guitar, indeed, the profoundly paradoxical history of that instrument first begins to register in the literature of the renaissance North. Saint-Gelais records that a 'guiterne espaignole' was presented to Charles de Valois (d. 1545), who apparently did not disdain such a gift, and the poet celebrates a lady's *guiterre* inscribed with the names of so many admirers that he fancies it will need to be as large as the Earth to accommodate them all.[5] The woman in question was Hélène de Clermont, who married Antoine de Gramont, comte de Guiche (1526–76). This is certainly to exchange the street for the aristocratic chamber.

It was not classical epic, but rather the lyric voice of Horace and Pindar that the poets of the Pléiade associated with the lute and the guitar. In the poetry of Pierre de Ronsard, the guitar of the later sixteenth century becomes the lyre of Horace or indeed of Anacreon. The 'trained thumb' or *doctus pollex* that Horace had seen plucking the lyre now strums the four-course renaissance guitar in the verse of Guillaume de Salluste Du Bartas, rendered thus into English by 1611:

---

[3] *Ibid.*

[4] Pike, 'An Urban Minority: The Moriscos of Seville'; for Riberyro Chiado, see Budasz, 'Black Guitar-Players'.

[5] Stone, ed., *Mellin de Saint-Gelais*, vol. II, 38.

> And, (in one instant) as the quaverings
> Of a quick Thumb, moues all the divers strings
> Of a sweet Guittern; and, its skill to grace,
> Causeth a Trebble sound, a Mean, a Base . . .[6]

In Ronsard, the guitar becomes a material embodiment of the lighter and more amorous vein of the lyric imagination, whence the instrument can be formally addressed like a Muse, a patron or a dear friend. For Jacques Tahureau, in his *Premières poesies* of 1555, the guitar can be celebrated as

> Ma guiterre qui jadis,
> Par ces chansons nompareils
> Ouvroyt un beau Paradis
> Aux plus friandes oreilles . . .[7]

My guitar that once, through its unrivalled songs, opened a fair paradise to the most pleasure-loving ears . . .

The words *guiterne* and *guiterre* were so frequently used by French poets of the sixteenth century that Maurice de la Porte included both terms in his manual for writers, *Les epithetes* of 1571:

Guiterne ou Guiterre. Hauteine, gentile, resonnante, damerette, ioyeuse, mignarde ou mignonne, portatiue, hebenine, plaisante, babillarde, chansonniere, amoureuse, cheuillee. La guiterne est comme vn diminutif du Luth.[8]

De la Porte's search for words to capture the ethos of the guitar has here produced one of the most fulsome attempts to characterise a musical instrument to be found in any renaissance source. So often associated with songs of love, the guitar is *chansonniere* and *amoureuse*; for the first time in the instrument's long history, it is celebrated for being portable (*portatiue*) and therefore accommodating to many different social contexts. It is essentially feminine, *damerette*, indeed perhaps effeminate in the sense that a man who dresses in a very refined manner 'et se parfumant fort' might be said to be *damerette*.[9] Other epithets reveal the paradoxical nature of the guitar's appeal. It is *hauteine*, a description that deftly combines the sense of 'noble', implying a consciousness of the right to pride, with the sense 'high-pitched' as befits a predominantly treble instrument; yet the guitar is also *babillarde*, prone to idle chatter. A well-informed reader of the sixteenth century would have recalled that *babillarde* is the epithet given to the swallow in Ronsard's famous imitation of Anacreon, 'Tay toy babillarde Arondelle', and in Remy Belleau's imitation of the same

---

[6] Sylvester, *Du Bartas his deuine weekes & workes translated & dedicated to the Kings most excellent Maiestie* (edition of 1611), 585.

[7] Peach, ed., *Poésies complètes*, 149. There are abundant references to the guitar in Tahureau's verse; see in this edition 72, 149, 154, 169, 221 and 275.

[8] Rouget, ed., *Les epithetes*, 285.

[9] Huguet, *Dictionnaire*, vol. II, sv 'damerette': 'Il estoit fort damaret, s'habillant tousjours fort bien et se parfumant fort.'

Greek model, 'Ha vraiment je vous puniray/Babillarde . . .'.[10] The guitar is therefore likened to these small springtime visitors whose 'gayes chansons nouvelles' are sometimes a delight and sometimes not; Ronsard and Belleau are calling for the swallow to be silent, not to sing. Above all, the guitar is *mignarde ou mignonne*, both seminal terms in the vocabulary of the Pléiade and used to evoke whatever is young, light and fresh, the very antithesis of the dull and ponderous, as in Belleau's 'Beuvons, et que chacun tortille', where a young girl

> Fredonnant dessus sa Guiterre,
> Dance d'un pié mignardelet.[11]

. . . melodiously sounding her guitar dances with a mignardelet foot.

The diminutive in *mignardelet* introduces a fundamental marker of style when the poets of the Pléiade write in this vein. The suffix *-et(te)* lightens, prettifies and causes everything in its vicinity to be viewed with a joyous regard.[12] That is the key to the correct interpretation of de la Porte's final line, 'La guiterne est comme vn diminutif du Luth': not just that the guitar is a small lute but that it can be regarded as a 'lute-ette', so to speak. By virtue of its size, pitch, repertoire and ethos it embodies the poets' wish, when writing in the *mignard* manner, to abjure whatever is sombre and dull.

---

[10] Céard, *et al.*, eds., *Pierre de Ronsard*, vol. I, 985; Demerson, ed., *Œuvres poétiques: Remy Belleau*, vol. I, 90.

[11] Demerson, ed., *Œuvres poétiques: Remy Belleau*, vol. I, 85.   [12] Joukovsky, *Le bel objet*, 163ff.

Raphe Bowle

Tablature for a six-course lute, with one item, probably for gittern, that was never completed, may be found on the parchment flyleaves of London, British Library, MS Stowe 389, a fourteenth-century volume of statutes in Latin and Anglo-Norman. A prefatory note to the lute tablature reads 'The xviijth daie of maye the same writtin by one Raphe Bowle to learne to playe on his Lutte in anno 1558.' As a result of this note, and the interest of the music on the leaves, Bowle has become an established figure in lute research, but much of what is commonly assumed to be knowledge about him is supposition, and is open to question. The use of third person in the inscription ('to play on *his* Lutte') and the indefinite article ('by *one* Raphe Bowle') should indicate that the note is not in Bowle's hand, and that the scribe did not know him. Indeed, it may indicate that the tablatures are not in Bowle's hand either; the pieces were perhaps transcribed into Stowe 389 from a larger collection of Bowle's, now lost, bearing a prefatory note that the scribe chose to retain. In that case, the date of 18 May 1558 may identify the day when the scribe added the note, not when Bowle copied the music. This is consistent with the layout of the inscription, correctly reported in *RISM*, Bvii, 192, where the information about Raphe Bowle forms – should one wish to read it so – a parenthesis between two elements of the scribe's dating note:

> The xviijth daie of maye
> the same writtin by one Raphe Bowle to learne to playe on his Lutte
> in anno 1558

Even on this interpretation, however, whereby we would no longer have anything in Raphe Bowle's hand, nor any date save 18 May 1558 as a *terminus ad quem* for his original (and lost) copy of the tablature, he remains a lutenist who made an important collection of pieces, and his identity therefore continues to be a matter of considerable interest. A likely candidate is the Ralph Bowle of St Lawrence in Thanet, for whom Administration was granted in 1575–6.[1] It is not clear how he is related to any other recorded Kentish Bowle/Bowles/Bolles. W. H. Bowles, in his

---

[1] Canterbury Probate Registry, Consistory Act Book, vol. vii, f. 129. See H. Ridge, ed., *Index of Wills and Administrations now preserved in the Probate Registry at Canterbury* (London, 1920), vol. ii, 18.

privately printed family history, *Records of the Bowles Family* (Derby and London, 1918), 4, notes that the earliest recorded Kentish Bowles were in Shalmesford Street, a hamlet in the parish of Chartham, near Canterbury, where there was a manor of 'Bolles Hall'. One of this family was John Bolles (d. 1461), a London grocer, of All Hallows Barking, who in his will refers to 'the grete place in Shalmesford' and lands in Chartham, Chilham, Canterbury and Faversham. The 1619–21 Visitation of Kent includes a Bowle pedigree, tracing the descendants of one Thomas Bowle, whose eldest son William died at Bromley in 1609. The second son, John, was settled at Brasted.[2] There is no Ralph in this pedigree. In the seventeenth and eighteenth centuries there are numerous people called Bowle/Bowles who are associated with Deal and Walmer and are probably related in some way to the Shalmesford Bowles. The only Ralph Bowle/Bowles recorded at either Oxford or Cambridge is one Ralph Bowles who matriculated Fellow-Commoner from King's College, Cambridge in Easter 1573, and graduated LL.B. from Trinity Hall in 1579, as Bowes (Venn, *Alumni Cantabrigienses*, vol. I, 192). This is too late. There is no Ralph Bowle in any of the admission registers of the Inns of Court. There are Bowles in other parts of the country, such as Hampshire, Hertfordshire, Lincolnshire and South Wales, but none of the pedigrees I have been able to consult contains a Ralph of the right date. So for the moment Ralph Bowle of St Lawrence in Thanet seems the best (or at least a likely) contender to be the Raphe Bowle whose tablatures found their way, perhaps by an indirect route, into Stowe 389.

---

[2] R. Hovendon, ed., *The Visitation of Kent, Taken in the Years 1619–1621* (London, 1898), 114.

Bibliography

PRIMARY SOURCES: MANUSCRIPT

Bristol, Record Office

P.St JB/ChW/7/b 233

Brussels, National Archives

MS Audience, n° 384

Cambridge, Magdalene College, Pepys Library

MS 2502

Cambridge, University Archives, Vice-Chancellor's Court

VCCt Invs. 2
VCCt Invs. 5
VCCt Original Wills/1

Cambridge, University Library

MS Microfilm 8315 (Stationers' Register)
University Archives, VCCt Invs. 7

Canterbury, Cathedral Archives

PRC32/27/1

Chelmsford, Essex County Record Office

D/DP/A4
D/DP/A10
D/DP/A17

Chester, Cheshire Records Office

DLT/B33

Lancashire Records Office

DDKE/acc. 7840 HMC/f.10d

Leicester, Leicestershire, Leicester and Rutland Record Office

PR/1/7

London, Bethlem Royal Hospital Archives and Museum

bcb–01
bcb–02

London, British Library

Add. MS 30513 (The Mulliner Book)
MS Stowe 389 (Raphe Bowle)

London, Drapers' Company

MB 5
MB 7

London, Lambeth Palace

MS Tenison 807/1

London, Metropolitan Archives

P 69/AND4/A/001/MS04107/001

London, The National Archives

Chancellor and Council of the Duchy of Lancaster, Records of

DL 44/96

Chancery: Inquisitions post mortem

C 142/121/120

Chancery and Supreme Court of Judicature: Patent Rolls

C 66/920

Exchequer: King's Remembrancer: Particulars of Customs Accounts

E 122/225/96

Exchequer: King's Remembrancer: Port Books

E 190/4/2
E 190/6/3
E 190/8/1
E 190/8/2
E 190/594/2
E 190/642/10
E 190/643/18
E 190/747/5
E 190/747/18
E 190/747/20
E 190/747/26

Prerogative Court of Canterbury and related Probate
Jurisdictions: Will Registers: Probate

PROB 11/4/362
PROB 11/48/191
PROB 11/64/107
PROB 11/74/150
PROB 11/108/533

Records assembled by the State Paper Office

SP 12/24/39
SP 70/48

London, Royal Academy of Music, Robert Spencer Collection

161921–1001

Newport, Isle of Wight Record Office

JER/WA/36/7

Norwich, Archive Centre

DN/INV 2/114
DN/INV 2/134

Oxford, Bodleian Libraries

MS Eng. Misc. c. 330

Reading, Berkshire Record Office

D/A2/c.40

Rochester, Archives of the Rochester Bridge Trust

E 01/01/001
E 01/02/008
F 01/102
F 01/103
F 01/105

Swindon, Wiltshire and Swindon History Centre

1178/245

Washington, DC, Folger Shakespeare Library

L.b.550

Winchester, Hampshire Record Office

1559B/020/1–2

Non-archival MSS

Cambridge, Trinity College

O.2.53.

Chicago, Newberry Library

Case MS VM C.25: 'Compositione di meser Vincenzo Capirola, gentil homo
  bresano'

Oxford, Bodleian Library

MS Tanner 103*, ff. 177–9v

*Yale, University Library, Beinecke Rare Book
and Manuscript Library*

Osborn Music MS 13 (The Osborn Commonplace Book)

Electronic (excluding catalogues)

Early English Books Online http://eebo.chadwyck.com
Early English Prose Fiction http://collections.chadwyck.co.uk
Early Music Online http://digirep.rhul.ac.uk
English Poetry 600–1900 http://collections.chadwyck.co.uk
English Short Title Catalogue http://estc.bl.uk
Fellowship of Makers and Researchers of Historical Instruments, Bulletins and
    Communications www.fomrhi.org
Lexicons of Early Modern English http://leme.library.utoronto.ca
Middle English Dictionary http://quod.lib.umich.edu/m/med/
Oxford Dictionary of National Biography www.oxforddnb.com
Oxford English Dictionary www.oed.com
Patrologiae Cursus Completus http://pld.chadwyck.co.uk
Petrucci Music Library http://imslp.org
Tinctoris, Johannes, online text of works http://earlymusictheory.org/Tinctoris
Yale, University Library, digital library of the Beinecke Rare Book and Manuscript
    Library http://beinecke.library.yale.edu

PRIMARY SOURCES: PRINTED BOOKS OF THE SIXTEENTH AND SEVENTEENTH CENTURIES

NOTE: Items in square brackets have not survived, and in some cases may never have been printed. The place of publication for all sixteenth-century books is London, unless otherwise specified.

Alford, J. (trans.), *A Briefe and easye instru[c]tion to learne the tableture to conducte
    and dispose thy hande vnto the lute.* See Le Roy, Adrian
Anonymous, *Cyuile and uncyuile life* (1579)
    La maniere de bien et iustement entoucher les Lucz et Guiternes (Poitiers, 1556).
    Facsimile in Saint-Arroman and Dugot, *Méthodes et Traités, Luth*, vol. i,
    25–53
    *The Psalter or Psalmes of Dauid Corrected and pointed as they shal be song in
    Churches* (1563)
    [*The Scyence of lutynge*]. Known only from a 1565/6 entry in the Stationers'
    Register
Archdeacon, Daniel, *A true Discourse of the Armie which the King of Spaine caused
    to bee assembled in the Hauen of Lisbon, in the Kingdome of Portugall, in the
    yeare 1588 against England* (1588)
Ascham, Roger, *Toxophilvs, the schole of shootinge conteyned in tvvo bookes. To all
    Gentlemen and yomen of Englande, pleasaunte for theyr pastyme to rede, and
    profitable for theyr use to folow, both in war and peace* (1545)
Averell, W., *A meruailous combat of contrarieties* (1588)
[Ballard, Robert, *An exhortation to all kynde of men how they shulde lerne
    to playe of the lute*]. Known only from a 1567 entry in the Stationers'
    Register
Barberiis, Melchiore de, *Opera intitolata contina/Intabolatura de lauto . . . Fantasie
    per sonar sopra la Chitara da sette corde* (Venice, 1549)
Barley, William, *A new booke of Citterne Lessons* (1593)

A new Booke of Tabliture, Containing sundrie easie and familiar Instructions, showing how to attain to the knowledge, to guide and dispose thy hand to play on sundry Instruments, as the Lute, Orpharion, *and* Bandora (1596)

A new Booke of Tabliture for the Bandora: Contayning sundrie sorts of lessons (1596)

A new Booke of Tabliture for the Orpharion: Contayning sundrie sorts of lessons (1596)

Barwick, Hunfrey, *A breefe discourse, concerning the force and effect of all manuall weapons of fire and the disability of the long bowe or archery, in respect of others of greater force now in vse* (1592)

Becon, Thomas, *A pleasaunt newe Nosegaye, full of many godly and swete floures* (1542)

Bermudo, Juan, *Declaracion de instrumentos musicales* (Osuna, 1555)

Blundeville, Thomas, *M. Blundevile his exercises containing sixe treatises* (1594)

Bonde, William, *The Pylgrimage of perfection* (1526)

Bonnecase, Robert Alcide de, *Remarques sur les principales difficultez de la langue françoise* (Paris, 1673)

Bonner, Edmund, *A profitable and necessarye doctrine with certayne homelyes adioyned therunto set forth by the reuerend father in God, Edmunde Byshop of London* (1555)

Braham, H., *The institucion of a gentleman* (1555)

Bright, Timothie, *A Treatise of Melancholie* (1586)

Bruto, Giovanni Michele, *The Necessarie, Fit, and Conuenient Education of a yong Gentlewoman*, trans. W. P. (1598)

Bullein, William, *A Dialogve bothe plesaunte and pietifull wherein is a goodly regimente against the feuer Pestilence* (1564)

Calendar of State Papers (Domestic), 1547–80

Calendar of State Papers (Spain), 1568–79

Case, John, *The Praise of Mvsicke: Wherein besides the antiquitie, dignitie, delectation, and vse thereof in ciuill matters, is also declared the sober and lawfull vse of the same in the congregation and Church of God* (1586)

Chillester, James (trans.), *A most excellent Hystorie Of the Institution and firste beginning of Christian Princes and the Originall of Kingdomes . . . First written in Latin by Chelidonius Tigurinus . . . and now englished by Iames Chillester, Londoner* (1571)

Cooper, Thomas, *Thesaurus Linguae Romanae et Britannicae* (1578)

Coplande, Robert, *Here foloweth the maner of dauncynge of bace dances after the vse of fraunce and other places translated out of french in englysshe.* Appended to Alexander Barclay, *Here begynneth the introductory to wryte and to pronounce French* (1521)

Copley, Anthony, *Wits Fittes and Fancies. Fronted and entermedled with Presidentes of Honour and Wisdome* (1595)

Cotgrave, Randle, *A Dictionarie of the French and English Tongues* (1611)

Davison, Francis, *A Poetical Rapsody Containing Diuerse Sonnets, Odes, Elegies, Madrigalls, and other Poesies both in Rime, and Measured Verse* (1602)

de Vries, Hans Vredeman, *Panoplia seu armamentarium* (Antwerp, 1572)

Digby, Kenelm, *Two treatises in the one of which the nature of bodies, in the other, the nature of mans soule is looked into in way of discovery of the immortality of reasonable soules* (Paris, 1644)

Dowland, Robert, *Varietie of Lute-Lessons* (1610)

Duwes, Giles, *An introductorie for to lerne to rede, to pronounce, and to speake Frenche trewely* (1533?)

Dymoke, Tailboys, *Caltha poetarum: or The bumble bee* (1599)

Eden, Richard, *The History of Trauayle in the West and East Indies, and other countreys . . . done into Englyshe by Richarde Eden. Newly set in order, augmented, and finished by Richarde Willes* (1577)

Elyot, Thomas, *Bibliotheca Eliotae. Eliotis librarie* (1542)

  The boke named the Gouernour (first edition, 1531)

  The Dictionary of syr Thomas Eliot knyght (1538)

Erasmus, Desiderius, *The praise of Folie. Moriae Encomivm a booke made in latine by that great clerke Erasmus Roterodame. Englisshed by sir Thomas Chaloner knight* (1549)

Fraunce, Abraham, *The Lawiers Logike, exemplifying the praecepts of Logike by the practise of the common Lawe* (1588)

Fulke, William, *A Goodly Gallerye with a Most Pleasaunt Prospect, into the garden of naturall contemplation, to behold the naturall causes of all kynde of Meteors* (1563)

Fulwell, Ulpian, *An Enterlude Intituled Like Wil to like quod the Deuel to the Colier, very godly and ful of plesant mirth* (1568)

Galilei, Vincenzo, *Dialogo di Vincentio Galilei nobile della musica antica e della moderna* (Florence, 1581)

Gascoigne, George, *A Hundreth sundrie Flowres bounde vp in one small Poesie* (1573)

  Certayne Notes of Instruction concerning the making of verse or ryme in English, in *The Posies of George Gascoigne Esquire* (1575), Sig. Tij–Uiij[v]

Greene, R., *A Dispvtation between a Hee Conny-catcher and a Shee Conny-catcher* (1592)

  A Quip for an Vpstart Courtier (1592)

Guevara, Antonio de, *The dial of princes, compiled by the reuerend father in God, Don Antony of Gueuara, Byshop of Guadix* (1568)

  R. P. D. Antonii de Guevara Episcopi Mondiniensis . . . Epistolae (Cologne, 1614)

Hakluyt, Richard, *The Principal Nauigations, Voyages, Traffiqves and Discoueries of the English Nation* (1599–1600)

Hales, John, *A compendious or briefe examination of certayne ordinary complaints, of diuers of our country men in these our dayes* (1581)

Harrison, Stephen and Kip, William, *The Arch's of Triumph Erected in honor of the High and mighty prince James the first of that name* (first edition, 1604)

Hellowes, Edward (trans.), *The Familiar Epistles of Sir Anthony of Gueuara* (1574)

Heywood, Jasper, *The seconde tragedie of Seneca entituled Thyestes faithfully Englished by Iasper Heywood* (1560)

Heywood, John, *An hundred Epigrammes. Inuented and made by John Heywood* (1550)

Hill, Thomas (trans.), *A briefe and pleasaunt treatise, entituled, Naturall and Artificiall conclusions: Written first by sundrie scholers of the Uniuersitie of Padua in Italie . . . And now Englished by Thomas Hyll Londoner* (1584)

Holme, R., *The Academy of Armory* (1688)

Huloet, Richard, *Dictionarie newelye corrected, amended, set in order and enlarged* (1572)

Hunnis, William, *Certayne Psalmes chosen out of the psalter of Dauid, and drawen furth into Englysh meter by William Hunnis seruant to the ryght honorable syr Wyllyam Harberde knight* (1550)

Jones, Inigo and Davenant, William, *Britannia triumphans a masque, presented at White Hall, by the Kings Majestie and his lords, on the Sunday after Twelfth-night, 1637. By Inigo Iones surveyor of his Majesties workes, and William Davenant her Majesties servant* (1638)

Jonson, Ben, *The Gypsies Metamorphosed*. See Knowles

Junius, Hadrianus, *Nomenclator omnium rerum propria nomina variis linguis explicata indicans* (Antwerp, 1583)

Ke, F. (trans.), *A briefe and plaine Instruction to set all Musicke of eight diuers tunes in Tableture for the Lute*. See Le Roy, Adrian

Langham, Robert, *A Letter: whearin. part of the entertainment vntoo the Queenz Maiesty, at Killingwoorth Castl, in warwik Sheer in this soomerz Progress 1575. is signified: from a freend officer attendant in Coourt vntoo hiz freend a Citizen, and Merchaunt of London* (1575)

Le Challeux, Nicolas, *A true and perfect description, of the last voyage or Nauigation . . . into Terra Florida, this yeare past* (1565)

Le Roy, Adrian, *Breve et facile instrvction povr apprendre la tablatvre, a bien accorder, condvire et disposer la main svr le cistre* (1565)

   A Briefe and easye instru[c]tion to learne the tableture to conducte and dispose thy hande vnto the Lute englished by I. Alford Londenor (1568)

   A briefe and plaine instruction for to learne the Tablature, to Conduct and dispose the hand vnto the Gitterne (?1569)

   A briefe and plaine Instruction to set all Musicke of eight diuers tunes in Tableture for the Lute (1574)

   [*Briefve et facile instruction pour apprendre la tabulature a bien accorder, conduire et disposer la main sur la Guiterne*] (1567)

   'An instruction to the Gitterne'. See *A briefe and plaine instruction for to learne the Tablature, to Conduct and dispose the hand vnto the Gitterne*

   Premier livre de tabulature de guiterre (1551)

Legh, Gerard, *The Accedens of Armory* (1562)

Lesse, Nicholas (trans.), *A worke of the predestination of saints wrytten by the famous doctor S. Augustine byshop of Carthage, and translated out of Latin into Englysshe, by Nycolas Lesse, Londoner* (1550)

Lever, Ralph, *The most noble, auncient, and learned playe, called the Phi[l]osophers game* (1563)

Lorkin, Thomas, *Recta Regula et victus ratio pro studiosis et literatis* (1562)

Maunsell, Andrew, *Catalogue of English Printed Bookes*, 2 vols. (1595)

Menage, Gilles, *Observations . . . sur la langue françoise* (Paris, 1672)

Mersenne, Marin, *Harmonie universelle, contenant la théorie et la pratique de la musique* (Paris, 1636)

Milton, John, *Areopagitica: a Speech of Mr. John Milton For the Liberty of Vnlicens'd Printing, To the Parliament of England* (1644)

Moya, Juan Pérez de, *Philosofia secreta: Donde debaxo de historias fabulosa* (Saragossa, 1585)

Mudarra, Alonso, *Tres Libros de Mvsica en Cifras para Vihvela* (Seville, 1546)

Munday, Anthony, *Banquet of Daintie Conceits* (1588)

North, George, *The Philosopher of the Court, written by Philbert of Vienne in Champaigne, and Englished by George North, gentleman* (1575)

Painter, William, *The second Tome of the Palace of Pleasure* (1567)

Palsgrave, John, *The Dictionary of syr Thomas Elyot knyght* (1538)
Lesclarcissement de la Langue Francoyse (1530)

Parker, Matthew, *The whole Psalter translated into English Metre, which contayneth an hundreth and fifty Psalmes* (?1567)

Phalèse, Pierre, *Selectissima elegantissimaque gallica italica et latina in guiterna ludenda carmina* (1570)

Playford, John, *A Booke of New Lessons for the Cithern and Gittern* (1652)
Musick's delight on the Cithren (1666)

Praetorius, Michael, *Syntagma Musicum,* vol. II, *De Organographia* (Wolfenbüttel, 1618–20)

Preston, Thomas, *A lamentable tragedy mixed ful of pleasant mirth* (1570)

Purchas, Samuel, *Purchas his pilgrimes In fiue books* (edition of 1625)

Puttenham, George (attrib.), *The Arte of English Poesie* (1589)

Rhodes, Hugh, *The boke of nurtur for men seruauntes and children* (edition of 1560)

Rich, B., *Allarme to England foreshewing what perilles are procured, where the people liue without regarde of martial laws* (1578)

Rivius, Johann, *A Notable discourse of the happinesse of this our age, and of the ingratitude of men to God for his benefites* (1578)

Robinson, Thomas, *The Schoole of Musicke: Wherein is Tavght, the Perfect Method, of Trve Fingering of the* Lute, Pandora, Orpharion, *and* Viol de Gamba (1603)

Roman y Zamora, Hieronymo, *Republicas del mundo,* 3 vols. (Salam, 1595)

Rosset, François de and d'Audiguier, Vital (trans.), *Cervantes: Les Novvelles de Migvel de Cervantes Saavedra* (Paris, 1633)

Rowbothum, James (trans.), *The Pleasaunt and vwittie Plaie of the Cheastes renewed* (1569)

R. P. (trans.), *The Second part of the Myrror of Knighthood* (1583)
A treatise of Schemes and Tropes very profytable for the better vnderstanding of good authors (1550)

Sherry, R., *A treatise of Schemes and Tropes very profytable for the better vnderstanding of good authors* (1550)

Shirrye, R. (trans.), *A verye fruitful Exposicion vpon the syxte Chapter of Saynte Iohn . . . translated into English by Richard Shirrye, Londoner* (1550)

Shute, John, *The First and Chief Groundes of Architectvre* (1563)

Stanihurst, Richard, *A treatise conteining a plaine and perfect description of Ireland, with an Introduction to the better vnderstanding of the histories apperteining to that Iland*, in Ralph Holinshed, *The Second volume of Chronicles: Conteining the description, conquest, inhabitation, and troblesome estate of Ireland; first collected by Raphaell Holinshed* (1586)

Sternhold, Thomas, *Certayne Psalmes chosen out of the Psalter of Dauid, and drawen into Englishe Metre by Thomas Sternhold grome of þᵉ kynges magesties Roobes* (?1548)
and Hopkins, J., *The Whole Booke of Psalmes, collected into Englysh metre by T. Starnhold I. Hopkins and others* (1562)
et al., Psalmes of Dauid in Englishe Metre, by Thomas Sterneholde and others: conferred with the Ebrue, and in certeine places corrected, as the sense of the Prophete required: and the Note ioyned withal. Very Mete to be Vsed of all sorts of

*people priuatly for their godly solace and confort, laiyng aparte all vngodly
songes and ballades, which tende only to the norishing of vice, and corrupting
of youth* (1560)

Strype, John, *Ecclesiastical Memorials*, 3 vols. (1721)

Sylvester, Josuah, *Du Bartas his deuine weekes & workes translated & dedicated to the
Kings most excellent Maiestie* (edition of 1611)

Thomas, William, *The historie of Italie* (1549)

Tottel's 'Miscellany' (= *Songes and Sonettes, written by the right honorable Lorde
Henry Haward late Earle of Surrey, and other*) (1557 and subsequently). Cited
from the edition of Holton and MacFaul (q.v.), by poem number

Vienne, Philibert de, *Le philosophe de court* (Paris, 1547)

Virdung, S., *Musica getutscht* (Basle, 1511)

Vreedman, Sebastian, *Nova Longeque Elegantissima Cithara Ludenda* (1568)

Webbe, William, *A Discourse of English Poetrie* (1586)

Wilson, Thomas, *The Arte of Rhetorique* (1553)

Wright, T., *The Passions of the Minde in Generall* (1604)

Young, Bartholomew (trans.), *Diana of George of Montemayor: Translated out of
Spanish into English by Bartholomew Yong of the Middle Temple Gentleman*
(1598)

MODERN EDITIONS AND TRANSLATIONS

Alexander, G., ed., *'The Defence of Poesy' and Selected Renaissance Literary Criticism*
(London, 2004)
   ed., *William Scott: The Model of Poesy* (Cambridge, 2013)

Anderson, J. J., ed., *Records of Early English Drama: Newcastle upon Tyne*
(Manchester, 1982)

Arber, E., ed., *A Transcript of the Registers of the Company of Stationers of London,
1554–1640, A.D.*, 5 vols. (London, 1875–94)

Baines, A., 'Fifteenth-Century Instruments in Tinctoris's *De Inventione et Usu
Musicae*', *GSJ*, 3 (1950), 19–26

Baldwin, E., Clopper, L. M. and Mills, D., eds., *Records of Early English Drama:
Cheshire including Chester*, 2 vols. (Toronto, 2007)

Bannerman, W. B., ed., *The Visitations of Kent taken in the Years 1530–1 by
Thomas Benolte, Clarenceux, and 1574 by Robert Cooke, Clarenceux*, 2 vols.
(London, 1923–4)

Bevington, D., Butler, M. and Donaldson, I., eds., *The Cambridge Edition of the
Works of Ben Jonson*, 5 vols. (Cambridge, 2012)

Boyd, P., ed., *Roll of the Drapers' Company of London* (Croydon, 1934)

Briquet, C.-M., ed., *Les filigranes: Dictionnaire historique des marques du papier dès
leur apparition vers 1282 jusqu'en 1600* (Amsterdam, 1968)

Caldwell, J., ed., *The Mulliner Book*, Musica Britannica, I (London, 2011)

Céard, J., Ménager, D. and Simonin, M., eds., *Pierre de Ronsard: Œuvres
complètes*, 2 vols. (Paris, 1993–94)

Chance, J., ed., *The Assembly of Gods* (Kalamazoo, 1999)

Chrimes, S. B., ed. and trans., *Sir John Fortescue: De Laudibus Legum Anglie*
(Cambridge, 1942)

Crookes, D. Z., trans., *Michael Praetorius: Syntagma Musicum, De Organographia,
Parts I and II* (Oxford, 1986)

Demerson, G., ed., *Œuvres poétiques complètes de Remy Belleau: Édition critique avec introductions, variantes et notes*, 6 vols. (Paris, 1995–2003)

Dietz, B., ed., *The Port and Trade of Early Elizabethan London* (London, 1972)

Duncan-Jones, K., ed., *Sir Philip Sidney: The Old Arcadia* (Oxford, 1985)

Earwaker, J. P., ed., *Lancashire and Cheshire Wills and Inventories*, 3 vols. (Manchester, 1884–97)

Ellinwood, L., ed., *Thomas Tallis: English Sacred Music*, 2 vols., rev. P. Doe, Early English Church Music, vols. xii and xiii (London, 1973–4)

Elliott, J. R., Nelson, A. H., Johnston, A. F. and Wyatt, D., eds., *Records of Early English Drama: Oxford*, 2 vols. (Toronto, 2004)

Fenn, R. D., 'William Percy's *Faery Pastorall*: An Old Spelling Edition', unpublished doctoral dissertation, University of British Columbia (1997)

Ferrero, G. G., ed., *Novelle di Matteo Bandello* (Turin, 1974)

Fisher, F. J., ed., *The State of England Anno Dom. 1600 by Thomas Wilson* (London, 1936)

Fowler, J. T., 'The Account Book of William Wray', *The Antiquary*, 32 (1896), 54–7, 76–81, 117–20, 178–81, 212–14, 242–44, 278–81, 316–17, 346–47 and 369–74

Furnivall, F. J., ed., *Queene Elizabethes Achademy* (London, 1869)

Gairdner, G. and Brodie, R. H., eds., *Letters and Papers Foreign and Domestic of the Reign of Henry VIII*, vols. xvi (London, 1898) and xvii (London, 1900)

Gibson, J. M., ed., *Records of Early English Drama. Kent: Diocese of Canterbury*, 3 vols. (Toronto and London, 2002)

Goldring, E., *et al.*, eds., *John Nichols's The Progresses and Public Processions of Queen Elizabeth I: A New Edition of the Early Modern Sources*, 5 vols. (Oxford, 2004)

Goodwin, C., ed., *The English Lute Song Before Dowland,* vol. i, *Songs from the Dallis Manuscript c.1583* (The Lute Society, 1996)

ed., *The English Lute Song Before Dowland,* vol. ii, *Songs from Additional Manuscript 4900 and Other Early Sources* (The Lute Society, 1997)

Gray, T., ed., *Devon Household Accounts*, 2 vols. Devon and Cornwall Record Society, vols. xxxviii and xxxix (1995–6)

Hamrick, S., ed., *Tottel's* Songes and Sonettes *in Context* (Farnham, 2013)

Harland, J., ed., *The House and Farm Accounts of the Shuttleworths of Gawthorpe Hall in the County of Lancaster, at Smithils and Gawthorpe: from September 1582 to October 1621*, 4 vols. (Manchester, 1856–80)

Hartley, T. E., ed., *Proceedings in the Parliaments of Elizabeth I*, 3 vols. (London, 1981 and 1995)

Havinden, M. A., ed., *Household and Farm Inventories in Oxfordshire, 1550–1590* (London, 1965)

Holton, A. and MacFaul, T., eds., *Tottel's Miscellany: Songs and Sonnets of Henry Howard, Earl of Surrey, Sir Thomas Wyatt and Others* (London, 2011)

Hopwood, C. H., ed., *A Calendar of Middle Temple Records* (London, 1903)

Middle Temple Records, 4 vols. (London, 1904–5)

Hovendon, R., ed., *The Visitation of Kent, Taken in the Years 1619–1621* (London, 1898)

Howard, J. J. and Armytage, G. J., eds., *The Visitation of London in the Year 1568* (London, 1869)

Hudson, W. and Tingey, J. C., eds., *The Records of the City of Norwich*, 2 vols. (Norwich, 1906–10)

Hughey, R., ed., *The Arundel Harrington Manuscript of Tudor Poetry*, 2 vols. (Columbus, Ohio, 1960)

Jackson, J. L., ed., *Three Elizabethan Fencing Manuals* (Delmar, 1972)

Jacquot, J., *et al.*, eds., *Œuvres d'Adrian Le Roy: Les instructions pour le Luth (1574)*, 2 vols. (Paris, 1977)

Jas, E., ed., *Motets on texts from the Old Testament, 4, Texts from the Psalms 3, The Collected Works of Josquin des Prez*, vol. XVII (2 vols. in one) (Utrecht, 2008)

Jones, E., ed., *Henry Howard, Earl of Surrey: Poems* (Oxford, 1964)

Kershaw, A., ed., *A Handefull of pleasant delites by Clement Robinson and divers others* (London, 1926)

Knowles, J., ed., *The Gypsies Metamorphosed*, in Bevington, Butler and Donaldson, 465–80

Kuin, R. J. P., ed., *Robert Langham: A Letter* (Leiden, 1983)

Lawson, J. A., ed., *The Elizabethan New Year's Gift Exchanges 1559–1603* (Oxford, 2013)

Lilly, J., ed., *A Collection of Seventy-Nine Black Letter Ballads and broadsides printed in the reign of Queen Elizabeth, between the years 1559 and 1597. Accompanied with an introduction and illustrative notes* (London, 1867)

Maclean, J., ed., *The Life and Times of Sir Peter Carew* (London, 1857)

McQuillan, R., ed., *Thomas Whythorne: Songes for Five Voyces*, Antico Edition, AE 38 (Newton Abbot, 1999)

   ed., *Thomas Whythorne: Songes for Four Voyces*, Antico Edition, AE 39 (Newton Abbot, 2004)

   ed., *Thomas Whythorne: Songes for Three Voyces*, Antico Edition, AE 31 (Newton Abbot, 1992)

Meads, M., ed., *The Diary of Lady Margaret Hoby 1599–1605* (London, 1930)

Menghini, M., ed., *Le rime di Serafino de' Ciminelli dall'Aquila*, vol. I (Bologna, 1894)

Metcalfe, W. C., ed., *The Visitation of Wiltshire 1565* (Exeter, 1897)

Millican, P., ed., *The Register of the Freemen of Norwich 1548–1713* (Norwich, 1934)

Milsom, J., ed., *A Tallis Anthology: 17 Anthems and Motets* (Oxford, 1992)

Morehen, J. and Mateer, D., eds., *Thomas Ravenscroft: Rounds, Canons and Songs from Printed Sources*, Musica Britannica, vol. XCIII (London, 2012)

Morfill, W. R. and Furnivall, F. J., eds., *Ballads from Manuscripts*, 2 vols. (1868 and 1873)

Nichols, J. G., ed., *The Diary of Henry Machyn* (London, 1848)

Osborn, J. M., ed., *The Autobiography of Thomas Whythorne* (Oxford, 1961)

   ed., *The Autobiography of Thomas Whythorne: Modern Spelling Edition* (Oxford, 1962)

Peach, T., ed., *Alonso Mudarra: Tres Libros de música en cifra para vihuela* (Barcelona, 1949)

   ed., *Poésies complètes: Jacques Tahureau* (Geneva, 1984)

Raine, J., ed., *Wills and Inventories from the Registry of the Archdeaconry of Richmond* (Durham, 1853)

   ed., *Wills and Inventories Illustrative of the History, Manners, Language Statistics, etc. of the Northern Counties of England*, vol. I (London, 1834)

Rebholz, R. A., ed., *The Complete Poems of Sir Thomas Wyatt* (New Haven, 1981)

Roberts, E. and Parker, K., eds., *Southampton Probate Inventories, 1447–1575*, 2 vols. (Southampton, 1992)

Rouget, F., ed., *Les epithetes (1571): Maurice de la Porte* (Paris, 2009)

Rye, W., ed., *The Visitacion of Norfolk (1563, 1589 and 1613)* (London, 1891)

Saint-Arroman, J. and Delume, C., eds., *Méthodes et Traités, 18, série I, France 1600–1800, Guitare* (2 vols.), vol. I (Courlay, 2003)

    and Dugot, J., *Méthodes et Traités, 19, série I, France 1600–1800, Luth* (2 vols.), vol. I (Courlay, 2004)

Simpson, C. M., ed., *The British Broadside Ballad and its Music* (New Brunswick, 1966)

Smith, G. G., ed., *Elizabethan Critical Essays*, 2 vols. (Oxford, 1904)

Smith, P. M., ed., *Philibert de Vienne: Le philosophe de court* (Geneva, 1990)

Somerset, J. A. B., ed., *Four Tudor Interludes* (London, 1974)

Spencer, R., ed., *The Burwell Lute Tutor* (Leeds, 1974)

Starkey, D., *et al.*, eds., *The Inventory of King Henry VIII: Society of Antiquaries MS 129 and British Library MS Harley 1419*, 2 vols. (London, 1998)

Statutes of the Realm, 1101–1713, 11 vols. in 12 (London, 1810–28)

Stone, D., Jr., ed., *Mellin de Saint-Gelais: Œuvres poétiques françaises*, 2 vols. (Paris, 1993)

Sturgess, H. A. C., ed., *Register of Admissions to the Honourable Society of the Middle Temple*, 3 vols. (London, 1949–)

Tydeman, W., ed., *Four Tudor Comedies* (Harmondsworth, 1984)

Tyler, J., ed., *Adrian le Roy and Robert Ballard: Five Guitar Books (1551–1555)*, Editions Chanterelle (Monaco, 1979)

    ed., *Alonso Mudarra: Tres Libros de Musica en Cifras para Vihuela (1546)*, Editions Chanterelle (Monaco, 1980)

    ed., *Simon Gorlier and Guillaume Morlaye: Four Guitar Books* (Editions Chanterelle (Monaco, 1980)

Vanes, J., ed., *Documents Illustrating the Overseas Trade of Bristol in the Sixteenth Century* (Bristol, 1979)

Way, A., ed., *Promptuarium parvulorum sive clericorum*, 3 vols. (London, 1843–53)

Weaver, F. W., ed., *The Visitations of the County of Somerset, in the years 1531 and 1575, together with additional pedigrees, chiefly from the Visitation of 1591* (Exeter, 1885)

Whigham, F. and Rebhorn, W. A., eds., *The Art of English Poesy by George Puttenham* (Ithaca and London, 2007)

Whythorne, T., *A book of songs and sonets*. See Osborn

Willan, T. S., ed., *A Tudor Book of Rates* (Manchester, 1962)

Wrightson, J., ed., *The Wanley Manuscripts*, Recent Researches in the Music of the Renaissance, 99–101 (Madison, 1995)

SECONDARY SOURCES: BOOKS, ARTICLES AND THESES

Abbot, D. and Segerman, E., 'The Cittern in England Before 1700', *LSJ*, 17 (1975), 24–48

Alcalde, A. B. F. C., 'The Players and Performance Practice of the Vihuela and its Related Instruments, the Lute and the Guitar from c1450 to c1650 as

Revealed by a Study of Musical, Theoretical and Archival Sources', unpublished doctoral dissertation, King's College London, 1999

'The Vihuela and Guitar in Sixteenth-Century Spain: A Critical Appraisal of Some of the Existing Evidence', *LSJ*, 30 (1990), 3–24

Aldis, H. G., *et al.*, *A Dictionary of Printers and Booksellers in England, Scotland and Ireland, and of Foreign Printers of English Books 1557–1640* (London, 1910)

Alford, S., *The Watchers: A Secret History of the Reign of Elizabeth I* (London, 2012)

Anderson, J. C., *A Short Chronicle concerning the Parish of Croydon in the County of Surrey* (Edinburgh and London, 1882)

Archer, I. W., *The History of the Haberdashers' Company* (Chichester, 1991)

Archer, J. E., Goldring, E. and Knight, S., eds., *The Intellectual and Cultural World of the Early Modern Inns of Court* (Manchester, 2011)

Arkell, T., 'Interpreting Probate Inventories', in Arkell, *et al.*, eds., *When Death do us Part: Understanding and Interpreting the Probate Records of Early Modern England* (Oxford, Leopard's Head Press, 2000), 72–102

Ashbee, A., 'Groomed for Service: Musicians in the Privy Chamber at the English Court' c.1495–1558', *EM*, 25 (1997), 185–97

Attridge, D., *Moving Words: Forms of English Poetry* (Oxford, 2013)

Well-Weighed Syllables: Elizabethan Verse in Classical Metres (Cambridge, 1974)

Baker, J. H., 'The Third University 1450–1550: Law School or Finishing School?', in Archer, Goldring and Knight, 8–24

Ball, J. N., *Merchants and Merchandise: The Expansion of Trade in Europe 1500–1630* (London, 1977)

Bartlett, K. R., 'The English Exile Community in Italy and the Political Opposition to Queen Mary I', *Albion: A Quarterly Journal Concerned with British Studies*, 13 (1981), 223–41

The English in Italy 1525–1558: A Study in Culture and Politics (Geneva, 1991)

'"The Misfortune that is wished for him": The Life and Death of Edward Courtenay, Earl of Devon', *Canadian Journal of History*, 14 (1979), 1–28

Bartoletti, M., ed., *Il coro ligneo della Cattedrale di Savona* (Milan, 2008)

Bayley, J., *The History and Antiquities of the Tower of London, with Memoirs of Royal and Distinguished Persons*, 2 vols. (London, 1821–25)

Bedford, R., David, L. I. and Kelly, P., eds., *Early Modern English Lives: Autobiography and Self-Representation 1500–1660* (Aldershot, 2007)

Beier, A. L., *Masterless Men: the Vagrancy Problem in England 1560–1640* (London, 1987)

'Social Problems in Elizabethan London', *Journal of Interdisciplinary History*, 9 (1978), 203–21

Beier, P., 'Right-Hand Position in Renaissance Lute Technique', *JLSA*, 12 (1979), 5–24

Ben-Amos, I. K., 'Failure to Become Freemen: Urban Apprentices in Early Modern England', *Social History*, 16 (1991), 155–72

Bergeron, D. M., 'Harrison, Jonson and Dekker: The Magnificent Entertainment for King James (1604)', *Journal of the Warburg and Courtauld Institutes*, 31 (1968), 445–48

Bernstein, J., 'An Index of Polyphonic Chansons in English Manuscript Sources, c. 1530–1640', *RMARC*, 21 (1988), 21–36

Bindoff, S. T., *The House of Commons 1509–1558*, 3 vols. (London, 1982)

Blanchard, I., *The International Economy in the 'Age of Discoveries', 1470–1570: Antwerp and the English Merchants' World* (Stuttgart, 2009)

Blank, P., '"niu ureiting": The Prose of Language Reform in the English Renaissance', in Fowler and Greene, 31–47

Blayney, P. M., *The Stationers' Company and the Printers of London*, 2 vols. (Cambridge, 2013)

Bloom, G., *Voice in Motion: Staging Gender, Shaping Sound in Early Modern England* (Philadelphia, 2007)

Boffey, J., 'Wynkyn de Worde, Richard Pynson, and the English Printing of Texts Translated from French', in Britnell and Britnell, 171–83

Boswell, J. C. and Braden, G. M., *Petrarch's English Laurels 1475–1700: A Compendium of Printed References and Allusions* (Farnham, 2012)

Bourciez, E., *Les mœurs polies et la littérature de cour sous Henri II* (Paris, 1886)

Bowers, R., 'To Chorus from Quartet: The Performing Resource for English Church Polyphony, c. 1390–1559', in Morehen, 1–47

Bray, R., 'Music and the Quadrivium in Early Tudor England', *ML*, 76 (1995), 1–18

Brenner, R., *Merchants and Revolution: Commercial Change, Political Conflict, and London's Overseas Traders, 1550–1653* (Cambridge, 1993)

Brigden, S., *Thomas Wyatt: The Heart's Forest* (London, 2012)

Britnell, J., and Britnell, R., eds., *Vernacular Literature and Current Affairs in the Early Sixteenth Century: France, England and Scotland* (Aldershot, 2000)

Brown, H. M., *Instrumental Music Printed before 1600: A Bibliography* (Cambridge, Mass., 1965)

   'St. Augustine, Lady Music, and the Gittern in Fourteenth-Century Italy', *Musica Disciplina*, 38 (1984), 25–65

Bryan, J., '"Verie sweete and artificiall": Lorenzo Costa and the Earliest Viols', *EM*, 36 (2008), 3–17

Budasz, R., 'Black Guitar-Players and Early African-Iberian Music in Portugal and Brazil', *EM*, 35 (2007), 3–21

Burzik, M., *Quellenstudien zur europäischen Zupfinstrumentenformen* (Kassel, 1995)

Cambers, A., 'Readers' Marks and Religious Practice: Margaret Hoby's Marginalia', in King, 211–31

Campbell, M., *The English Yeoman under Elizabeth and the Early Stuarts* (New Haven, 1942)

Cardamone, D. G., *The* canzone villanesca alla napolitana *and Related Forms, 1537–1570*, 2 vols. (Ann Arbor, 1981)

   The canzone villanesca alla napolitana: *Social, Cultural and Historical Contexts* (Aldershot, 2008)

   'The Prince of Salerno and the Dynamics of Oral Transmission in Songs of Political Exile', *Acta Musicologica*, 67 (1995), 77–108

   and Cesare, C., 'The Canzone Villanesca and Comic Culture: The Genesis and Evolution of a Mixed Genre (1537–1557)', *EMH*, 25 (2006), 59–104

Casey, W. S., 'Printed English Lute Instruction Books 1568–1610', unpublished doctoral dissertation, University of Michigan, 1960

Charlton, K., '"False Fonde Bookes, Ballades and Rimes": An Aspect of Informal Education in Early ModernEngland', *History of Education Quarterly*, 27 (1987), 449–71

Cheles, L., 'The Inlaid Decorations of Federico da Montefeltro's Urbino Studiolo: An Iconographic Study', *Mitteilungen des Kunsthistorischen Institutes in Florenz*, 26 (1982), 1–46

Coelho, V. A., ed., *Performance on Lute, Guitar and Vihuela* (Cambridge, 1997)

Collins, D., 'A 16th-Century Manuscript in Wood: The Eglantine Table at Hardwick Hall', *EM*, 4 (1976), 275–79

Collinson, P., *Birthpangs of Protestant England* (New York, 1988)

Coogan, R., 'Petrarch's *Trionfi* and the English Renaissance', *Studies in Philology*, 67 (1970), 270–91

Cooper, T., *Citizen Portrait: Portrait Painting and the Urban Elite of Tudor and Jacobean England and Wales* (New Haven and London, 2012)

Corbett, M. and Lightbown, R., *The Comely Frontispiece: The Emblematic Title-Page in England, 1550–1660* (London, 1979)

Cormack, B. and Mazzio, C., *Book Use, Book Theory 1500–1700* (Chicago, 2005)

Coromines, J., ed., *Diccionari etimològici complementari de la Llengua Catalana*, 10 vols. (Barcelona, 1980–2001)

   and Pascual, A., *Diccionario crítico etimológico castellano e hispánico*, 6 vols. (Madrid, 1980–1991)

Craig-McFeely, J., *English Lute Manuscripts and Scribes 1530–1630*. Book version of a doctoral dissertation, awarded by Oxford in 1993; available at www.ramesescats.co.uk/thesis/

Cressy, D., *Birth, Marriage and Death: Ritual, Religion and the Life-Cycle in Tudor and Stuart England* (Oxford, 1997)

Crossley, E. W., 'A Templenewsam Inventory, 1565', *Yorkshire Archaeological Journal*, 25 (1920), 91–100

Cullum, J., 'The History and Antiquities of Hawsted', in Nichols, J., ed., *Bibliotheca topographica Britannica*, 8 vols. (London, 1745–1826), VIII, 139.

Dalai Emiliani, M., ed., *La Prospettiva rinascimentale: Codificazioni e trasgressioni* (Florence, 1980)

Danner, P., 'Dd.4.23 or English Cittern Music Revisited', *JLSA*, 3 (1970), 1–12

Daybell, J. 'Secret Letters in Elizabethan England', in Daybell, J. and Hinds, P., eds., *Material Readings of Early Modern Culture: Texts and Social Practices 1580–1730* (Basingstoke, 2010), 47–64

Dean, A., 'The Five-Course Guitar and Seventeenth-Century Harmony: Alfabeto and Italian Song', unpublished doctoral dissertation, University of Rochester, 2009

   'Strumming in the Void: A New Look at the Guitar and Rhythm in Early 17th-Century Canzonettas', *EM*, 42 (2014), 55–72

Dobbins, F., *Music in Renaissance Lyons* (Oxford, 1992)

Dobson, C., Segerman, E. and Tyler, J., 'The Tunings of the Four-Course French Cittern', *LSJ*, 16 (1974), 17–23

Downing, J., 'The Guitar and Praetorius's Finger', *FoMRHI Bulletin* 119 (2013), Communication 195

Du Verdier, A. and La Croix du Maine, F. G. sieur de, *Les bibliothèques françoises, nouvelle edition*, 6 vols. (Paris, 1772)

Dugot, J., and Ballot, N., eds., *Aux origines de la guitare: La vihuela da mano* (Mayenne, 2004)

Dumitrescu, T., *The Early Tudor Court and International Musical Relations* (Aldershot, 2007)

Durant, D. N., *Bess of Hardwick: Portrait of an Elizabethan Dynast*, rev. edn (London, 1999)

Eastwell, M., 'Twenty-First Century Lute Technique: A Compromise Too Far?', *Lute News*, 101 (March, 2010), 16–21

Edgerton, S. Y., *The Renaissance Rediscovery of Linear Perspective* (New York, 1975)

Edgerton, W. L., 'The Date of *Roister Doister*', *Philological Quarterly*, 44 (1965), 555–60

Edwards, A. S. G., 'Manuscripts of the Verse of Henry Howard, Earl of Surrey', *Huntington Library Quarterly*, 67 (2004), 283–293

Eisenhardt, L., 'Baroque Guitar Accompaniment: Where is the Bass?', *EM*, 42 (2014), 73–84

Emmison, F. G., 'John Petre's Account Books', *GSJ*, 14 (1961), 73–5
   Tudor Secretary: Sir William Petre at Court and Home (London, 1961)

Evett, D., 'Some Elizabethan Allegorical Paintings: A Preliminary Enquiry', *Journal of the Warburg and Courtauld Institutes*, 52 (1989), 140–66

Ewing, E., 'Marketing Art in Antwerp, 1460–1560: Our Lady's Pand', *The Art Bulletin*, 72 (1990), 558–84

Farmer, A. B. and Lesser, Z., 'What is Print Popularity? A Map of the Elizabethan Book Trade', in Kesson and Smith, 19–54

Fink, M., 'A Newly-Discovered Stringing for the Four-Course Guitar and its Implications for Performance', *Lute Society of America Quarterly*, 42 (2012), 7–25

Fisher, R. M., 'Privy Council Coercion and Religious Conformity at the Inns of Court', *Recusant History*, 15 (1979–81), 305–24

Fleming, J., 'Damask Papers', in Kesson and Smith, 179–91
   Graffiti and the Writing Arts of Early Modern England (London, 1967)

Fleming, M., 'John Rose', entry in Milnes, J., ed., *Musical Instruments in the Ashmolean Museum* (Berkhamstead, 2011)
   'An "Old Violl" and "Other Lumber": Musical Remains in Provincial, Non-Noble England c. 1580–1660', *GSJ*, 58 (2005), 89–99
   'Some Points Arising from a Survey of Wills and Inventories', *GSJ*, 53 (2000), 301–11

Flynn, J., 'Thomas Mulliner: An Apprentice of John Heywood?', in Boynton, S. and Rice, E., eds., *Young Choristers 650–1700* (Woodbridge, 2008), 173–94

Foister, S., 'Paintings and Other Works of Art in Sixteenth-Century English Inventories', *The Burlington Magazine* (May, 1981), 273–82

Forman, B., 'Continental Furniture Craftsmen in London: 1511–1625', *Furniture History*, 8 (1971), 94–120

Forrester, P., 'Citterns and their Fingerboards', *LSJ*, 23 (1983), 15–20
   Various communications regarding the cittern. Available only on the FoMRHI website, www.fomrhi.org/pages/all-bulletins
   'Wood, Wire and Geometry', in Lustig, M., ed., *Gitarre und Zister: Im Auftrag der Stiftung Kloster Michaelstein* (Michaelstein, 2004), 33–50

Fowler, E. and Greene, R., eds., *The Project of Prose in Early Modern Europe and the New World* (Cambridge, 1997)

Freeman, J. I., 'Anthony Scoloker: The "*Just Reckoning* Printer", and the Earliest Ipswich Printing', *Transactions of the Cambridge Bibliographical Society*, 9/5 (1990), 476–96

Frye, R. M., 'Ways of Seeing in Shakespearean Drama and Elizabethan Painting', *Shakespeare Quarterly*, 31 (1980), 323–42

Gage, J., *The History and Antiquities of Hengrave in Suffolk* (London, 1822)

Gair, W. R., *The Children of Paul's: The Story of a Theatre Company 1553–1608* (Cambridge, 1982)

Garrard, R., 'English Probate Inventories and their Use in Studying the Significance of the Domestic Interior, 1570–1700', in Van der Woude, A. and Schuurman, A., eds., *Probate Inventories: A New Source for the Historical Study of Wealth, Material Culture and Agricultural Development* (Utrecht, 1980), 55–81

Gent, L., '"The Rash Gazer": Economies of Vision in Britain 1550–1660', in Gent, L., ed., *Albion's Classicism: The Visual Arts in Britain, 1550–1660* (New Haven, 1995), 377–93

Gill, D., *Gut-Strung Plucked Instruments Contemporary with the Lute* (The Lute Society, 1976)
  'The Seventeenth-Century Gittern and the Englisch Zitterlein', *LSJ*, 35 (1995), 76–86
  'Vihuelas, Violas and the Spanish Guitar', *EM*, 9 (1981), 455–62
  Wire-Strung Plucked Instruments Contemporary with the Lute (The Lute Society, 1977)

Godefroy, F., ed., *Dictionnaire de l'ancienne langue française, et de tous ses dialectes du IXe au XVe siècle*, 10 vols. (Paris, 1881–1902)

Goldring, E., '"A mercer ye wot az we be": The Authorship of the Kenilworth Letter Reconsidered', *English Literary Renaissance*, 38 (2008), 245–69

Goodwin, C., 'The Earliest English Lute Manuscript?', *Lute News*, 61 (2002), 10–24
  'A Few More Discoveries in Elizabethan Song', *The Lute*, 44 (2004), 58–73
  'Philip van Wilder's English Songs', *The Lute*, 43 (2003), 63–77
  'Some Recent Discoveries in Elizabethan Song', *The Lute*, 40 (2000), 32–50

Greer, D. and Robinson, J. H., 'A Fragment of Tablature in the Marsh Library', *The Lute*, 49 (2009), 30–5

Griffiths, J., 'L'essor et le déclin de la vihuela', in Dugot and Ballot, 8–15
  'Strategies for the Recovery of Guitar Music', in Veneziano, 59–81
  'The Vihuela: Performance Practice, Style, and Context', in Coelho, 158–79

Griffiths, P., *Lost Londons: Change, Crime and Control in the Capital City, 1550–1660* (Cambridge, 2008)
  Youth and Authority: Formative Experiences in England, 1560–1640 (Oxford, 1996)

Grijp, L. P., 'Fret Patterns of the Cittern', *GSJ*, 34 (1981), 62–97

Gunn, S., 'Anglo-Florentine Contacts in the Age of Henry VIII: Political and Social Contacts', in Sicca and Waldman, 19–47

Hall, M., *Baroque Guitar Stringing: A Survey of the Evidence* (The Lute Society, 2003)
  'A Few More Observations on Baroque Guitar Stringing', *The Lute*, 48 (2008), 71–82
  'The *Guitarra española* of Joan Carles Amat', *EM*, 6 (1978), 362–73
  ed., *Guitarra española: Introduction to Facsimile Edition* (Editions Chanterelle, 1980)
  and Yakeley, M. J., 'El estilo castellano y el estilo catalan: An Introduction to Spanish Guitar Chord Notation', *Lute*, 35 (1995), 28–61

Handschin, J., 'Aus der alten Musiktheorie. V. Zur Instrumentenkunde', *Acta Musicologica*, 16/17 (1944/1945), 1–10

Hanham, A., 'The Musical Studies of a Fifteenth-Century Wool Merchant', *The Review of English Studies*, New Series, 8 (1957), 270–74

Harrison, B. A., *The Tower of London Prisoner Book: A Complete Chronology of the Persons Known to have been Detained at Their Majesties' Pleasure 1100–1941* (London, 2004)

Harwood, I., *Wire Strings at Helmingham Hall* (The Lute Society, 2005)

Hasted, E., The *Historical and Topographical Survey of the County of Kent*, 12 vols. (1793)

Hazard, M. E., *Elizabethan Silent Language* (Lincoln, Nebraska, 2000)

Heal, A., *The London Goldsmiths 1200–1800: A Record of the Names and Addresses of the Craftsmen, their Shop Signs and Trade-Cards* (Cambridge, 1935)

Heale, E., 'Misogyny and the Complete Gentleman in Early Elizabethan Printed Miscellanies', *The Yearbook of English Studies*, 33 (2003), 233–47

Heartz, D., 'An Elizabethan Tutor for the Guitar', *GSJ*, 16 (1963), 3–21
'Parisian Music Publishing under Henry II: A Propos of Four Recently Discovered Guitar Books', *MQ*, 46 (1960), 448–67

Hellinga, L. and Trapp, J. B., eds., *The Cambridge History of the Book in Britain, III: 1400–1557* (Cambridge, 1999)

Hellwig, F., 'Lute-Making in the Later 15th and 16th Century', *LSJ*, 16 (1974), 21–38

Helms, D., *Heinrich VIII. und die Musik: Überlieferung, musikalische Bildung des Adels und Kompositionstechniken eines Königs* (Eisenach, 1998)

Hill, J. W., 'L'accompagnamento *rasgueado* di chitarra: Un possibile modello per il basso continuo dello stile recitativo?' In Veneziano, 35–57

Hodgkin, K., 'Thomas Whythorne and the Problems of Mastery', *History Workshop*, 29 (1990), 20–41

Hollstein, F. W. H., *Dutch and Flemish Etchings, Engravings and Woodcuts 1450–1700*, 58 vols. (Amsterdam, 1940)
The New Hollstein: Dutch & Flemish Etchings, Engravings and Woodcuts 1450–1700 (Amsterdam, 1993). In progress

Holman, P., *Four and Twenty Fiddlers: The Violin at the English Court, 1540–1690* (Oxford, 1993)

Howard, M., 'Inventories, Surveys and the History of Great Houses 1480–1640', *Architectural History*, 41 (1998), 14–29

Hudson, R., 'Chordal Aspects of the Italian Dance Style 1500–1650', *JLSA*, 3 (1970), 35–52
The Folia, the Saraband, the Passacaglia, and the Chaconne: The Historical Evolution of Four Forms that Originated in Music for the Five-Course Spanish Guitar, 4 vols., American Institute of Musicology, Musicological Studies and Documents, 35 (Neuhausen-Stuttgart, 1982)
'The Music in Italian Tablatures for the Five-Course Spanish Guitar', *JLSA*, 4 (1971) 21–42

Huguet, E., *Dictionnaire de la langue française du seizième siècle*, 7 vols. (Paris, 1925–67)

Hunt, A., *The Art of Hearing: English Preachers and their Audiences 1590–1640* (Cambridge, 2010)

Jackson, W. A., 'Variant Entry Fees of the Stationers' Company', in Jackson, W. A., *Records of a Bibliographer* (Cambridge, Mass., 1967), 107–13

James, M. R., *A Descriptive Catalogue of the Manuscripts in the Library of Sidney Sussex College* (Cambridge, 1895)

Jeffery, B., 'The Idea of Music in Ronsard's Poetry', in Cave, T., ed., *Ronsard the Poet* (London, 1973), 209–39

Johnson, A. H., *The History of the Worshipful Company of the Drapers of London*, 5 vols. (Oxford, 1914–22)

Johnson, F. R., 'Notes on English Retail Book Prices, 1550–1640', *The Library*, 5th Series, 2 (1950), 83–112

  'Printers' "Copy Books" and the Black Market in the Elizabethan Book Trade', *The Library*, 5th Series, 2 (1946), 97–105

Jones, E., *Inside the Illicit Economy: Reconstructing the Smugglers' Trade of Sixteenth Century Bristol* (Farnham, 2012)

Jones, N., *Birth of the Elizabethan Age: England in the 1560s* (Oxford, 1993)

Joukovsky, F., *Le bel objet: Les paradis artificiels de la Pléiade* (Paris, 1991)

Kearney, H. F., *Scholars and Gentlemen: Universities and Society in Pre-Industrial Britain, 1500–1700* (London, 1970).

Keiser, G. F., 'Practical Books for the Gentleman', in Hellinga and Trapp, 470–94

Kesson, A. and Smith, E., eds., *The Elizabethan Top Ten: Defining Print Popularity in Early Modern England* (Farnham, 2013)

Kevin, P., *et al.*, 'A Musical Instrument Fit for a Queen: The Metamorphosis of a Medieval Citole', *The British Museum Technical Research Bulletin*, 2 (2008), 13–27

King, J. N., ed., *Tudor Books and Readers: Materiality and the Construction of Meaning* (Cambridge, 2010)

Kisby, F., 'Royal Minstrels in the City and Suburbs of Early-Tudor London: Professional Activities and Private Interests', *Early Music*, 25 (1997), 199–221

Kolsky, S. D, 'The Courtier as Critic: Vincenzo Calmeta's *Vita del facondo poeta vulgare Serafino Aquilano*', *Italica*, 67 (1990), 161–72

Kreisel, H., *Die Kunst des deutschen Möbels*, 3 vols. (Munich, 1968–73)

Kuhn, J. R., 'Measured Appearances: Documentation and Design in Early Perspective Drawing', *Journal of the Warburg and Courtauld Institutes*, 53 (1990), 114–32

Kury, G., '"Glancing Surfaces": Hilliard, Armour and the Italian Model', in Gent, ed., *Albion's Classicism*, 395–426

Lafargue, V., 'Adrian Le Roy: Those Accompaniments which Resemble Solo Music', *LSJ*, 38 (1998), 65–82

Lake, P. and Pincus, S., 'Rethinking the Public Sphere in Early Modern England', *Journal of British Studies*, 45 (2006), 270–92

Le Cocq, J., 'The Status of Le Roy's Publications for Voice and Lute or Guitar', *The Lute*, 35 (1995), 4–27

Leaver, R. A., *'Goostly Psalmes and Spirituall Songes': English and Dutch Metrical Psalms from Coverdale to Utenhove, 1535–1566* (Oxford, 1991)

Leedham-Green, E. S., *Books in Cambridge Inventories*, 2 vols. (Cambridge, 1986)

Lesure, F., 'La Facture instrumentale à Paris au seizième siècle', *GSJ*, 7 (1954), 11–52

  'La Guitare en France au XVIᵉ Siècle', *Musica Disciplina*, 4 (1950), 187–95

  and Thibault, G., *Bibliographie des éditions d'Adrian Le Roy et Robert Ballard, 1551–1598* (Paris, 1955)

Levey, S. M., *An Elizabethan Inheritance: The Hardwick Hall Textiles* (London, 1998)
    Of Household Stuffe: The 1601 Inventories of Bess of Hardwick (London, 2001)
Levy, F. J., 'How Information Spread Amongst the Gentry', *Journal of British Studies*, 21 (1982), 1–34
Lindley, D., 'Words for Music, Perhaps: Early Modern Songs and the Lyric', in Thain, M., ed., *Lyric Poem: Formations and Transformations* (Cambridge, 2013), 10–29
Luborsky, R. S. and Ingram, E. M., *Guide to English Illustrated Books, 1536–1603*, 2 vols. (1998)
Luu, L. B., 'Natural-Born versus Stranger-Born Subjects: Aliens and their Status in Elizabethan London', in Goose, N. and Luu, L. B., eds., *Immigrants in Tudor and Early Stuart England* (Brighton and Portland, 2005), 57–75
MacDowell, K. E., 'Il Mattaccino: Music and Dance of the Matachin and its Role in Italian Comedy', *EM*, 40 (2012), 659–70
Marsh, C., *Music and Society in Early Modern England* (Cambridge, 2010)
Martin, R., 'The Autobiography of Grace, Lady Mildmay', *Renaissance and Reformation*, 18 (1994), 33–81
Maslen, R. W., 'The Healing Dialogues of Doctor Bullein', *The Yearbook of English Studies*, 38 (2008), 119–35
Mateer, D., 'William Byrd, John Petre and Oxford, Bodleian MS Mus. Sch. E. 423', *RMARC*, 29 (1996), 21–46
May, W. and Wolfe, H., 'Manuscripts in Tudor England', in K. Cartwright, ed., *A Companion to Tudor Literature* (Oxford, 2010), 125–39
McGee, T. and Carter, S., eds., *Instruments, Ensembles and Repertory, 1300–1600: Essays in Honour of Keith Polk* (Turnhout, 2012)
McGrath, P. and Rowe, J., 'The Imprisonment of Catholics for Religion under Elizabeth I', *Recusant History*, 20 (1991), 415–35
McKerrow, R. B., *Printers' and Publishers' Devices in England and Scotland 1485–1640* (London, 1913)
McKitterick, D., *A History of Cambridge University Press*, 3 vols. (Cambridge, 1992–2004)
Mears, N., 'Courts, Courtiers, and Culture in Tudor England', *The Historical Journal*, 46 (2003), 703–22
Meucci, R., 'Da "chitarra italiana" a "chitarrone": Una nuova interpretazione', in *Enrico Radesca da Foggia e il suo tempo: Atti del Convegno di studi, Foggia 7–8 Aprile 2000* (Lucca, 2001), 30–57
Miller, R., *Securing Baritone, Bass-Baritone, and Bass Voices* (Oxford, 2008)
Milsom, J., 'Caustun's Contrafacta', *JRMA*, 132 (2007), 1–31
    'Sacred Songs in the Chamber', in Morehen, 161–79
    'Songs, Carols and Contrafacta in the Early History of the Tudor Anthem', *Proceedings of the Royal Musical Association*, 107 (1980–81), 34–45
    'Songs and Society in Early Tudor London', *EMH*, 16 (1997), 235–93
    and Fenlon, I., '"Ruled Paper Imprinted": Music Paper and Patents in Sixteenth-Century England', *JAMS*, 37 (1984), 139–63
Minamino, H., 'The Spanish Plucked Viola in Renaissance Italy', *EM*, 32 (2004), 177–192
Montagu, G. and Montagu, J., *Minstrels and Angels: Carvings of Musicians in Medieval English Churches* (Berkeley, 1998)

Morehen, J., ed., *English Choral Practice 1400–1650* (Cambridge, 1995)

Morris, R. K., "'I was never more in love with an Olde House now Never Newe Worke Could be Better Bestowed": The Earl of Leicester's Remodelling of Kenilworth Castle for Queen Elizabeth I', *The Antiquaries Journal*, 89 (2009), 241–305

Mousley, A., 'Renaissance Selves and Life Writing', *Forum for Modern Language Studies*, 26 (1990), 222–30

Muldrew, C., *The Economy of Obligation: The Culture of Credit and Social Relations in Early Modern England* (Basingstoke, 1998)

Mundy, V., 'An Inventory of the Contents of Markeaton Hall', *Derbyshire Archaeological Journal*, 51 (1930), 117–40

Nelson, K. M., 'Love in the Music Room: Thomas Whythorne and the Private Affairs of Tudor Music Tutors', *EM*, 40 (2012), 15–26

'Thomas Whythorne and the Social and Professional World of Tudor Musicians', unpublished doctoral dissertation, University of Warwick, 2010

Nevinson, J. L., 'A Show of the Nine Worthies', *Shakespeare Quarterly*, 14 (1963), 103–7

Newman, J., *The Buildings of England: West Kent and the Weald*, 2nd edn (London, 1976)

Nordstrom, L., 'Albert de Rippe Joueur de luth du Roy', *EM*, 7 (1979), 378–85

The Bandora: Its Music and Sources (Michigan, 1992)

Oras, A., 'Surrey's Technique of Phonetic Echoes: A Method and its Background', *JEGP*, 50 (1951), 289–308

Orlin, L. C., *Locating Privacy in Tudor London* (Oxford, 2007)

Overell, M. A., *Italian Reform and English Reformations, c.1535–c.1585* (Aldershot, 2008)

Page, C., 'The Fifteenth-Century Lute: New and Neglected Sources', *EM*, 9 (1981), 11–21

'Jerome of Moravia on the Rubeba and Viella', in Page, *Music and Instruments*, Essay VII

Music and Instruments of the Middle Ages: Studies on Texts and Performance (Aldershot, 1997)

'Le troisième accord pour vièle de Jérome de Moravia: Jongleurs et "anciens Pères de France"', in Page, *Music and Instruments*, Essay XIX

Voices and Instruments of the Middle Ages: Instrumental Practice and Songs in France 1100–1300 (London, 1987)

ed., Summa musicae: *A Thirteenth-Century Manual for Singers* (Cambridge, 1991)

Palmer, R. E., *Thomas Whythorne's Speech: The Phonology of a Sixteenth-Century Native of Somerset in London* (Copenhagen, 1969)

Parks, G. B., 'The Genesis of Tudor Interest in Italian', *PMLA*, 77 (1962), 529–35

Pearsall, E. S., 'Tudor Court Musicians 1485–1547: Their Number, Status and Function', unpublished doctoral dissertation, 2 vols., New York University, 1986

Pellini, G., *Strumenti musicali in tarsie italiane dal XIV al XVI secolo esistenti in Italia*, Scuola di Paleografia e Filologia Musicale di Cremona, Università di Pavia (Pavia, 1990)

Peters, G., *The Musical Sounds of Medieval French Cities: Players, Patrons, and Politics* (Cambridge, 2012)

Pettegree, A., *Foreign Protestant Communities in Sixteenth-Century London* (Oxford, 1986)

Pick, R., 'The Worthy Ladies of Hardwick Hall', *Theatre History Studies*, 113 (1993), 115–34

Pike, R., 'An Urban Minority: The Moriscos of Seville', *International Journal of Middle East Studies*, 2 (1971), 368–77

Polk, K., *German Instrumental Music of the Late Middle Ages: Players, Patrons, and Performance Practice* (Cambridge, 1992)

Poplawska, D. and Czechak, T., 'The Tuning and Playing of a Medieval Gittern and Fiddle from Elblag, Poland', *The Consort*, 58 (2002), 3–12

Potter, D., *Henry VIII and Francis I: The Final Conflict, 1540–1547* (Leiden, 2011)

Poulton, D., 'Graces of Play in Renaissance Lute Music', *EM*, 3 (1975), 107–14

Prest, W., 'Conflict, Change and Continuity: Elizabeth I to the Great Temple Fire', in O' Havery, H. R., ed., *History of the Middle Temple* (Oxford and Portland, 2011), 81–110

   The Inns of Court under Elizabeth and the Early Stuarts 1590–1640, corrected edn (Oxford, 1991)

Price, D. C., *Patrons and Musicians of the English Renaissance* (Cambridge, 1981)

Pringle, J., 'The Founder of English Viol-Making', *EM*, 6 (1978), 501–11

Prizer, W. F., 'Isabella d'Este and Lorenzo da Pavia, "Master Instrument-Maker"', *EMH*, 2 (1982), 87–127

   'Music at the Court of the Sforza: The Birth and Death of a Musical Center', *Musica Disciplina*, 43 (1989), 141–93

Quitslund, B., *The Reformation in Rhyme: Sternhold, Hopkins and the English Metrical Psalter, 1547–1603* (Aldershot, 2008)

Ramsay, G. D., *The City of London in International Politics at the Accession of Elizabeth Tudor* (Manchester, 1975)

   The Queen's Merchants and the Revolt of the Netherlands (Manchester, 1986)

Raven, J., *The Business of Books: Booksellers and the English Book Trade, 1450–1850* (New Haven and London, 2007)

Reader, F. W., 'Tudor Mural Paintings in the Lesser Houses in Bucks', *The Archaeological Journal*, 89 (1932), 116–73

Reeve, J. 'A Mid Sixteenth-Century Guide to Fret Placement', *LSJ*, 43 (2003), 44–61

Remnant, M., 'The Gittern in English Mediaeval Art', *GSJ*, 18 (1965), 104–19 and Marks, R., 'A Medieval Gittern', *British Museum Yearbook*, 1 (London, 1980), 83–134

Rey, P., 'La guitarra en la baja Edad Media – The Guitar in the Late Middle Ages', Catalogue of the Exhibition *La Guitarra Española – The Spanish Guitar*, Madrid, Sociedad Estatal Quinto Centenario (Madrid, 1991)

Reynard, P. C., 'Unreliable Mills: Maintenance Practices in Early Modern Papermaking', *Technology and Culture*, 40 (1999), 237–62

Richards, J., 'Useful Books: Reading Vernacular Regimens in Sixteenth-Century England', *Journal of the History of Ideas*, 73 (2012), 247–71

Ringler, W. A., Jr., *Bibliography and Index of English Verse in Manuscript, 1501–1558, Prepared and Completed by Michael Rudick and Susan J. Ringler* (London, 1992)

Roberts, P., 'Elizabethan Players and Minstrels and the Legislation of 1572 against Retainers and Vagabonds', in Fletcher, A. and Roberts, P., eds., *Religion,*

Culture and Society in Early Modern Britain: Essays in Honour of Patrick Collinson (Cambridge, 1994), 29–55

Robinson, J., 'Lute Music for Comic Actors, Fools, Buffoons and Matachins', Music Supplement to *Lute News*, 81 (April 2007)

Romanillos Vega, J. L. and Winspear, H. S., *The Vihuela de Mano and the Spanish Guitar: A Dictionary of the Makers of Plucked and Bowed Musical Instruments of Spain (1200–2002)* (Guijosa, 2002)

Ross, M. P., 'The Kytsons of Hengrave: A Study in Musical Patronage', unpublished doctoral dissertation, University of London, 1989

Ryding, E. S., review of Ward, *Music for Elizabethan Lutes*, in *Renaissance Quarterly*, 47 (1994), 441–2

Ryrie, A., *Being Protestant in Reformation Britain* (Oxford, 2013)

Sabol, A. J., 'A Three-Man Song in Fulwell's *Like Will to Like* at the Folger', *Renaissance News*, 10 (1957), 139–42

Sainéan, L., *Les sources indigènes de l'etymologie française*, 2 vols. (Paris, 1925)

Salzman, P., 'Placing Tudor Fiction', *The Yearbook of English Studies*, 38 (2008), 136–49

Sayce, L., review of Ward, *Music for Elizabethan Lutes, The Lute*, 32 (1992), 87–96

Sayle, C., *The Library of Thomas Lorkin* (New York, 1921)

Scammell, G., 'British Merchant Shipbuilding, *c*1500–1750', *IJMH*, 11 (1999), 27–52

Scheller, R. W., 'Gallia Cisalpina: Louis XII and Italy 1499–1508', *Simiolus: Netherlands Quarterly for the History of Art*, 15 (1985), 5–60

Schmidt, A. J., *The Yeoman in Tudor and Stuart England* (Washington, 1961)

Segerman, E., *Communications* on the cittern available on the FoMRHI website, www.fomrhi.org/pages/all–bulletins

   The Development of Western European Stringed Instruments (Northern Renaissance Instruments, Manchester, 2006)

   'Pitch Relativity in the Renaissance and the Sizes of Fiddles and Viols', *FoMRHI Communication*, undated, available from the FoMRHI website

   'A Short History of the Cittern', *GSJ*, 52 (1999), 77–107

   and Abbot, D., 'Stringed Instruments on the Eglantine Table', *EM*, 4 (1976), 485

Sessions, W. A., *Henry Howard: The Poet Earl of Surrey* (Oxford, 1999)

Seznec, J., 'Apollo and the Swans on the Tomb of St. Sebaldus', *Journal of the Warburg Institute*, 2 (1938), 7

Shaw, D., 'The Construction of the Private in Medieval London', *Journal of Medieval and Early Modern Studies*, 26 (1996), 447–66

Shepard, A., *Meanings of Manhood in Early Modern England* (Oxford, 2003)

Shephard, S. and Spicksley, J., 'Worth, Age, and Social Status in Early Modern England', *The Economic History Review*, 64 (2011), 493–530

Shepherd, M., 'The Interpretation of Signs for Graces in English Lute Music', *The Lute*, 36 (1996), 37–84

Sherman, W. H., 'Anatomising the Commonwealth: Language, Politics and the Elizabethan Social Order', in Fowler and Greene, 104–121

   Used Books: Marking Readers in Renaissance England (Philadelphia, University of Pennsylvania Press, 2008)

Shore, D. R., 'The Autobiography of Thomas Whythorne: An Early Elizabethan Context for Poetry', *Renaissance and Reformation*, 17 (1981), 72–86

'Whythorne's Autobiography and the Genesis of Gascoigne's Master F.J.', *Journal of Medieval and Renaissance Studies*, 12 (1982), 159–78

Shrank, C., '"Matters of Love as of Discourse": The English Sonnet, 1560–1580', *Studies in Philology*, 105 (2008), 30–49

Sicca, C. M. and Waldman, L. A., eds., *The Anglo-Florentine Renaissance: Art for the Early Tudors* (New Haven and London, 2012)

Sinisgalli, R., ed., *La prospettiva: Fondamenti teorici ed esperienze figurative dall'antichità al mondo moderno: Atti del convegno internazionale di studi: Istituto svizzero di Roma* (Florence, 1998)

Skura, M., *Tudor Autobiography: Listening for Inwardness* (Ithaca, 2008)

Smith, H., '"Whose heavenly Touch doth ravish human Sense"', *EM*, 41 (2013), 295–7

Smith, S. R., 'The London Apprentices as Seventeenth-Century Adolescents', *Past and Present*, 61 (1973), 149–61

Spiegel, G. S., 'Perfecting English Meter: Sixteenth-Century Criticism and Practice', *The Journal of English and Germanic Philology*, 79 (1980), 192–209

Spring, M., *The Lute in Britain: A History of the Instrument and its Music* (Oxford, 2001)

Spufford, M., 'The Limitations of the Probate Inventory', in Chartres, J. and Hey, D., eds., *English Rural Society, 1500–1800: Essays in Honour of Joan Thirsk* (Cambridge, 1990), 139–74

Stark, J. A., *Bel Canto: A History of Vocal Pedagogy* (Toronto and London, 1999)

Stauder, W., 'Zur Entwicklung der Cister', *Renaissance-Studien: Helmuth Osthoff zum 80. Geburtstag* (Tutzing, 1979), 233–35

Stephenson, M., *A List of Monumental Brasses in the British Isles* (London, 1926, repr. 1964)

Stern, T., '"On each Wall/And Corner Post": Playbills, Title-Pages, and Advertising in Early Modern London', *English Literary Renaissance*, 36 (2006), 57–85

Stevens, J., *Music and Poetry in the Early Tudor Court* (Cambridge, 1979)

Stevenson, C., *The City and the King: Architecture and Politics in Restoration London* (New Haven and London, 2013)

Strahle, G., *An Early Music Dictionary: Musical Terms from British Sources, 1500–1740* (Cambridge, 1995)

String, T., *Art and Communication in the Reign of Henry VIII* (Aldershot, 2008)

Strohm, R., *The Rise of European Music, 1380–1500* (Cambridge, 1993)

Suárez, S. D., 'The English Spelling Reform in the Light of the Works of Richard Mulcaster and John Hart', *Sederi*, 7 (1996), 115–26

Thomas, K., *The Ends of Life: Roads to Fulfilment in Early Modern England* (Oxford, 2009)

Thompson, W., 'Poets, Lovers, and Heroes in Italian Mythological Prints', *The Metropolitan Museum of Art Bulletin*, New Series, 61 (2004), 1–56

Thornton, M. J., '*Tarsie*: Design and Designers', *Journal of the Warburg and Courtauld Institutes*, 36 (1973), 377–82

Trésor de la langue française: Dictionnaire de la langue du XIXe et du XXe siècle (Paris, 1971–1994)

Tyler, J., 'The Mandore in the 16th and 17th Centuries', *EM*, 9 (1981), 22–3
'The Renaissance Guitar 1500–1650', *EM*, 3 (1975), 341–7

and Sparks, P., *The Guitar and its Music from the Renaissance to the Classical Era* (Oxford, 2002)

Unger, R. W., 'Shipping and Western European Economic Growth in the Late Renaissance: Potential Connections', *IJMH*, 18/2 (2006), 85–104

Vaccaro, J.-M., *La Musique de luth en France au XVIᵉ siècle* (Paris, 1981)

Vanhulst, H., 'Édition comparative des instructions pour le luth, le cistre et la guitare publiées à Louvain par Pierre Phalèse (1545–1570)', *Revue belge de Musicologie*, 34/35 (1980/1981), 81–105

'Les éditions de musique polyphonique et les traités musicaux mentionnés dans les inventaires dressés en 1569 dans les Pays-Bas espagnols sur ordre du duc d'Albe', *Revue belge de Musicologie*, 31(1977), 60–71

'A Fragment of a Lost Lutebook Printed by Phalèse (Louvain, c1575)', *Tijdschrift van de Vereniging voor Nederlandse Muziekgeschedenis*, 40 (1990), 57–80.

Veneziano, G., ed., *Rime e suoni alla spagnola: Atti della giornata internazionale di studi sulla chitarra barocca . . . 7 febbraio 2002* (Florence, 2003)

Venn, J. A., *Alumni Cantabrigienses: A Biographical List of All Known Students, Graduates and Holders of Office at the University of Cambridge, from the Earliest Times to 1900* (Cambridge, 1922–54)

Verney, P., *The Standard Bearer* (London, 1963)

Vigarello, *Concepts of Cleanliness: Changing Attitudes in France since the Middle Ages* (Cambridge, 1988)

Voss, P. J., 'Books for Sale: Advertising and Patronage in Late Elizabethan England', *The Sixteenth Century Journal*, 29 (1998), 733–56

Wagner, J. A., *The Devon Gentleman: The Life of Sir Peter Carew* (Hull, 1998)

Walker, G., *Writing Under Tyranny: English Literature and the Henrician Reformation* (Oxford, 2005)

Ward, J., 'A Dowland Miscellany', *JLSA*, 10 (1977)

'The English Measure', *EM*, 14 (1986), 15–21

'The Maner of Dauncying', *EM*, 4 (1976), 127–42

'The Morris Tune', *JAMS*, 39 (1986), 294–331

Music for Elizabethan Lutes, 2 vols. (Oxford, 1992)

'Music for "A Handefull of pleasant delites"', *JAMS*, 10 (1957), 151–80

Sprightly and Cheerful Musick: Notes on the Cittern, Gittern and Guitar in Sixteenth- and Seventeenth-Century England, *LSJ*, 21 (1978–81)

Warneke, S., 'A Taste for Newfangledness: The Destructive Potential of Novelty in Early Modern England', *Sixteenth Century Journal*, 4 (1995), 881–96

Warner, C. J., *The Making and Marketing of Tottel's Miscellany, 1557: Songs and Sonnets in the Summer of the Martyrs' Fires* (Ashgate, 2013)

Weiss, S. F., 'Didactic Sources of Musical Learning in Early Modern England', in Glaisyer, N. and Pennell, S., eds., *Didactic Literature in England, 1500–1800: Expertise Constructed* (Aldershot, 2003), 40–62

Wells-Cole, A., *Art and Decoration in Elizabethan and Jacobean England: The Influence of Continental Prints, 1558–1625* (London, 1997)

White, G., '"that whyche ys nedefoulle and nesesary": The Nature and Purpose of the Original Furnishings and Decoration of Hardwick Hall, Derbyshire', unpublished doctoral dissertation, University of Warwick, 2005

White, J., *The Birth and Rebirth of Pictorial Space*, 2nd edn (London, 1972)

Wiggins, M. and Richardson, C., *British Drama 1533–1642: A Catalogue,* vol. I, *1533–1566* (Oxford, 2011)

Willan, T. S., *The Inland Trade: Studies in English Internal Trade in the Sixteenth and Seventeenth Centuries* (Manchester, 1976)

Williams, G., *A Dictionary of Sexual Language and Imagery in Shakespearean and Stuart Literature*, 3 vols. (London, 1994)

Willis, J., *Church Music and Protestantism in Post-Reformation England: Discourses, Sites and Identities* (Farnham, 2010)

Wilson, B., 'The Keyboard Instruments of King Henry VIII', *The Organ Yearbook*, 13 (1982), 31–45

Winston, J., 'Lyric Poetry at the Early Elizabethan Inns of Court: Forming a Professional Community', in Archer, Goldring and Knight, 223–44

Woodcock, W. M., 'Shooting for England: Configuring the Book and the Bow in Roger Ascham's Toxophilus', *Sixteenth Century Journal*, 41 (2010), 1017–38

Woodfield, I., *The Early History of the Viol* (Cambridge, 1984)
  English Musicians in the Age of Exploration (Stuyvesant, NY, 1995)

Woodfill, W. L., *Musicians in English Society from Elizabeth to Charles I* (Princeton, 1953)

Worsley, R., *The History of the Isle of Wight* (London, 1781)

Wright, L., 'The Medieval Gittern and Citole: A Case of Mistaken Identity', *GSJ*, 30 (1977), 8–42

Wrightson, K., '"Sorts of People" in Tudor and Stuart England', in Barry, J. and Brooks, C., eds., *The Middling Sort of People: Culture, Society and Politics in England, 1550–1800* (Basingstoke, 1994), 28–51

Young, C., 'Zur Klassifikation und ikonographischen Interpretation mittelalterlicher Zupfinstrumente', *BJHM*, 8 (1984), 67–103

Youngs, D., *Humphrey Newton: An Early Tudor Gentleman* (Woodbridge, 2008)

Yu-Chiao Wang, 'Caxton's Romances and their Early Tudor Readers', *Huntington Library Quarterly*, 67 (2004), 173–88

Zaerr, L. M., *Performance and the Middle English Romance* (Woodbridge, 2012)

Zecher, C., 'The Gendering of the Lute in Sixteenth-Century French Love Poetry', *Renaissance Quarterly*, 53 (2000), 769–91
  'Ronsard's Guitar: A Sixteenth-Century Heir to the Horatian Lyre', *International Journal of the Classical Tradition*, 4 (1998), 532–54
  Sounding Objects: Musical Instruments, Poetry, and Art in Renaissance France (Toronto, 2007)

Zim, R., *English Metrical Psalms: Poetry as Praise and Prayer 1535–1601* (Cambridge, 1987)

Index

Printed in Great Britain
by Amazon

82170086R00154